D0440920

SET YOUR LIFE ON A SUCCESSFUL COURSE!

Sydney Omarr, America's most accurate astrologer, will help you turn all your dreams into wonderful realities. Beginning in July, 1991, his on-target horoscopes and sound advice will counsel you in all aspects of your future—from romance to health and career.

A year of heavenly possibilities awaits you. Look up your planets . . . find out what makes a lover of each sign stay around, stray or get jealous. . . . Know when to play it cool—and when to go for it! Discover the secrets to a great 1992 and make it your most fulfilling year ever!

SYDNEY OMARR'S DAY-BY-DAY ASTROLOGICAL GUIDES FOR YOU IN 1992

- ☐ **ARIES** ....(169980—$3.99)
- ☐ **TAURUS** ....(169999—$3.99)
- ☐ **GEMINI** ....(170008—$3.99)
- ☐ **CANCER** ....(170016—$3.99)
- ☐ **LEO** ....(170024—$3.99)
- ☐ **VIRGO** ....(170032—$3.99)
- ☐ **LIBRA** ....(170040—$3.99)
- ☐ **SCORPIO** ....(170059—$3.99)
- ☐ **SAGITTARIUS** ....(170067—$3.99)
- ☐ **CAPRICORN** ....(170075—$3.99)
- ☐ **AQUARIUS** ....(170083—$3.99)
- ☐ **PISCES** ....(170091—$3.99)

Price slightly higher in Canada.

SYDNEY OMARR'S

DAY-BY-DAY ASTROLOGICAL GUIDE FOR

AQUARIUS

JANUARY 20-FEBRUARY 18

·1·9·9·2·

A SIGNET BOOK

SIGNET
Published by the Penguin Group
Penguin Books USA Inc.,
375 Hudson Street, New York, New York 10014, U.S.A.
Penguin Books Ltd, 27 Wrights Lane,
London W8 5TZ, England
Penguin Books Australia Ltd, Ringwood,
Victoria, Australia
Penguin Books Canada Ltd,
2801 John Street, Markham, Ontario, Canada L3R 1B4
Penguin Books (N.Z.) Ltd, 182-190 Wairau Road,
Auckland 10, New Zealand

Penguin Books Ltd, Registered Offices:
Harmondsworth, Middlesex, England

First published by Signet,
an imprint of New American Library,
a division of Penguin Books USA Inc.

First Printing, July, 1991
10 9 8 7 6 5 4 3 2 1

REGISTERED TRADEMARK—MARCA REGISTRADA

Printed in the United States of America

Contents

Introduction

The scene is a New York courtroom in the year 1914. The woman on trial for fortune-telling is an astrologer, the proper Bostonian descendant of two American presidents, who learned her technique from a noted Boston physician who used astrology in his diagnoses. Into the courtroom she comes, laden with piles of reference books, tracing the history of astrology back to the ancient Babylonians. As the trial progresses, she challenges the skeptical judge to let her cast a chart to demonstrate the accuracy of astrology. The judge agrees and gives her the birth date, time, and place of an unnamed subject. Evangeline Adams consults her books of tables and draws up a chart, then confidently gives the first public reading of a horoscope in the United States.

The judge's verdict: not guilty. He needed no experts to verify the accuracy of the stunning insights into the character of the subject—the birth date he had given Miss Adams was that of his own son. That trial, which was reported in newspapers across the country, was the beginning of astrology consciousness in America.

Astrology has come a long way since that time. Now it has entered the high-tech era with computer programs, nationwide networks of astrologers, conventions, seminars, and lectures attended by thousands of astrology fans.

Who's following the stars in the 1990s? An estimated 32 million people, according to a recent Gallup Poll, believe that the movements of the planets affect their daily lives. And as national barriers break down, astrologers around the world are discovering a kinship. By the time this guide is published there will have been the first international conference of astrologers in Russia, where

7

an astrological community has survived through all the years of tumultuous political changes.

New areas of astrology are opening up as other professionals are incorporating astrological insights into their work. Psychotherapists are using astrological charts for accurate information about the personalities of their patients—and astrologers, in a fair turnabout, are becoming more aware of the techniques and responsibilities of being counselors. Businesses are analyzing the horoscopes of their employees for successful job matchups and financiers are retaining astrologers for advice on timing and markets.

This book is for you if you want to learn more about astrology and how to use it every day in your personal and professional life. There are tips on how to take control of your life and steer it on a successful course by moving in harmony with planetary cycles. You'll learn which are the most powerful planets in your chart and the special qualities that enhance your chances for success in your career. You'll not only learn about your sun sign, but about the nine other planets in your horoscope. You can find out what celebrities share your birthday, too.

Astrology can help you put the increasingly complicated lifestyle of the 1990s into perspective, help you achieve a more fulfilling love relationship, and guide you in timing and decision making. Let this be your guide to following the stars in 1992—and may you have a year of growth, happiness, and prosperity!

1

Clearing Up the
Mystery of Astrology

Over the years, I've gathered the most frequent questions asked about how astrology works. Once you get beyond sun signs, the symbols and terminology of this subject can often be confusing to the beginner. I'm also often asked about how to find an astrologer or if you can do astrology on your personal computer at home. The answers should help to solve some of astrology's mysteries for you. And you'll find that it's easy to get hooked on astrology: the more you know, the more deeply you'll want to investigate this fascinating subject.

What is the difference between sign and a constellation?
This is one of the most frequently asked questions. Everyone knows that the constellations of the zodiac are specific configurations of stars. But not everyone knows that the sign the constellation represents may be in a different place!

A sign is actually a 30-degree division of a circular belt of sky called the zodiac, which means "circle of animals" in Greek. Originally, each division was marked by a constellation, some of which were named after animals—a lion, a bull, a goat, a ram—or sea creatures—fish, a crab. But as the earth's axis changed over thousands of years, so did the signposts. Even though the "animals" have moved, however, the division of the circle—which is what astrologers call a "sign"— remains the same.

Then what is a sun sign?
That is the sign (or division of the zodiac) the sun was passing through at the time of your birth. This is really the foundation of your horoscope, the base of your astrological character. It takes on color and nuances with nine

9

other planets (the moon is most often referred to as a planet) and the signs in which they fall.

What does it mean that Pisces is a water sign, Aquarius is an air sign?

The definitions of the signs evolved systematically from four components, which interrelate. These four different criteria are: a sign's ELEMENT, its QUALITY, its POLARITY or sex, and its ORDER on the zodiac "belt." These all work together to tell us what the sign is like and how it behaves.

The system is magically mathematical: The number 12—as in the 12 signs of the zodiac—is divisible by 4, by 3, and by 2. Perhaps it is no coincidence that there are four elements, three qualities, and two polarities. The signs follow each other in sequence around the zodiac, starting with Aries.

The four elements (earth, air, fire, and water) are the "building blocks" of astrology. The use of an element to describe a sign probably dates from man's first attempts to categorize what and who he saw in the world. Ancient sages believed that all things were composed of combinations of earth, air, fire, and water. This included the human character, which was fiery/choleric, earthy/melancholy, airy/sanguine, or watery/phlegmatic. The elements also correspond to our emotional (water), physical (earth), mental (air), and spiritual (fire) natures. The energies of each of the elements were then observed to relate to the time of year when the sun was passing through a certain segment of the zodiac.

The fire signs—Aries, Leo, and Sagittarius—embody the characteristics of that element. Optimism, warmth, hot tempers, enthusiasm, and "spirit" are typical of these signs. Taurus, Virgo, and Capricorn are "earthy"—more grounded, physical, materialistic, organized, and deliberate than fire people. Air signs—Gemini, Libra, and Aquarius—are mentally oriented communicators. Water signs—Cancer, Scorpio, and Pisces—are emotional and creative.

Think of what each element does to the others: water puts out fire or evaporates heat. Air fans the flames or blows them out. Earth smothers fire, drifts and erodes with too much wind, becomes mud or fertile soil with water. Those are often perfect analogies for the relationships between signs of these elements! This astro-chemistry was one of the first ways man described his relationships. Fortunately, no one is entirely "air" or "fire." We all have a bit, or a lot, of each element in our horoscopes; it is this unique mix that defines each astrological personality.

Within each element there are three qualities that describe how the sign behaves, how it works. Cardinal signs are the activists, the go-getters. These signs—Aries, Cancer, Libra, and Capricorn—begin each season. Fixed signs are the builders that happen in the middle of the season. You'll find that Taurus, Leo, Scorpio, and Aquarius are gifted with concentration, stubbornness, and stamina. Mutable signs—Gemini, Virgo, Sagittarius, and Pisces—are catalysts for change at the end of each season; these are flexible, adaptable, mobile signs.

The polarity of a sign is its positive or negative "charge." It can be masculine, active, positive, and yang like the air and fire signs. Or feminine, reactive, negative, and yin like the water and earth signs.

Finally, we consider the sign's place in the order of the zodiac. This is vital to the balance of all the forces and the transmission of energy moving through the signs. You may have noticed that your sign is quite different from your neighboring sign on either side. Yet each seems to grow out of its predecessor like links in a chain and transmits a synthesis of energy gathered along the "chain" to the following sign, beginning with the fire-powered active positive charge of Aries.

What if a person has no planets in an element?
Usually that person will be especially challenged in the areas of that low-function element. For instance, someone who has no planets in earth signs may have to work very hard to manifest the material side of life. Or the person may overcompensate in that area and want to be around earthy things—near a beautiful garden, for instance.

It's appropriate here to remember that, in astrology, there are no pat answers. How a chart works out depends on the individual—a missing element could be an area of great self-expression and self-development, as well as a

11

difficult area. One example is a famous television commentator, renowned for his intellectual approach, who has no planets in air signs. The missing element could also be emphasized in the placement of the houses. Someone with no water might have a water sign in a powerful angular position.

Does my sign have a special planet?
Each sign has a "ruling planet" that is most compatible with its energies. Mars rules the fiery, assertive Aries. The sensual beauty and comfort-loving side of Venus rules Taurus, whereas the more idealistic side rules Libra. The quick-moving Mercury rules both Gemini and Virgo—showing its mental agility in Gemini, its critical analytical side in Virgo. Emotional Cancer is ruled by the moon, while outgoing Leo is ruled by the sun. Scorpio was originally given Mars, but when Pluto was discovered in this century, its powerful magnetic energies were deemed more suitable to Scorpio (though many astrologers still consider Mars the co-ruler of Scorpio). Disciplined Capricorn is ruled by Saturn, and expansive Sagittarius by Jupiter. Unpredictable Aquarius is ruled by Uranus and creative, impressionable Pisces by Neptune.

What does an astrologer need to know to cast a horoscope?
First, an astrologer needs to know the date and time of birth, as accurate as possible, and the subject's place of birth. A horoscope can be cast about anything that has a specific time and place.

An astrologer may use a book of tables called an ephemeris to determine the exact placement of the moon and planets at that moment. Today, however, many astrologers prefer to use one of several computer programs available that calculates the exact information very quickly, saving much time and effort.

Once the chart is set up, there is the matter of interpretation. Most astrologers have looked at hundreds of charts and have a ready frame of reference. Each will have a unique point of view, based on experience and interests. Some astrologers may be more literal, some more intuitive, whereas others are also trained psychotherapists. But, although some may seem to have an almost psychic ability, extrasensory perception or any other parapsychological talent is not necessary to be a good astrologer. You can draw a very accurate picture from factual data.

An astrologer may draw up several charts for each client or date—one for the time of birth, one for the current date, and a "progressed" chart showing the changes from that person's birth time to the present. According to your individual needs, there are many other possibilities, such as a chart for a different location, if you are contemplating a change of place.

An astrologer may also be called upon to interpret relationships. Then they will do a special "synastry" chart, which compares the chart of one date with the chart of another date. The relationship can be between any two people or things or events.

An astrologer will be particularly interested in transits—planets passing over the planets or sensitive points in your chart during the upcoming year. These will signal important times for you.

If someone has the same birthday as mine, why aren't our lives similar? What about twins?
Even a few moments difference in time can change a horoscope chart. However, the difference in development of the charts involves how the individual uses the energies. Over and over again, we point out that, though astrology may indicate certain strengths and weaknesses, every person can choose positive or negative ways to express them. We often see strikingly similar charts, belonging to people who bear little resemblance to each other, who have used their energies in radically different ways. Twins may often choose to express different facets of very similar charts, simply from the desire not to be alike.

Besides my "sun sign," how many other signs do I have?
In compiling your astrological data base, we consider eight planets, besides the moon and sun. The phrase "as above, so below" is often used to describe a chart as a microcosm of the universe. The three closest planets to the earth—Mercury, Mars, Venus—and the moon affect

13

your personal character. The next farthest out, Jupiter and Saturn, affect influences from others, turning points, and significant cycles in your life. As we get farther out, the slower-moving planets Uranus, Neptune, and Pluto deal with mass trends that affect your whole generation.

In the western systems of astrology, we confine our charts to the planets and stars within the zodiac. We would not consider the influence of the Big Dipper or Orion or black holes and supernovas.

What about the asteroids and Chiron?

Between Saturn and Uranus lies a ring of thousands of oddly shaped bodies, called asteroids. There is much conjecture about their origin. Some astronomers think they are pieces of a planet or several planets that exploded in the past. Others feel that these are random, floating pieces of matter that never came together to form a planet. Most asteroids are quite small; the larger ones are only about 200 miles in diameter. The asteroids have recently been noticed by astrologers who have begun to chart the effects of the larger asteroids in the horoscopes of clients and have found a correlation with the reemergence of feminine consciousness.

Many astrologers now use the four major asteroids—Pallas, Vesta, Ceres, and Juno—to supply an extra feminine dimension to the chart. Ceres, "the great mother," symbolizes the principle of nurturing, both of ourselves—in terms of self-love—and others. Pallas is the significator of creative intelligence, the healing arts, and the role of woman in a man's world. Vesta deals with the way we use our personal sexual energy and how we integrate it with our focus on work. Juno rules over intimate relationships and our lessons to learn from one-on-one commitments. Astrologer Demetra George has provided an in-depth study of the asteroids in her book *Asteroid Goddesses*, which also contains tables where you can look up the placements of sixteen asteroids.

Chiron is a small body orbiting the sun between Saturn and Uranus. Discovered in 1977, it is thought to be a comet. It travels slowly, taking between 49 and 51 years to make a full transit of the zodiac. In Greek mythology, Chiron was the chief centaur, half man and half horse, who was a teacher to both the Gods and man. In your natal chart, Chiron is thought to relate to your life quest. Its symbol, the key, reflects its power to unlock higher consciousness. As such a small body, Chiron has not been definitely assigned to any astrological sign. However, its teaching and healing energies are thought to be most related to Virgo. A definitive in-depth book on Chiron has been written by astrologer Barbara Hand Clow and is available at your nearest astrological bookstore.

With ten planets to juggle, what more do astrologers need? The answer could come from our quest for depth, richness, and a relationship to the issues of today, which emerges in the archetypes and symbolism of the most recent discoveries. Women's consciousness, deep psychological issues, healing, and ecology, as well as our approach to the afterlife, all have a place in astrological readings and can be clarified by the components discovered in our own time. Whatever is out there or whatever we put out there has a place in the energies that affect us all.

Will astrology conflict with my religious beliefs?
Many religious people disapprove of astrologers, first because they confuse modern-day astrologers with charlatans or fortune-tellers of the past or because they feel someone interested in astrology will turn away from religion. However, the study of astrology actually brings one closer to a religious understanding of the dynamic interchange between the universal plan, the material world, and man's place in it.

There is no religious dogma attached to astrology—although it has deep roots in all religions and can be found in the spiritual history of all races. It is an objective study with no definite rules for behavior, moral codes, or concept of a particular god. Most astrologers stress strongly that you are in charge of your horoscope. It is a diagnostic tool for enlightenment, a helpful method of analysis, but by no means an arbitrary dictator and should not conflict with other forms of spiritual self-development.

I own a personal computer and would like to use it to learn more about astrology by doing some charts for

friends. What kind of program would you recommend for a nonprofessional student of astrology?

If you have a PC, the world of astrology can really open up for you. No longer do you have to spend hours on tedious calculations or rely on guesswork when you set up a chart.

There is software available for every make of computer, at all levels of astrological expertise. Some will calculate a chart in a few seconds and provide pages of interpretations. Others simply run off a chart with technical information. Still others give you mind-boggling menus of different zodiacs, house systems, and types of charts to choose from.

If, like most of our readers, you will be using the program only occasionally for fun, then you don't need an expensive and complicated program. Many options are available that don't require a complicated computer setup to run. The easiest start at less than $100 and can be ordered from one of the several companies specializing in astrology programs. It's a good idea to contact one of these companies and tell them what your needs are and the type of hardware you use.

Some of the names to know are:

MATRIX SOFTWARE
315 Madison Avenue
Big Rapids, MI 49307
1-800-PLANETS, extension 22

ASTRO COMPUTING SERVICES
Dept. AA689, P.O. Box 34487
San Diego, CA 92103-0802

ASTROLABE
Department A.
P.O. Box 28
Orleans, MA 02653
1-800-843-6682

I would like to study astrology—how can I find a good teacher?

There are several ways to find a good teacher. You might

contact one of the regional astrology groups across the country, which have regular meetings; ask at your local metaphysical or "New Age" bookstore.

Astrological organizations such as the National Council for Geocosmic Research may also hold classes in your area. Several times a year, these organizations sponsor regional astrology conferences where you can meet some of the best teachers. Write to the N.C.G.R. for more information:

N.C.G.R. Headquarters
105 Snyder Avenue
Ramsey, NJ 07446

You can also investigate the study-by-mail courses offered by astrological computing services and astrology magazines.

2

How the Planets Operate

To decide who "you" are, an astrologer must weigh and balance nine other planets besides the sun (the moon is considered a "planet," too). Each planet represents a basic force in your life and the sign where it is placed represents how this force will manifest itself. It may be easier to imagine the planet as a person with a choice of twelve different roles to play. In some roles, the person will be more flamboyant or aggressive, in others the more thoughtful or spiritual side of his nature will be expressed.

Interpreting a planet's personality changes according to the different signs is one of the most basic skills in astrology. It's one you can begin to practice yourself with the help of the charts in the "Look Up Your Planets" chapter in this book and the following descriptions. Let's consider first the basic personality of the planet and its function in your life, then the possible roles it can play in each sign.

THE SUN

Because the sun shows your basic will and ego, it's always the strongest planetary personality in your chart. That is why sun sign astrology is so accurate for so many born under the same sign. In chart interpretation, the sun can also play the paternal role. It rules the sign of Leo, gaining strength though the pride, dignity, and confidence of the fixed fire personality. It is also strong in "me-first" Aries. In Aquarius, the sun-ego is strengthened through group participation and social consciousness rather than self-centeredness. In Libra, the sun needs the strength of a partner, an "other," for balance and self-expression.

THE MOON

The most emotional function in your chart is the moon, which represents your subconscious "hidden" side. The moon's function is to dig beneath the surface to reflect your needs, longings, the kind of mothering and childhood conditioning you had. The moon is strongest in Cancer and Taurus—both comforting, home-loving signs where the natural emotional energies of the moon are easily and productively expressed. But, when the moon is in the opposite signs, Capricorn and Scorpio, it leaves the comfortable nest and deals with emotional issues of power and achievement in the outside world. Those of you with the moon in these signs will find your emotional role more challenging in life.

(Because accurate moon tables are too extensive to include in this book, I suggest you consult an astrologer or have a computer chart made to determine your correct moon position.)

MERCURY

Mercury reveals your logical mind, how you think and speak. It stays close to the sun and often shares the same sign as the sun, reinforcing the sun's communicative talents. Mercury operates most easily in the sign it rules—Gemini and Virgo—naturally analytical signs. Yet Mercury in Sagittarius and Pisces, signs where logic often takes second place to visionary ideas, can, when this planet is properly harnessed, provide great visionary thinking and poetic expression.

Since Mercury never moves far from the sun, check the signs preceding and following your sun sign, to see which Mercury position is most applicable to you.

VENUS

Venus is the planet of romantic love, pleasure, and artistry. It shows what you react to, your tastes, what (or who) turns you on. It is strongest in Libra, the sign of partnerships, or Taurus, the sign of physical pleasures. In

Pisces, where Venus is exalted, this planet can go overboard, loving to the point of self-sacrifice.

You can find your Venus placement on the chart in this book. Look for the year of your birth in the left-hand column, then follow the line across the page until you read the time of your birthday. The sign heading that column will be your Venus. If you were born on a day when Venus was changing signs, check the signs preceding or following that day.

MARS

This planet is your driving force, your active sexuality. Mars is what makes you run. In Aries, Mars is at his most powerful. Yet this drive can be self-serving and impetuous. In Libra, Mars demands cooperation in a relationship. In Capricorn, Mars becomes an ambitious achiever, headed for the top—but in Cancer, Mars' aggression becomes tempered by feelings, which are always considered. The end can never justify the means, for Mars in Cancer. To find your Mars, refer to the Mars chart in this book and the description later in this chapter.

JUPITER

Jupiter is often viewed as the Santa Claus of the horoscope, a jolly happy planet that brings good luck, gifts, success, and opportunities. Jupiter also embodies the functions of the higher mind, where you do complex, expansive thinking, and deal with the big overall picture rather than the specifics (the province of Mercury). Jupiter functions naturally in Sagittarius, the sign of the philosopher. In Gemini, Jupiter can be a scattered jack-of-all-trades or a lighthearted, effective communicator. In Cancer, Jupiter becomes the protective "big brother." In Capricorn, Jupiter is brought down to earth, its vision harnessed to practical goals.

Be sure to look up your Jupiter "lucky spot" in the tables in this book. But bear in mind that Jupiter gives growth without discrimination or discipline. It's also the place where you could have too much of a good thing, resulting in extravagance, excess pounds, laziness, or carelessness.

SATURN

Saturn has suffered from a bad reputation, always cast as the "heavy" in the chart. The flip side of Saturn is the teacher, however, the one whose class is the toughest in school, but, when you graduate, has taught you lessons you'll never forget. And the tests of Saturn, which come at regular seven-year "exam periods," are the ones you need to pass to survive as a conscious, independent adult. Saturn gives us the grade we've earned—so, if we have studied and prepared for our tests, we needn't be afraid of the "big bad wolf." Saturn in Capricorn is comfortable with this sign's emphasis on structure and respect for authority. In Cancer, however, it suggests both that feeling must become responsible and that authority cannot operate effectively without concern for the heart.

Your Saturn position can illuminate your fears, your hang-ups, your important lessons in life. Remember that Saturn is concerned with your maturity, what you need to know to survive in the world. Be sure to look it up in the Saturn chart in this book.

THE OUTER PLANETS

The three outer planets, Uranus, Neptune, and Pluto are slow-moving but powerful forces in your life. Since they stay in a sign at least seven years, you'll share the sign placement with everyone you went to school with and probably your brothers and sisters. However, the specific place (house) in the horoscope where each one operates is yours alone, and depends on your "moment in time" —the exact time you were born. That's why it is important to have an accurate birth chart.

URANUS

Uranus shakes us out of a rut and propels us forward. When Uranus hits a critical area of your life, such as when it passes another planet, or moves into a new area of your chart, nothing is ever the same again. Uranus strikes hardest at the fixed signs, where a shakeup is sometimes desperately needed. Uranus is right at home

21

in the fixed air sign of Aquarius, where brilliant ideas have universal applications, but in the fixed fire sign of Leo, Uranus breaks up rigid patterns and seems to thumb its nose at proud, sometimes pompous Leo. In Scorpio, its insights lead to transformation, but in Taurus, Uranus becomes focused on revolutionizing earthly affairs, turning daily life topsy-turvy.

NEPTUNE

With Neptune, what you see is not what you get. Neptune is the planet of glamour, dissolution (it dissolves hard reality), illusion, makeup! Neptune is not interested in the world at face value—it dons tinted glasses or blurs the facts with the haze of an intoxicating substance. Where Neptune is, you don't see things quite clearly. This planet's function is to express our visions, and it is most at home in Pisces. In Virgo, Neptune can put visions to practical service. In Cancer, Neptune blends personal feelings and sensitivity on an elevated level, but in the opposite sign of Capricorn, where it is passing through this year, Neptunian glamour fogs over the impersonal structures of society and the workplace. Since Neptune has been in Capricorn for several years, we can witness this in the dissolution of Capricorn areas—big business and government scandals. Neptune can work for some of us while in Capricorn by bringing great creativity to the workplace as well.

PLUTO

Pluto deals with the underside of our personality, digging out our secrets to effect a total transformation. Pluto brings our deep subconscious feelings to the surface through painful probing. Nothing escapes—or is sacred—with Pluto. Because Pluto was discovered only recently, the signs of its exaltation and fall are still debated. But in Scorpio, which Pluto rules, we have been able to witness its effect in the past several years. Pluto symbolizes death and rebirth, violence, elimination, and renewal. Those with strong Scorpio influences in their chart—such as a Scorpio ascendant, sun, or other planets—have probably experienced a transformation in their life in some area.

Planets in Aries

In Aries, each planet will show its most assertive and powerful form.

Moon in Aries—Emotionally, you are independent and ardent. You love the challenge of an emotional pursuit and difficult situations in love only intensify your excitement. But once you attain your goal or conquer your pursuit, your ardor cools. To avoid continuous "treat 'em rough" situations, work on developing patience and tolerance.

Mercury in Aries—You say what you think, even if it provokes confrontation, and you have an active, assertive nature. Your mind is sharp, alert, impatient, though you may not think things through. You may need to develop thoroughness in your analytical processes.

Venus in Aries—You love the sense of challenge that adds spice to life, and might even pick a fight now and then to charge the atmosphere. Since a good chase revs up your romantic motor, you could abandon a romance if the going becomes too smooth. You're first on the block with the newest styles. And first out the door if you're bored or ordered around.

Mars in Aries—You run in high gear, showing the full force of Mars energy. You have a fiery explosive disposition, but are also very courageous, with enormous drive. You'll tackle problems head on and mow down anything that stands in your way. Though you're supercharged and can jump-start others, you are short on perseverance, especially when the situation requires diplomacy, patience, and tolerance.

Jupiter in Aries—You have big ambitions and won't settle for second place. You are luckiest when you are pioneering an innovative project, when you are pushing to be "first." You can break new ground with this placement, but watch a tendency to be pushy and arrogant.

You'll also need to learn patience and perseverance in the house where Jupiter falls in your horoscope.

Saturn in Aries—There's no pushing you around! Saturn puts the brakes on Aries' natural drive and enthusiasm. You'll have to learn to cooperate, tone down self-centeredness.

Uranus in Aries—With a powerful mixture of fire and electricity powering your generation, you were creative pioneers, developing the airplane, the computer, the cyclotron. You never let anything hold you back from exploring the unknown. You have a surprise in store for everyone, and your life can be jolted by sudden, unpredictable changes.

NEPTUNE and PLUTO were not in ARIES in this century.

Planets in Taurus

Planets in Taurus add stability and practicality to your chart.

Moon in Taurus—Solid, secure, comfortable situations and relationships appeal to you. You need displays of affection and gravitate to those who provide you with material comforts and sensual pleasures. Your emotions are steady and nurturing in this strong moon sign, but you could lean toward stubbornness when pushed. You could miss out on some of life's excitement by sticking to the safe straight and narrow road.

Mercury in Taurus—You are deliberate, thorough, with good concentration. You'll take the slow, methodical approach and leave no stone unturned. You'll see a problem through to the end, stick with a subject until you become an expert. You may talk very slowly, with a melodious or very distinctive voice.

Venus in Taurus—Venus is literally "at home" in Taurus. It's a terrific placement for a "Material Girl" or boy, an interior designer, or a musician. You love to surround yourself with the very finest smells, tastes, sounds, visuals, textures. You'd run from an austere lifestyle or uncomfortable surroundings. Creature comforts turn you on. And so does a beautiful, secure nest—and nest egg. Not one to rush about, you take time to enjoy your pleasures and treasures.

Mars in Taurus—Persistence is a great advantage of those with Mars in Taurus. Gifted with stamina and focus, this Mars may not be first out of the gate, but you're sure to finish. You tend to wear away or outlast your foes rather than bowl them over. This Mars is super-sensual sexually—you take your time and enjoy yourself all the way.

Jupiter in Taurus—You have expensive tastes and like to surround yourself with the luxuries money can buy, acquire beauty and comfort in all its forms. You could tend to expand physically—from overindulgence in good tastes! Dieting could be a major challenge. Land and real estate are especially lucky for you.

Saturn in Taurus—"How am I going to pay the rent?" You'll have to weather some lean periods, get control of your material life. Learn to use your talents to their fullest potential. In the same boat, Ben Franklin had the right idea: "A penny saved is a penny earned."

Uranus in Taurus—Your generation were the hippies who rejected the establishment values. You who were intent on doing your own thing are natural entrepreneurs—you'd probably like to be self-employed if you are not already on your own. However, it's likely that you've also had many sudden financial shake-ups. This is one of Uranus' most unstable positions.

NEPTUNE and PLUTO were not in TAURUS in this century.

Planets in Gemini

Planets in Gemini add a versatile, intellectual dimension to your chart.

Moon in Gemini—You need constant emotional stimulation and enjoy an outgoing, diversified lifestyle. You could have difficulty with commitment, and therefore marry more than once or have a love life of changing partners. An outgoing, interesting, talented partner could merit your attention, however. Don't spread yourself too thin to accomplish major goals—and watch a tendency to be emotionally fragmented. Find a creative way to express the range of your feelings.

Mercury in Gemini—This phase is a quick study. You can handle many subjects at once, jumping from one to the other with ease. You may, however, spread yourself too thin. You express yourself well both verbally and in writing. You are a "people person" who enjoys communicating with a large audience.

Venus in Gemini—You're a sparkler who "Loves the Night Life," with constant variety, a frequent change of scenes—and loves. You like lots of stimulation, a varied social life, and are better at light flirtations than serious romances. You may be attracted to younger playful lovers who have the pep and energy to keep up with you.

Mars in Gemini—"Two loves are better than one" is a philosophy that could get this Mars in trouble. Your restless nature searches out stimulation and will switch rather than fight. Your life gets complicated—but that only makes it more interesting for you. You have a way with words and can "talk" with your hands. Since you tend to go all over the lot in your interests, you may have to work hard to develop focus and concentration.

Jupiter in Gemini—You love to be in the center of a whirlwind of activity, talking a blue streak, with all phone lines busy. You have great facility in expressing yourself verbally or in writing. Work that involves communicating or manual dexterity is especially lucky for you. Watch a tendency to be too restless—slow down from time to time. Try not to spread yourself too thin.

Saturn in Gemini—You're a deep thinker, with lofty ideals—a good position for scientific studies. You may be quite shy, speak slowly, or have fears or difficulty communicating. You'll take shelter in abstract ideas when dealing with emotional issues.

Uranus in Gemini—You are the first generation of the information era. Electronic mass communication developed at breakneck speed in your lifetime. You were watching TV since childhood, and now stock up on fax machines, modems, car telephones, not to mention the most sophisticated home telephone systems. You are the generation that popularized the talk show—you are forever reaching out in new ways.

NEPTUNE was not in GEMINI in this century.

Pluto in Gemini—A time of mass suggestion and breakthroughs in communication. Many brilliant writers, such as Ernest Hemingway and F. Scott Fitzgerald, were born in this phase. Henry Miller, James Joyce, and D. H. Lawrence scandalized the world with explicit sex in literature. Muckraking journalism and psychoanalysis (talk therapy) transformed both journalism and mental health fields.

Planets in Cancer

These planets are more nurturing, sensitive, and emotionally self-protective.

Moon in Cancer—The moon is strongest here, making you the zodiac nurturer—one who needs to be needed. You have an excellent memory and an intuitive understanding of the needs of others. You are happiest at home and may work in a home office or turn your corner of the company into a home away from home. Work that supplies food and shelter, occult studies, and psychology could take advantage of this lunar position.

Mercury in Cancer—You have empathy for others—can read their feelings. You are intuitive, rather than logical. And your thoughts are always colored by your emotions. You have an excellent memory and imagination.

Venus in Cancer—You can be "Daddy's girl" or "Mama's boy," like the late Liberace. You love to be babied, coddled, and protected in a cozy, secure home. Men with this position are attracted to old-fashioned femininity, Victorian lace fantasies. Women are attracted to those who make you feel secure, well provided for. You could also have a secret love life or clandestine arrangement with a sugar daddy. You love to mother others as well.

Mars in Cancer—You are given to moods and can be quite crabby. This may be due to a fragile sense of security. You are quite self-protective and secretive about your life, which might make you appear untrustworthy or manipulative to others. Try not to take things so much to heart—cultivate a sense of impersonality or detachment. Sexually, you are tender and sensitive, a very protective lover.

Jupiter in Cancer—This Jupiter has a big safe-deposit box, an attic piled to overflowing with boxes of treasures. You may still have your christening dress or your beloved high school sweater. This Jupiter loves to accumulate things, to save for a rainy day, or gather collections. Negatively, you could be a hoarder with closets full of things you'll never use. This protective, nurturing Jupiter often has many mouths to feed— human or animal. Naturally, this placement produces great restaurateurs and hotel managers. The shipping business is also a good bet.

Saturn in Cancer—Some very basic fears could center on your early home environment, overcoming a negative childhood influence to establish a sense of security. You may fear being mothered or smothered—and be tested in your female relationships. You may have to learn to be objective and distance yourself emotionally when threatened or when dealing with negative feelings such as jealousy or guilt.

Uranus in Cancer—Your generation grew up at a time when women's roles were being redefined and the concept of the tight-knit nuclear family was changing. This was also the time of the family shows on electronic media, such as "I Love Lucy," "I Remember Mama," "Father Knows Best." Since divorce became commonplace with your generation, you probably have some unusual ideas about marriage and family. Your generation matured at the time of New Age movements, renewed interest in dreams, psychic phenomena.

Neptune in Cancer—Those with this placement were born in the first quarter of the century. This was a time when family ties extended to the nation—motherhood, the homeland, flag-waving patriotism characterizes this Neptune. Many of you, such as Julia Child and Dr. Spock, have found ways to glamorize and profit from homemaking and child rearing.

Pluto in Cancer—A time of mass manipulation by emotional appeals. Dictators pushed patriotism to extremes. Women's rights legislation transformed the role of women. You who have this placement are deeply sentimental, place great value on emotional and financial security, because this was the time of the Great Depression.

Planets in Leo

These planets show their boldest, most flamboyant showbiz side.

Moon in Leo—You need to be treated like royalty! Strong support, loyalty, and loud applause win your heart. You rule over your territory, and resent anyone who intrudes on your turf. Your attraction to the finer things in people and in your lifestyle could give you a snobbish outlook. But basically you have a warm, passionate, loyal, emotional nature that gives generously to those you deem worthy.

Mercury in Leo—You express yourself dramatically and hold the attention of others. You think "big"—and prefer to skip the details. You are a good salesperson and public speaker.

Venus in Leo—You're an "Uptown Girl" or boy who loves "Putting on the Ritz," where you can consort with elegant people, dress extravagantly, and be the center of attention. Think of Coco Chanel, who piled on the jewelry and decorated tweed suits with gold braid. You dress and act like a star, but you may be attracted to hangers-on and flatterers rather than relationships with solid value.

Mars in Leo—This phase fills you with self-confidence and charisma. You come on strong, with show-biz flair. In fact you'll head right for the spotlight. Sexually, you're a giver—but you do demand the royal treatment in return. You enjoy giving orders and can create quite a scene if you're disobeyed. At some point, you may have to learn some lessons in humility.

Jupiter in Leo—Naturally warm, romantic, and playful, you can't get too much attention or applause. Politics or show business—anywhere you can perform for an audience —are lucky for you. You love the good life and are happy to share your wealth with others. Negatively, you could be extravagant and tend to hog center stage. Let others take a bow from time to time. Also, be careful not to overdo or overspend.

Saturn in Leo—This phase can bring ego problems. Because you have not received the love you crave, you could be an overly strict, dictatorial parent. You may demand respect and a position of leadership at any cost. You may have to watch a tendency toward rigidity and withholding affection. Learn to relax, have fun, lighten up!

Uranus in Leo—This period coincided with the rise of rock and roll and the heydey of Hollywood. Self-expression (Leo) led to the exhibitionism of the sixties. Electronic media was used skillfully for self-promotion. This "thirty-something" generation may have a very eccentric kind of charisma and a life sparked by unusual love affairs. Your children also may be out of the ordinary in some way. Where this planet falls in your chart, you'll show the full force of your personality in a unique way, like tennis great Martina Navratilova.

Neptune in Leo—Here was the glamour of the twenties, the beginning of the "star system" in Hollywood. Lavish spending blurred the harsh realities of the day. When Neptune left Leo in 1929, this coincided with the stock market crash. Those born with this placement have a flair for drama but may idealize fame without realizing there's a price to pay.

Pluto in Leo—This is the do-your-own-thing generation—who place extreme emphasis on self-expression. Flamboyant performers swayed the masses and those born during this time—such as Mick Jagger and John Lennon and the rock-and-roll stars—transformed the entertainment business. You born in this generation reflect this powerful Pluto's star quality, creativity, and self-centeredness.

Planets in Virgo

These planets show their most practical analytical side.

Moon in Virgo—This moon often draws you to situations in which you play the role of healer, teacher, or critic. You may find it difficult to accept others as they are or enjoy what you have. The Virgo moon, negatively, can be hard on others and yourself—you may have impossible standards and be constantly judging others to see if they "measure up." Take it easy!

Mercury in Virgo—You are a natural critic. You pay attention to details and have a talent for thorough analysis, although you tend to focus on the practical side of things. Teaching and editing come naturally to you.

Venus in Virgo—This Venus is attracted to perfect order, but underneath your pristine white dress is some naughty black lace! You fall for those who you can "make over" or improve in some way. You may also like those in the medical profession. Here Venus may express itself best through some kind of service—giving loving support. You may find it difficult to show your true feelings, to really let go in intimate moments.

Mars in Virgo—You are a worker bee, a "Felix Unger" character who notices every detail. This is a thorough, painstaking Mars who worries a great deal about making mistakes—this "worrier" tendency may lead to very tightly strung nerves under your controlled facade. Your energy can be expressed positively in a field such as teaching or editing; however, your tendency to find fault could make you a hard-to-please lover. Learning to delegate and praise, rather than do everything perfectly yourself, could make you easier to live with. You enjoy a good mental companionship, with less emphasis on sex and no emotional turmoil.

Jupiter in Virgo—You like to work! In fact, work can be more interesting than play for you. You have a sharp eye for details and notice every flaw! Be careful not to get caught up in nitpicking. You expect nothing short of perfection from others. Finding practical solutions to problems and helping others make the most of themselves are better uses for this Jupiter. Consider some form of health work, nutrition, medicine, or education.

Saturn in Virgo—You can be very hard on yourself, making yourself sick by worrying about every little detail. You must learn to set priorities, discriminate, and laugh!

Uranus in Virgo—Your generation came at a time of student rebellions, the civil rights movement, and mass acceptance of health foods. You'll be concerned with pollution and cleaning up the environment. You could revolutionize the healing arts, making nontraditional methods acceptable. This generation has also campaigned against the use of dangerous pesticides and cigarette smoking.

Neptune in Virgo—This Neptune glamorizes health and fitness (e.g., Jane Fonda). This generation invented fitness videos, marathon running, television sports. You may include psychotherapy as part of your mental health regime. You glamorized the workplace, and your devotion to working overtime and weekends inspired the term *workaholics*.

Pluto in Virgo—This is the "Yuppie" generation that sparked a mass movement toward fitness, health, career. During this generation, machines were invented to process the detail work efficiently. Inventions took a practical turn: answering machines, sophisticated telephones, office copiers, which helped transform the workplace.

Planets in Libra

These planets are concerned with relationships, aesthetics, and ideals.

Moon in Libra—Your emotional role is partnership-oriented. You may find it difficult to do things alone. You need the emotional balance of a strong "other." You thrive in an elegant, harmonious atmosphere, where you get attention and flattery. This moon needs to keep it light. Heavy emotions cause your Libran moon's scales to swing precariously. So does an overly possessive or demanding partner.

Mercury in Libra—You are a smooth talker, with a graceful gift of gab. Though skilled in diplomacy and debate, you may vacillate in making decisions, forever juggling the pros and cons. You speak in elegant, well-modulated tones.

Venus in Libra—"I Feel Pretty" sings this Venus. You love a beautiful, harmonious, luxurious atmosphere. Many artists and musicians thrive with this Venus, with its natural feeling for the balance of colors and sounds. In love, you make a very compatible partner in a supportive relationship where there are few confrontations. You can't stand arguments or argumentative people. The good looks of your partner may also be a deciding factor.

Mars in Libra—You are a passive aggressor who avoids confrontations and charms people into doing what you want. You do best in a position where you can exercise your great diplomatic skills. Mars is in its detriment in Libra, and expends much energy deciding which course of action to take. However, setting a solid goal in life, perhaps one that expresses your passion for beauty, justice, or art, could give you the vantage point you need to achieve success. In love, like Michael Douglas, you'll seek beauty in your partner and surroundings.

Jupiter in Libra—You function best when you have a stimulating partner. You also need harmonious, beautiful surroundings. Chances are, you have closets full of fashionable clothes. The serious side of this Jupiter has an excellent sense of fair play, and often plays the diplomat or judge. Careers in law, the arts, or fashion are favored.

Saturn in Libra—You may have your most successful marriage (or your first) later in life, because you must learn to stand on your own first. How to relate to others is one of your major lessons. Your great sense of fairness makes you a good judge or lawyer, or a prominent diplomat like former Secretary of State Henry Kissinger.

Uranus in Libra—Born at a time when the divorce rate soared and the women's lib movement gained ground, this generation will have some revolutionary ideas about marriage and partnerships. You may have an on-again, off-again relationship, choose unusual partners, or prefer to stay uncommitted. You'll also pioneer concepts in justice and revolutionize the arts.

Neptune in Libra—Born at a time when "Ozzie and Harriet" was the marital ideal, this generation went on to glamorize "relating" in ways that idealized equality and is still trying to find its balance in marriage. There have been many divorces as this generation tries to adapt traditional marriage concepts to modern times—and allow both sexes free expression.

Pluto in Libra—As this generation now begins to assert itself, we will see the reflection of the time of their birth—the 1970s and early 1980s. Attitudes toward relationships were transformed during this time from an emphasis on open relationships to more committed and safe partnerships. Landmark legislation on gay rights, euthanasia, and the ERA took place. Marital partnerships emphasized equal sharing.

Planets in Scorpio

These planets function in a very intense, focused, emotional way.

Moon in Scorpio—You take disappointments very hard and are often drawn to extreme situations, dealing with issues of power and control. You need a stable, secure emotional life, because you are especially vulnerable to jealousy. Meaningful work could provide a healthy outlet to diffuse your intense needs. Medicine, occult work, police work, and psychology are good possibilities.

Mercury in Scorpio—You have a sharp mind and can be sarcastic and prone to making cutting remarks. You have a penetrating insight and will stop at nothing to get to the heart of matters. You are an excellent and thorough researcher or detective. You enjoy problems that challenge your investigative skills.

Venus in Scorpio—Here, Venus wants "Body and Soul." Your attraction to the dark and mysterious could involve you with the wrong people—just to figure them out. You know how to keep a secret and have quite a few of your own. This is a very intense placement, where you can be preoccupied with sex and power. Living dangerously adds spice to your life, but don't get burned. All that's intense appeals to you—heady perfume, deep rich colors, dark woods, spicy foods.

Mars in Scorpio—You have a powerful drive (relax, sometimes!) that could become an obsession. So learn to use this energy wisely and well. For Mars in Scorpio hates to compromise, loves with "all or nothing" fever (while it lasts), and can become jealous or manipulative if you don't get your way! But your powerful concentration and nonstop stamina is an asset in challenging fields like medicine or scientific research. You're the Master Planner, a super-strategist who, when well-directed, can achieve important goals.

Jupiter in Scorpio—This phase loves the power of handling other people's money—or lives! Others see you as having nerves of steel. You have luck in detective work, sex-related ventures, psychotherapy, research, the occult, or tax matters—anything that involves a mystery. At least one great master spy has this placement. You're always going to extremes, testing the limits gives you a thrill. Your timing is excellent—you'll wait for the perfect moment to make your moves. Negatively this Jupiter could use power to achieve selfish ends.

Saturn in Scorpio—Your tests arise when you handle situations involving the control of others. You could fear depending on others financially or sexually—or there could be a blurring of the lines between sex and money. Sexual tests, periods of celibacy (resulting from fear of "merging" with another), sex for money are some ways this could manifest itself.

Uranus in Scorpio—Uranus here shook up our sexual ideas, and this generation (now adults) will have unorthodox sex lives, will delve beneath the surface to explore life after death, mediumship, transformation of any sort. This time signaled public awareness of the New Age. Body and mind control will be an issue with this generation—and they may explore innovative high-tech methods to do it, making breakthroughs in medicine and scientific research.

Neptune in Scorpio—Because of their healing, regenerative powers, this generation will be involved in rescuing the planet from the effects of the abuse of power. Born at a time that glamorized sex and drugs, this generation matured at a time when the price was paid in sexually transmitted diseases and abuses of drugs like cocaine. The emphasis on transformative spiritual power is especially heightened in their lives.

Pluto in Scorpio—Since August 1984, Pluto has been moving through its ruling sign of Scorpio, coming as close to the earth as its orbit will allow, and giving us the full force of its transformative power. Devastating, sexually transmitted diseases such as AIDS, nuclear power controversies, extreme turnabouts in international politics are signs of this tiny planet's force. It may be helpful to remember that Pluto clears the decks in order to start anew. It's the phoenix rising from the ashes that should hearten those of you who are undergoing Pluto transformations in your life. Babies born now will reflect Scorpio concerns such as sex, birth and death (and transcending death), nuclear power.

Planets in Sagittarius

Planets here expand personal freedom and elevate their energies.

Moon in Sagittarius—This moon needs freedom—you can't stand to be possessed by anyone. You have emotional wanderlust and may need a constant dose of mental and spiritual stimulation. But you cope with the fluctuations of life with good humor and a spirit of adventure. You may find great satisfaction in exotic situations, foreign travels, and spiritual studies, rather than in intense relationships.

Mercury in Sagittarius—You have a great sense of humor but a tendency toward tactlessness. You enjoy telling others what you see as the truth "for their own good." You can be dogmatic when you feel you're in the right, and you can expound endlessly on your own ideas. Watch a tendency to puff up ideas unrealistically (however, this talent could serve you well in sales positions).

Venus in Sagittarius—Travel, athletics, New Age philosophies, and a casual and carefree lifestyle appeal to you. You are attracted to exciting idealistic types who give you plenty of space. Large animals, especially horses, are part of your life. You probably have a four-wheel-drive vehicle—or a motorized skateboard—anything to keep moving.

Mars in Sagittarius—In Sagittarius, the "conquering hero" sets off on a crusade. You're great at getting things off the ground! Your challenge is to consider the consequences of your actions. In love with freedom, you don't always make the best marriage partner. Love 'em and leave 'em could be your motto. You may also gravitate toward risk and adventure and may have great athletic skill. You're best off in a situation where you can express your love of adventure, philosophy, and travel or where you can use artistic talents to elevate the lives of others, like Johann Sebastian Bach.

Jupiter in Sagittarius—In its natural place, Jupiter compels you to expand your mind, travel far from home, collect college degrees. This is the placement of the philosopher, the gambler, the animal trainer, the publisher. You have an excellent sense of humor and a cheerful disposition. This placement often works with animals, especially horses.

Saturn in Sagittarius—This phase accepts nothing at face value. You are the opposite of the "happy-go-lucky" Sagittarius. With Saturn here, your beliefs must be fully examined and tested. Firsthand experience, without the guidance of dogma, gurus, or teachers is your best education. This Saturn has little tolerance for another authority. You won't follow a "dream" unless you understand the idea behind it.

Uranus in Sagittarius—Those born in the 1980s could be the first generation to travel in outer space! Uranus (electronic innovation) in Sagittarius (long trips) tempts us to make speculations like this. Earlier in this century, the Wright brothers and Charles Lindberg began to fly during this transit. It's for sure that this generation will make some unusual modes of religion, philosophy, and higher education as well as long-distance travel.

Neptune in Sagittarius—In the 1970s and early 1980s, the New Age was born and astronaut travel became a reality. The Neptune influence glamorized mysticism, meditation, new approaches to religion—with gurus, and mind expansion via drugs. This generation will take a creative and imaginative approach to spiritual and philosophical life, with emphasis on mysticism, clairvoyance. Perhaps they will develop new spiritually oriented schools. They will also redefine the use of petroleum (Neptune-ruled) in travel.

Pluto in Sagittarius—Pluto moves into Sagittarius on January 17, 1995, a day to mark on your calendar! This should signal a time of great expansion and transformation physically, mentally, and spiritually. Perhaps Pluto, the planet of extremes, will make space travel (or space visitors) a reality. There will be new emphasis on publishing, higher education, religion, animal rights. And we'll be concerned with elevating our lives with a higher sense of purpose—something to look forward to at the close of the century!

Planets in Capricorn

Planets here function in their most organized, result-oriented way.

Moon in Capricorn—In its detriment, the moon here is cool and calculating. You get serious about matters of prestige and position, rather than romance. Although you are dutiful toward those you love, you expend most of your emotion on your climb to the top of the business or social ladder. Improving your position in life gives you the most satisfaction.

Mercury in Capricorn—This phase has excellent mental discipline. You take a serious, orderly approach and play by the rules. You have a super-organized mind that grasps structures easily, though you may lack originality. You have a dry sense of humor.

Venus in Capricorn—This ambitious Venus may seem calculating, but underneath you're insecure and want a substantial relationship you can count on. However, it wouldn't hurt if your beloved could help you up the ladder professionally. This Venus is often attracted to objects and people of a different generation (you could marry someone much older—or younger)—antiques, traditional clothing (sometimes worn in a very "today" way), and dignified conservative behavior are trademarks.

Mars in Capricorn—Mars is exalted in Capricorn, a "chief executive" placement that gives you a drive for success and the discipline to achieve it. You deliberately aim for status and a high position in life, and you'll keep climbing, despite the odds. This Mars will work for what you get. You are well organized and persistent—a winning combination. Sexually, you have a strong, earthy drive—but may prefer someone who can be useful to you rather than someone flashy or superficially fascinating.

Jupiter in Capricorn—You are luckiest working in an established situation, within a traditional structure. In the sign of caution and restraint, Jupiter is thrifty rather than a big spender. You accumulate duties and responsibilities, which is fine for business leadership. You'll expand in those areas where you can achieve respect, prestige, or social position. People with this position are especially concerned that nothing be wasted. You might have great success in a recycling or renovation business.

Saturn in Capricorn—You are sensitive to public opinion and achieving a high-status image. You are not a big risk taker, because you do not want to compromise your position. In its most powerful place, Saturn is the teacher par excellence, giving structure and form to your life. Your persistence will assure you a continual climb to the top.

Uranus in Capricorn—Passing through Capricorn since 1988, Uranus will be shaking up our lives in this area until 1996. During this time expect the foundations of traditional structures to rattle, if not crumble like the Berlin Wall. High-tech (Uranus) practical gadgets are revolutionizing our daily lives. Home and portable computers and fax machines bring new independence to the workplace. Increasing numbers of us will be working on our own. Those born with this placement will take an independent, innovative approach to their careers. They'll also have the task of reconciling tradition with change.

Neptune in Capricorn—Beginning in 1984 and continuing until 1998, this has been a time when material values are first glamorized, then dashed on the rocks of reality. As first Saturn, then Uranus, pass by, Neptune performs its dissolving magic on Capricorn's walls of tradition and structure everywhere. In the marketplace, we should see some especially disillusioned management as Neptune dissolves traditional corporate structures.

PLUTO will not be in CAPRICORN in this century.

Planets in Aquarius

Planets here show their most independent, original, and humanitarian functions.

Moon in Aquarius—This is a gregarious moon, happiest when surrounded by people. You're everybody's buddy—as long as no one gets too close. You'd rather stay pals. You make your own rules in emotional situations, may have a radically different life or love-style. Intimate relationships may feel too confining—and you need plenty of space.

Mercury in Aquarius—This phase has a highly original point of view, combined with good mental focus. You are an independent thinker, who would break the rules to make your point. You are, however, fixed mentally, and are reluctant to change your mind once it is made up—and you could come across as a know-it-all.

Venus in Aquarius—You love to be surrounded by people, but are uncomfortable with intense emotions (steer clear of Venus in Scorpio!). You like a spontaneous lifestyle, full of surprises. You make your own rules in everything you do, including love. The avant garde, high technology, and possible unusual sexual experiences attract you.

Mars in Aquarius—This phase is a visionary and often a revolutionary who stands out from the crowd. You are innovative and highly original in your methods. Sexually, you could go for out-of-the-ordinary relationships. You have a rebellious streak and like to shake people up a bit. Intimacy can be a problem—you may keep lots of people around you or isolate yourself to prevent others from getting too close.

Jupiter in Aquarius—This phase is lucky when doing good in the world. You are extremely idealistic and think in the most expansive terms about improving society at large—an excellent position for a politician or labor leader.

You're "everybody's buddy" who can relate to people of diverse backgrounds. You are luckiest when you can operate away from rigid rules and conservative organizations.

Saturn in Aquarius—Saturn here can make you feel like an outsider, one who doesn't fit into the group. There may be a lack of trust in others, a kind of defensiveness that could engender defensiveness in return. Not a superficial social butterfly, your commitment to groups must have depth and humanitarian meaning.

Uranus in Aquarius—At home in its own sign, Uranus produced great innovative minds such as Orson Welles and Leonard Bernstein, plus many breakthroughs in science and technology. It will once again enter Aquarius in 1995–2002, when we can expect the unexpected, because this planet will be at its most revolutionary, eccentric, and brilliant. This generation will be much concerned with global issues that unite humanity, and with experimentation on every level.

NEPTUNE and PLUTO will not be in AQUARIUS in this century.

Planets in Pisces

These planets show their most sensitive, emotional side.

Moon in Pisces—This watery moon needs an emotional anchor to help you keep grounded in reality. Otherwise, you tend to escape through fantasies or intoxicating substances. Creative work could give you a far more productive way to express yourself and get away from it all. Working in a healing or helping profession is also good for you because you get satisfaction from helping the underdog. You naturally attract people with sob stories, but you should also cultivate friends with a positive, upbeat point of view.

Mercury in Pisces—This phase has a poetic mind that is receptive to psychic, intuitive influences. You may be vague and forgetful of details and find it difficult to work within a structure, but you are strong on creative expression. You'll express yourself in a very sympathetic, caring way. You should find work that uses your imaginative talents.

Venus in Pisces—"Why not take all of me," sings this exalted Venus, who loves to give. You may have a collection of stray animals, lost souls, the underprivileged, the lonely. Try to assess their motives in a clear light. You're a natural for theater, film, anything involving fantasy. Psychic or spiritual life also fascinates you, as does selfless service for a needy cause.

Mars in Pisces—You like to play different roles. Your ability to tune in and project others' emotions makes you a natural actor—many film and television personalities have this placement, such as Mary Tyler Moore, Jane Seymour, Cybill Shepherd, Burt Reynolds, and Jane Fonda. You understand how to use glamour and illusion for your own benefit. You can switch emotions on and off quickly, and you're especially good at getting sympathy. You'll go for romance, though real-life relationships never quite live up to your fantasies.

Jupiter in Pisces—You work best in a creative field or in one where you are helping the downtrodden. You exude sympathy and gravitate toward the underdog. Beware a tendency to be too self-sacrificing and overly emotional. You should also be careful not to overindulge in alcohol or drugs. Some lucky work areas: oil, fragrances, dance, footwear, alcohol, pharmaceuticals, and the arts, especially film.

Saturn in Pisces—This phase generates a sense of helplessness, of vulnerability, of feeling like a victim of circumstances. You could underestimate yourself or subordinate yourself to a powerful institution. This placement can give great wisdom, however, if you can manage to look inward to contemplation and meditation—like

Edgar Cayce—rather than outward, for solutions. You have the ability to cope!

Uranus in Pisces—Many of the early well-known TV personalities were born with this placement, because this generation was the first to exploit the electronic media. This was the time of Prohibition (Pisces rules alcohol) and the development of the film industry (also Pisces ruled). The next go-round, in the early 2000s, could bring on the Hollywood of the twenty-first century!

NEPTUNE and PLUTO will not be in PISCES in this century.

3

Look Up Your Planets

The following tables are provided so that you can look up the signs of seven major planets—Venus, Mars, Saturn, Jupiter, Uranus, Neptune, and Pluto. We do not have room for tables for the moon and Mercury, which change signs often.

How to Use the Venus Table

Find the year of your birth in the vertical column on the left, then follow across the page until you find the correct date. The Venus sign is at the top of that column.

How to Use the Mars, Saturn, and Jupiter Tables

Find the year of your birth date on the left side of each column. The dates the planet entered each sign are listed on the right side of each column. (Signs are abbreviated to the first three letters.) Your birthday should fall on or between each date listed, and your planetary placement should correspond to the earlier sign of that period.

How to Use the Uranus, Neptune, and Pluto Tables

Find your birthday in the list following each sign.

LOOK UP YOUR URANUS PLACEMENT by finding your birthday on the following lists:

URANUS IN ARIES BIRTH DATES:

March 31–November 4, 1927
January 13, 1928–June 6, 1934
October 10, 1934–March 28, 1935

URANUS IN TAURUS BIRTH DATES:

June 6, 1934–October 10, 1935
March 28, 1935–August 7, 1941
October 5, 1941–May 15, 1942

URANUS IN GEMINI BIRTH DATES:

August 7–October 5, 1941
May 15, 1942–August 30, 1948
November 12, 1948–June 10, 1949

URANUS IN CANCER BIRTH DATES:

August 30–November 12, 1948
June 10, 1949–August 24, 1955
January 28–June 10, 1956

URANUS IN LEO BIRTH DATES:

August 24, 1955–January 28, 1956
June 10, 1956–November 1, 1961
January 10–August 10, 1962

VENUS SIGNS 1901–2000

	Aries	Taurus	Gemini	Cancer	Leo	Virgo
1901	3/29-4/22	4/22-5/17	5/17-6/10	6/10-7/5	7/5-7/29	7/29-8/23
1902	5/7-6/3	6/3-6/30	6/30-7/25	7/25-8/19	8/19-9/13	9/13-10/7
1903	2/28-3/24	3/24-4/18	4/18-5/13	5/13-6/9	6/9-7/7	7/7-8/17 9/6-11/8
1904	3/13-5/7	5/7-6/1	6/1-6/25	6/25-7/19	7/19-8/13	8/13-9/6
1905	2/3-3/6 4/9-5/28	3/6-4/9 5/28-7/8	7/8-8/6	8/6-9/1	9/1-9/27	9/27-10/21
1906	3/1-4/7	4/7-5/2	5/2-5/26	5/26-6/20	6/20-7/16	7/16-8/11
1907	4/27-5/22	5/22-6/16	6/16-7/11	7/11-8/4	8/4-8/29	8/29-9/22
1908	2/14-3/10	3/10-4/5	4/5-5/5	5/5-9/8	9/8-10/8	10/8-11/3
1909	3/29-4/22	4/22-5/16	5/16-6/10	6/10-7/4	7/4-7/29	7/29-8/23
1910	5/7-6/3	6/4-6/29	6/30-7/24	7/25-8/18	8/19-9/12	9/13-10/6
1911	2/28-3/23	3/24-4/17	4/18-5/12	5/13-6/8	6/9-7/7	7/8-11/8
1912	4/13-5/6	5/7-5/31	6/1-6/24	6/24-7/18	7/19-8/12	8/13-9/5
1913	2/3-3/6 5/2-5/30	3/7-5/1 5/31-7/7	7/8-8/5	8/6-8/31	9/1-9/26	9/27-10/20
1914	3/14-4/6	4/7-5/1	5/2-5/25	5/26-6/19	6/20-7/15	7/16-8/10
1915	4/27-5/21	5/22-6/15	6/16-7/10	7/11-8/3	8/4-8/28	8/29-9/21
1916	2/14-3/9	3/10-4/5	4/6-5/5	5/6-9/8	9/9-10/7	10/8-11/2
1917	3/29-4/21	4/22-5/15	5/16-6/9	6/10-7/3	7/4-7/28	7/29-8/21
1918	5/7-6/2	6/3-6/28	6/29-7/24	7/25-8/18	8/19-9/11	9/12-10/5
1919	2/27-3/22	3/23-4/16	4/17-5/12	5/13-6/7	6/8-7/7	7/8-11/8
1920	4/12-5/6	5/7-5/30	5/31-6/23	6/24-7/18	7/19-8/11	8/12-9/4
1921	2/3-3/6 4/26-6/1	3/7-4/25 6/2-7/7	7/8-8/5	8/6-8/31	9/1-9/25	9/26-10/20
1922	3/13-4/6	4/7-4/30	5/1-5/25	5/26-6/19	6/20-7/14	7/15-8/9
1923	4/27-5/21	5/22-6/14	6/15-7/9	7/10-8/3	8/4-8/27	8/28-9/20
1924	2/13-3/8	3/9-4/4	4/5-5/5	5/6-9/8	9/9-10/7	10/8-11/12
1925	3/28-4/20	4/21-5/15	5/16-6/8	6/9-7/3	7/4-7/27	7/28-8/21

Libra	Scorpio	Sagittarius	Capricorn	Aquarius	Pisces
8/23-9/17	9/17-10/12	10/12-1/16	1/16-2/9	2/9	3/5-3/29
			11/7-12/5	12/5-1/11	
10/7-10/31	10/31-11/24	11/24-12/18	12/18-1/11	2/6-4/4	1/11-2/6
					4/4-5/7
8/17-9/6	12/9-1/5			1/11-2/4	2/4-2/28
11/8-12/9					
9/6-9/30	9/30-10/25	1/5-1/30	1/30-2/24	2/24-3/19	3/19-4/13
		10/25-11/18	11/18-12/13	12/13-1/7	
10/21-11/14	11/14-12/8	12/8-1/1/06			1/7-2/3
8/11-9/7	9/7-10/9	10/9-12/15	1/1-1/25	1/25-2/18	2/18-3/14
	12/15-12/25	12/25-2/6			
9/22-10/16	10/16-11/9	11/9-12/3	2/6-3/6	3/6-4/2	4/2-4/27
			12/3-12/27	12/27-1/20	
11/3-11/28	11/28-12/22	12/22-1/15			1/20-2/14
8/23-9/17	9/17-10/12	10/12-11/17	1/15-2/9	2/9-3/5	3/5-3/29
			11/17-12/5	12/5-1/15	
10/7-10/30	10/31-11/23	11/24-12/17	12/18-12/31	1/1-1/15	1/16-1/28
				1/29-4/4	4/5-5/6
11/19-12/8	12/9-12/31		1/1-1/10	1/11-2/2	2/3-2/27
9/6-9/30	1/1-1/4	1/5-1/29	1/30-2/23	2/24-3/18	3/19-4/12
	10/1-10/24	10/25-11/17	11/18-12/12	12/13-12/31	
10/21-11/13	11/14-12/7	12/8-12/31		1/1-1/6	1/7-2/2
8/11-9/6	9/7-10/9	10/10-12/5	1/1-1/24	1/25-2/17	2/18-3/13
	12-6/12-30	12/31			
9/22-10/15	10/16-11/8	1/1-2/6	2/7-3/6	3/7-4/1	4/2-4/26
		11/9-12/2	12/3-12/26	12/27-12/31	
11/3-11/27	11/28-12/21	12/22-12/31		1/1-1/19	1/20-2/13
8/22-9/16	9/17-10/11	1/1-1/14	1/15-2/7	2/8-3/4	3/5-3/28
		10/12-11/6	11/7-12/5	12/6-12/31	
10/6-10/29	10/30-11/22	11/23-12/16	12/17-12/31	1/1-4/5	4/6-5/6
11/9-12/8	12/9-12/31		1/1-1/9	1/10-2/2	2/3-2/26
9/5-9/30	1/1-1/3	1/4-1/28	1/29-2/22	2/23-3/18	3/19-4/11
	9/31-10/23	10/24-11/17	11/18-12/11	12/12-12/31	
10/21-11/13	11/14-12/7	12/8-12/31		1/1-1/6	1/7-2/2
8/10-9/6	9/7-10/10	10/11-11/28	1/1-1/24	1/25-2/16	2/17-3/12
	11/29-12/31				
9/21-10/14	1/1	1/2-2/6	2/7-3/5	3/6-3/31	4/1-4/26
	10/15-11/7	11/8-12/1	12/2-12/25	12/26-12/31	
11/3-11/26	11/27-12/21	12/22-12/31		1/1-1/19	1/20-2/12
8/22-9/15	9/16-10/11	1/1-1/14	1/15-2/7	2/8-3/3	3/4-3/27
		10-12/11-6	11/7-12/5	12/6-12/31	

VENUS SIGNS 1901–2000

	Aries	Taurus	Gemini	Cancer	Leo	Virgo
1926	5/7-6/2	6/3-6/28	6/29-7/23	7/24-8/17	8/18-9/11	9/12-10/5
1927	2/27-3/22	3/23-4/16	4/17-5/11	5/12-6/7	6/8-7/7	7/8-11/9
1928	4/12-5/5	5/6-5/29	5/30-6/23	6/24-7/17	7/18-8/11	8/12-9/4
1929	2/3-3/7 4/20-6/2	3/8-4/19 6/3-7/7	7/8-8/4	8/5-8/30	8/31-9/25	9/26-10/19
1930	3/13-4/5	4/6-4/30	5/1-5/24	5/25-6/18	6/19-7/14	7/15-8/9
1931	4/26-5/20	5/21-6/13	6/14-7/8	7/9-8/2	8/3-8/26	8/27-9/19
1932	2/12-3/8	3/9-4/3	4/4-5/5 7/13-7/27	5/6-7/12 7/28-9/8	9/9-10/6	10/7-11/1
1933	3/27-4/19	4/20-5/28	5/29-6/8	6/9-7/2	7/3-7/26	7/27-8/20
1934	5/6-6/1	6/2-6/27	6/28-7/22	7/23-8/16	8/17-9/10	9/11-10/4
1935	2/26-3/21	3/22-4/15	4/16-5/10	5/11-6/6	6/7-7/6	7/7-11/8
1936	4/11-5/4	5/5-5/28	5/29-6/22	6/23-7/16	7/17-8/10	8/11-9/4
1937	2/2-3/8 4/14-6/3	3/9-4/17 6/4-7/6	7/7-8/3	8/4-8/29	8/30-9/24	9/25-10/18
1938	3/12-4/4	4/5-4/28	4/29-5/23	5/24-6/18	6/19-7/13	7/14-8/8
1939	4-25/5/19	5/20-6/13	6/14-7/8	7/9-8/1	8/2-8/25	8/26-9/19
1940	2/12-3/7	3/8-4/3	4/4-5/5 7/5-7/31	5/6-7/4 8/1-9/8	9/9-10/5	10/6-10/31
1941	3/27-4/19	4/20-5/13	5/14-6/6	6/7-7/1	7/2-7/26	7/27-8/20
1942	5/6-6/1	6/2-6/26	6/27-7/22	7/23-8/16	8/17-9/9	9/10-10/3
1943	2/25-3/20	3/21-4/14	4/15-5/10	5/11-6/6	6/7-7/6	7/7-11/8
1944	4/10-5/3	5/4-5/28	5/29-6/21	6/22-7/16	7/17-8/9	8/10-9/2
1945	2/2-3/10 4/7-6/3	3/11-4/6 6/4-7/6	7/7-8/3	8/4-8/29	8/30-9/23	9/24-10/18
1946	3/11-4/4	4/5-4/28	4/29-5/23	5/24-6/17	6/18-7/12	7/13-8/8
1947	4/25-5/19	5/20-6/12	6/13-7/7	7/8-8/1	8/2-8/25	8/26-9/18
1948	2/11-3/7	3/8-4/3	4/4-5/6 6/29-8/2	5/7-6/28 8/3-9/7	9/8-10/5	10/6-10/31
1949	3/26-4/19	4/20-5/13	5/14-6/6	6/7-6/30	7/1-7/25	7/26-8/19
1950	5/5-5/31	6/1-6/26	6/27-7/21	7/22-8/15	8/16-9/9	9/10-10/3
1951	2/25-3/21	3/22-4/15	4/16-5/10	5/11-6/6	6/7-7/7	7/8-11/9

Libra	Scorpio	Sagittarius	Capricorn	Aquarius	Pisces
10/6-10/29	10/30-11/22	11/23-12/16	12/17-12/31	1/1-4/5	4/6-5/6
11/10-12/8	12/9-12/31	1/1-1/7	1/8	1/9-2/1	2/2-2/26
9/5-9/28	1/1-1/3	1/4-1/28	1/29-2/22	2/23-3/17	3/18-4/11
	9/29-10/23	10/24-11/16	11/17-12/11	12/12-12/31	
10/20-11/12	11/13-12/6	12/7-12/30	12/31	1/1-1/5	1/6-2/2
8/10-9/6	9/7-10/11	10/12-11/21	1/1-1/23	1/24-2/16	2/17-3/12
	11/22-12/31				
9/20-10/13	1/1-1/3	1/4-2/6	2/7-3/4	3/5-3/31	4/1-4/25
	10/14-11/6	11/7-11/30	12/1-12/24	12/25-12/31	
11/2-11/25	11/26-12/20	12/21-12/31		1/1-1/18	1/19-2/11
8/21-9/14	9/15-10/10	1/1-1/13	1/14-2/6	2/7-3/2	3/3-3/26
		10/11-11/5	11/6-12/4	12/5-12/31	
10/5-10/28	10/29-11/21	11/22-12/15	12/16-12/31	1/1-4/5	4/6-5/5
11/9-12/7	12/8-12/31		1/1-1/7	1/8-1/31	2/1-2/25
9/5-9/27	1/1-1/2	1/3-1/27	1/28-2/21	2/22-3/16	3/17-4/10
	9/28-10/22	10/23-11/15	11/16-12/10	12/11-12/31	
10/19-11/11	11/12-12/5	12/6-12/29	12/30-12/31	1/1-1/5	1/6-2/1
8/9-9/6	9/7-10/13	10/14-11/14	1/1-1/22	1/23-2/15	2/16-3/11
	11/15-12/31				
9/20-10/13	1/1-1/3	1/4-2/5	2/6-3/4	3/5-3/30	3/31-4/24
	10/14-11/6	11/7-11/30	12/1-12/24	12/25-12/31	
11/1-11/25	11/26-12/19	12/20-12/31		1/1-1/18	1/19-2/11
8/21-9/14	9/15-10/9	1/1-1/12	1/13-2/5	2/6-3/1	3/2-3/26
		10/10-11/5	11/6-12/4	12/5-12/31	
10/4-10/27	10/28-11/20	11/21-12/14	12/15-12/31	1/1-4/4	4/6-5/5
11/9-12/7	12/8-12/31		1/1-1/7	1/8-1/31	2/1-2/24
9/3-9/27	1/1-1/2	1/3-1/27	1/28-2/20	2/21-3/16	3/17-4/9
	9/28-10/21	10/22-11/15	11/16-12/10	12/11-12/31	
10/19-11/11	11/12-12/5	12/6-12/29	12/30-12/31	1/1-1/4	1/5-2/1
8/9-9/6	9/7-10/15	10/16-11/7	1/1-1/21	1/22-2/14	2/15-3/10
	11/8-12/31				
9/19-10/12	1/1-1/4	1/5-2/5	2/6-3/4	3/5-3/29	3/30-4/24
	10/13-11/5	11/6-11/29	11/30-12/23	12/24-12/31	
11/1-1/25	11/26-12/19	12/20-12/31		1/1-1/17	1/18-2/10
8/20-9/14	9/15-10/9	1/1-1/12	1/13-2/5	2/6-3/1	3/2-3/25
		10/10-11/5	11/6-12/5	12/6-12/31	
10/4-10/27	10/28-11/20	11/21-12/13	12/14-12/31	1/1-4/5	4/6-5/4
11/10-12/7	12/8-12/31		1/1-1/7	1/8-1/31	2/1-2/24

VENUS SIGNS 1901–2000

	Aries	Taurus	Gemini	Cancer	Leo	Virgo
1952	4/10-5/4	5/5-5/28	5/29-6/21	6/22-7/16	7/17-8/9	8/10-9/3
1953	2/2-3/13	3/4-3/31	7/8-8/3	8/4-8/29	8/30-9/24	9/25-10/18
	4/1-6/5	6/6-7/7				
1954	3/12-4/4	4/5-4/28	4/29-5/23	5/24-6/17	6/18-7/13	7/14-8/8
1955	4/25-5/19	5/20-6/13	6/14-7/7	7/8-8/1	8/2-8/25	8/26-9/18
1956	2/12-3/7	3/8-4/4	4/5-5/7	5/8-6/23	9/9-10/5	10/6-10/31
			6:24-8/4	8/5-9/8		
1957	3/26-4/19	4/20-5/13	5/14-6/6	6/7-7/1	7/2-7/26	7/7-8/19
1958	5/6-5/31	6/1-6/26	6/27-7/22	7/23-8/15	8/16-9/9	9/10-10/3
1959	2/25-3/20	3/21-4/14	4/15-5/10	5/11-6/6	6/7-7/8	7/9-9/20
					9/21-9/24	9/25-11/9
1960	4/10-5/3	5/4-5/28	5/29-6/21	6/22-7/15	7/16-8/9	8/10-9/2
1961	2/3-6/5	6/6-7/7	7/8-8/3	8/4-8/29	8/30-9/23	9/24-10/17
1962	3/11-4/3	4/4-4/28	4/29-5/22	5/23-6/17	6/18-7/12	7/13-8/8
1963	4/24-5/18	5/19-6/12	6/13-7/7	7/8-7/31	8/1-8/25	8/26-9/18
1964	2/11-3/7	3/8-4/4	4/5-5/9	5/10-6/17	9/9-10/5	10/6-10/31
			6/18-8/5	8/6-9/8		
1965	3/26-4/18	4/19-5/12	5/13-6/6	6/7-6/30	7/1-7/25	7/26-8/19
1966	5/6-6/31	6/1-6/26	6/27-7/21	7/22-8/15	8/16-9/8	9/9-10/2
1967	2/24-3/20	3/21-4/14	4/15-5/10	5/11-6/6	6/7-7/8	7/9-9/9
					9/10-10/1	10/2-11/9
1968	4/9-5/3	5/4-5/27	5/28-6/20	6/21-7/15	7/16-8/8	8/9-9/2
1969	2/3-6/6	6/7-7/6	7/7-8/3	8/4-8/28	8/29-9/22	9/23-10/17
1970	3/11-4/3	4/4-4/27	4/28-5/22	5/23-6/16	6/17-7/12	7/13-8/8
1971	4/24-5/18	5/19-6/12	6/13-7/6	7/7-7/31	8/1-8/24	8/25-9/17
1972	2/11-3/7	3/8-4/3	4/4-5/10	5/11-6/11	9/9-10/5	10/6-10/30
			6/12-8/6	8/7-9/8		
1973	3/25-4/18	4/18-5/12	5/13-6/5	6/6-6/29	7/1-7/25	7/26-8/19
1974						
	55-5/31	6/1-6/25	6/26-7/21	7/22-8/14	8/15-9/8	9/9-10/2
1975	2/24-3/20	3/21-4/13	4/14-5/9	5/10-6/6	6/7-7/9	7/10-9/2
					9/3-10/4	10/5-11/9

Libra	Scorpio	Sagittarius	Capricorn	Aquarius	Pisces
9/4-9/27	1/1-1/2	1/3-1/27	1/28-2/20	2/21-3/16	3/17-4/9
	9/28-10/21	10/22-11/15	11/16-12/10	12/11-12/31	
10/19-11/11	11/12-12/5	12/6-12/29	12/30-12/31	1/1-1/5	1/6-2/1
8/9-9/6	9/7-10/22	10/23-10/27	1/1-1/22	1/23-2/15	2/16-3/11
	10/28-12/31				
9/19-10/13	1/1-1/6	1/7-2/5	2/6-3/4	3/5-3/30	3/31-4/24
	10/14-11/5	11/6-11/30	12/1-12/24	12/25-12/31	
11/1-11/25	11/26-12/19	12/20-12/31		1/1-1/17	1/18-2/11
8/20-9/14	9/15-10/9	1/1-1/12	1/13-2/5	2/6-3/1	3/2-3/25
		10/10-11/5	11/6-12/16	12/7-12/31	
10/4-10/27	10/28-11/20	11/21-12/14	12/15-12/31	1/1-4/6	4/7-5/5
11/10-12/7	12/8-12/31		1/1-1/7	1/8-1/31	2/1-2/24
9/3-9/26	1/1-1/2	1/3-1/27	1/28-2/20	2/21-3/15	3/16-4/9
	9/27-10/21	10/22-11/15	11/16-12/10	12/11-12/31	
10/18-11/11	11/12-12/4	12/5-12/28	12/29-12/31	1/1-1/5	1/6-2/2
8/9-9/6	9/7-12/31		1/1-1/21	1/22-2/14	2/15-3/10
9/19-10/12	1/1-1/6	1/7-2/5	2/6-3/4	3/5-3/29	3/30-4/23
	10/13-11/5	11/6-11/29	11/30-12/23	12/24-12/31	
11/1-11/24	11/25-12/19	12/20-12/31		1/1-1/16	1/17-2/10
8/20-9/13	9/14-10/9	1/1-1/12	1/13-2/5	2/6-3/1	3/2-3/25
		10/10-11/5	11/6-12/7	12/8-12/31	
10/3-10/26	10/27-11/19	11/20-12/13	2/7-2/25	1/1-2/6	4/7-5/5
			12/14-12/31	2/26-4/6	
11/10-12/7	12/8-12/23		1/1-1/6	1/7-1/30	1/31-2/23
9/3-9/26	1/1	1/2-1/26	1/27-2/20	2/21-3/15	3/16-4/8
	9/27-10/21	10/22-11/14	11/15-12/9	12/10-12/31	
10/18-11/10	11/11-12/4	12/5-12/28	12/29-12/31	1/1-1/4	1/5-2/2
8/9-9/7	9/8-12/31		1/1-1/21	1/22-2/14	2/15-3/10
9/18-10/11	1/1-1/7	1/8-2/5	2/6-3/4	3/5-3/29	3/30-4/23
	10/12-11/5	11/6-11/29	11/30-12/23	12/24-12/31	
	11/25-12/18	12/19-12/31		1/1-1/16	1/17-2/10
10/31-11/24					
8/20-9/13		1/1-1/12	1/13-2/4	2/5-2/28	3/1-3/24
		10/9-11/5	11/6-12/7	12/8-12/31	
			1/30-2/28	1/1-1/29	
10/3-10/26	10/27-11/19	11/20-12/13	12/14-12/31	3/1-4/6	4/7-5/4
			1/1-1/6	1/7-1/30	1/31-2/23
11/10-12/7	12/8-12/31				

VENUS SIGNS 1901–2000

	Aries	Taurus	Gemini	Cancer	Leo	Virgo
1976	4/8-5/2	5/2-5/27	5/27-6/20	6/20-7/14	7/14-8/8	8/8-9/1
1977	2/2-6/6	6/6-7/6	7/6-8/2	8/2-8/28	8/28-9/22	9/22-10/17
1978	3/9-4/2	4/2-4/27	4/27-5/22	5/22-6/16	6/16-7/12	7/12-8/6
1979	4/23-5/18	5/18-6/11	6/11-7/6	7/6-7/30	7/30-8/24	8/24-9/17
1980	2/9-3/6	3/6-4/3	4/3-5/12	5/12-6/5	9/7-10/4	10/4-10/30
			6/5-8/6	8/6-9/7		
1981	3/24-4/17	4/17-5/11	5/11-6/5	6/5-6/29	6/29-7/24	7/24-8/18
1982	5/4-5/30	5/30-6/25	6/25-7/20	7/20-8/14	8/14-9/7	9/7-10/2
1983	2/22-3/19	3/19-4/13	4/13-5/9	5/9-6/6	6/6-7/10	7/10-8/27
					8/27-10/5	10/5-11/9
1984	4/7-5/2	5/2-5/26	5/26-6/20	6/20-7/14	7/14-8/7	8/7-9/1
1985	2/2-6/6	6/8-7/6	7/6-8/2	8/2-8/28	8/28-9/22	9/22-10/16
1986	3/9-4/2	4/2-4/26	4/26-5/21	5/21-6/15	6/15-7/11	7/11-8/7
1987	4/22-5/17	5/17-6/11	6/11-7/5	7/5-7/30	7/30-8/23	8/23-9/16
1988	2/9-3/6	3/6-4/3	4/3-5/17	5/17-5/27	9/7-10/4	10/4-10/29
			5/27-8/6	8/6-9/7		
1989	3/23-4/16	4/16-5/11	5/11-6/4	6/4-6/29	6/29-7/24	7/24-8/18
1990	5/4-5/30	5/30-6/25	6/25-7/20	7/20-8/13	8/13-9/7	9/7-10/1
1991	2/22-3/18	3/18-4/13	4/13-5/9	5/9-6/6	6/6-7/11	7/11-8/21
					8/21-10/6	10/6-11/9
1992	4/7-5/1	5/1-5/26	5/26-6/19	6/19-7/13	7/13-8/7	8/7-8/31
1993	2/2-6/6	6/6-7/6	7/6-8/1	8/1-8/27	8/27-9/21	9/21-10/16
1994	3/8-4/1	4/1-4/26	4/26-5/21	5/21-6/15	6/15-7/11	7/11-8/7
1995	4/22-5/16	5/16-6/10	6/10-7/5	7/5-7/29	7/29-8/23	8/23-9/16
1996	2/9-3/6	3/6-4/3	4/3-8/7	8/7-9/7	9/7-10/4	10/4-10/29
1997	3/23-4/16	4/16-5/10	5/10-6/4	6/4-6/28	6/28-7/23	7/23-8/17
1998	5/3-5/29	5/29-6/24	6/24-7/19	7/19-8/13	8/13-9/6	9/6-9/30
1999	2/21-3/18	3/18-4/12	4/12-5/8	5/8-6/5	6/5-7/12	7/12-8/15
					8/15-10/7	10/7-11/9
2000	4/6-5/1	5/1-5/25	5/25-6/13	6/13-7/13	7/13-8/6	8/6-8/31

Libra	Scorpio	Sagittarius	Capricorn	Aquarius	Pisces
9/1-9/26	9/26-10/20	1/1-1/26	1/26-2/19	2/19-3/15	3/15-4/8
		10/20-11/14	11/14-12/6	12/9-1/4	
10/17-11/10	11/10-12/4	12/4-12/27	12/27-1/20		1/4-2/2
8/6-9/7	9/7-1/7			1/20-2/13	2/13-3/9
9/17-10/11	10/11-11/4	1/7-2/5	2/5-3/3	3/3-3/29	3/29-4/23
		11/4-11/28	11/28-12/22	12/22-1/16	
10/30-11/24	11/24-12/18	12/18-1/11			1/16-2/9
8/18-9/12	9/12-10/9	10/9-11/5	1/11-2/4	2/4-2/28	2/28-3/24
			11/5-12/8	12/8-1/23	
10/2-10/26	10/26-11/18	11/18-12/12	1/23-3/2	3/2-4/6	4/6-5/4
			12/12-1/5		
11/9-12/6	12/6-1/1			1/5-1/29	1/29-2/22
9/1-9/25	9/25-10/20	1/1-1/25	1/25-2/19	2/19-3/14	3/14-4/7
		10/20-11/13	11/13-12/9		
10/16-11/9	11/9-12/3	12/3-12/27			1/4-2/2
8/7-9/7	9/7-1/7			1/20-3/13	2/13-3/9
9/16-10/10	10/10-11/3	1/7-2/5	2/5-3/3	3/3-3/28	3/28-4/22
		11/3-11/28	11/28-12/22	12/22-1/15	
10/29-11/23	11/23-12/17	12/17-1/10			1/15-2/9
8/18-9/12	9/12-10/8	10/8-11/5	1/10-2/3	2/3-2/27	2/27-3/23
			11/5-12/10	12/10-1/16	
10/1-10/25	10/25-11/18	11/18-12/12	1/16-3/3	3/3-4/6	4/6-5/4
			12/12-1/5		
8/21-12/6	12/6-12/31	12/21-1/25/92		1/5-1/29	1/29-2/22
8/31-9/25	9/25-10/19	10/19-11/13	1/25-2/18	2/18-3/13	3/13-4/7
			11/13-12/8	12/8-1/3	
10/16-11/9	11/9-12/2	12/2-12/26	12/26-1/19		1/3-2/2
8/7-9/7	9/7-1/7			1/19-2/12	2/12-3/8
9/16-10/10	10/10-11/13	1/7-2/4	2/4-3/2	3/2-3/28	3/28-4/22
		11/3-11/27	11/27-12/21	12/21-1/15	
10/29-11/23	11/23-12/17	12/17-1/10/97			1/15-2/9
8/17-9/12	9/12-10/8	10/8-11/5	1/10-2/3	2/3-2/27	2/27-3/23
			11/5-12/12	12/12-1/9	
9/30-10/24	10/24-11/17	11/17-12/11	1/9-3/4	3/4-4/6	4/6-5/3
11/9-12/5	12/5-12/31	12/31-1/24		1/4-1/28	1/28-2/21
8/31-9/24	9/24-10/19	10/19-11/13	1/24-2/18	2/18-3/12	3/13-4/6
			11/13-12/8	12/8	

1901	MAR	1	Leo		APR	28	Gem
	May	11	Vir		JUN	11	Can
	JUL	13	Lib		JUL	27	Leo
	AUG	31	Scp		SEP	12	Vir
	OCT	14	Sag		OCT	30	Lib
	NOV	24	Cap		DEC	17	Scp
1902	JAN	1	Aqu	1907	FEB	5	Sag
	FEB	8	Pic		APR	1	Cap
	MAR	19	Ari		OCT	13	Aqu
	APR	27	Tau		NOV	29	Pic
	JUN	7	Gem	1908	JAN	11	Ari
	JUL	20	Can		FEB	23	Tau
	SEP	4	Leo		APR	7	Gem
	OCT	23	Vir		MAY	22	Can
	DEC	20	Lib		JUL	8	Leo
1903	APR	19	Vir		AUG	24	Vir
	MAY	30	Lib		OCT	10	Lib
	AUG	6	Scp		NOV	25	Scp
	SEP	22	Sag	1909	JAN	10	Sag
	NOV	3	Cap		FEB	24	Cap
	DEC	12	Aqu		APR	9	Aqu
1904	JAN	19	Pic		MAY	25	Pic
	FEB	27	Ari		JUL	21	Ari
	APR	6	Tau		SEP	26	Pic
	MAY	18	Gem		NOV	20	Ari
	JUN	30	Can	1910	JAN	23	Tau
	AUG	15	Leo		MAR	14	Gem
	OCT	1	Vir		MAY	1	Can
	NOV	20	Lib		JUN	19	Leo
1905	JAN	13	Scp		AUG	6	Vir
	AUG	21	Sag		SEP	22	Lib
	OCT	8	Cap		NOV	6	Scp
	NOV	18	Aqu		DEC	20	Sag
	DEC	27	Pic	1911	JAN	31	Cap
1906	FEB	4	Ari		MAR	14	Aqu
	MAR	17	Tau		APR	23	Pic

	JUN	2	Ari		MAY	4	Tau
	JUL	15	Tau		JUN	14	Gem
	SEP	5	Gem		JUL	28	Can
	NOV	30	Tau		SEP	12	Leo
1912	JAN	30	Gem		NOV	2	Vir
	APR	5	Can	1918	JAN	11	Lib
	MAY	28	Leo		FEB	25	Vir
	JUL	17	Vir		JUN	23	Lib
	SEP	2	Lib		AUG	17	Scp
	OCT	18	Scp		OCT	1	Sag
	NOV	30	Sag		NOV	11	Cap
1913	JAN	10	Cap		DEC	20	Aqu
	FEB	19	Aqu	1919	JAN	27	Pic
	MAR	30	Pic		MAR	6	Ari
	MAY	8	Ari		APR	15	Tau
	JUN	17	Tau		MAY	26	Gem
	JUL	29	Gem		JUL	8	Can
	SEP	15	Can		AUG	23	Leo
1914	MAY	1	Leo		OCT	10	Vir
	JUN	26	Vir		NOV	30	Lib
	AUG	14	Lib	1920	JAN	31	Scp
	SEP	29	Scp		APR	23	Lib
	NOV	11	Sag		JUL	10	Scp
	DEC	22	Cap		SEP	4	Sag
1915	JAN	30	Aqu		OCT	18	Cap
	MAR	9	Pic		NOV	27	Aqu
	APR	16	Ari	1921	JAN	5	Pic
	MAY	26	Tau		FEB	13	Ari
	JUL	6	Gem		MAR	25	Tau
	AUG	19	Can		MAY	6	Gem
	OCT	7	Leo		JUN	18	Can
1916	MAY	28	Vir		AUG	3	Leo
	JUL	23	Lib		SEP	19	Vir
	SEP	8	Scp		NOV	6	Lib
	OCT	22	Sag		DEC	26	Scp
	DEC	1	Cap	1922	FEB	18	Sag
1917	JAN	9	Aqu		SEP	13	Cap
	FEB	16	Pic		OCT	30	Aqu
	MAR	26	Ari		DEC	11	Pic

1923	JAN	21	Ari		JUN	26	Tau
	MAR	4	Tau		AUG	9	Gem
	APR	16	Gem		OCT	3	Can
	MAY	30	Can		DEC	20	Gem
	JUL	16	Leo	1929	MAR	10	Can
	SEP	1	Vir		MAY	13	Leo
	OCT	18	Lib		JUL	4	Vir
	DEC	4	Scp		AUG	21	Lib
1924	JAN	19	Sag		OCT	6	Scp
	MAR	6	Cap		NOV	18	Sag
	APR	24	Aqu		DEC	29	Cap
	JUN	24	Pic	1930	FEB	6	Aqu
	AUG	24	Aqu		MAR	17	Pic
	OCT	19	Pic		APR	24	Ari
	DEC	19	Ari		JUN	3	Tau
1925	FEB	5	Tau		JUL	14	Gem
	MAR	24	Gem		AUG	28	Can
	MAY	9	Can		OCT	20	Leo
	JUN	26	Leo	1931	FEB	16	Can
	AUG	12	Vir		MAR	30	Leo
	SEP	28	Lib		JUN	10	Vir
	NOV	13	Scp		AUG	1	Lib
	DEC	28	Sag		SEP	17	Scp
1926	FEB	9	Cap		OCT	30	Sag
	MAR	23	Aqu		DEC	10	Cap
	MAY	3	Pic	1932	JAN	18	Aqu
	JUN	15	Ari		FEB	25	Pic
	AUG	1	Tau		APR	3	Ari
1927	FEB	22	Gem		MAY	12	Tau
	APR	17	Can		JUN	22	Gem
	JUN	6	Leo		AUG	4	Can
	JUL	25	Vir		SEP	20	Leo
	SEP	10	Lib		NOV	13	Vir
	OCT	26	Scp	1933	JUL	6	Lib
	DEC	8	Sag		AUG	26	Scp
1928	JAN	19	Cap		OCT	9	Sag
	FEB	28	Aqu		NOV	19	Cap
	APR	7	Pic		DEC	28	Aqu
	MAY	16	Ari	1934	FEB	4	Pic

	MAR 14 Ari		NOV 19 Pic
	APR 22 Tau	1940 JAN 4 Ari
	JUN 2 Gem		FEB 17 Tau
	JUL 15 Can		APR 1 Gem
	AUG 30 Leo		MAY 17 Can
	OCT 18 Vir		JUL 3 Leo
	DEC 11 Lib		AUG 19 Vir
1935 JUL 29 Scp		OCT 5 Lib
	SEP 16 Sag		NOV 20 Scp
	OCT 28 Cap	1941 JAN 4 Sag
	DEC 7 Aqu		FEB 17 Cap
1936 JAN 14 Pic		APR 2 Aqu
	FEB 22 Ari		MAY 16 Pic
	APR 1 Tau		JUL 2 Ari
	MAY 13 Gem	1942 JAN 11 Tau
	JUN 25 Can		MAR 7 Gem
	AUG 10 Leo		APR 26 Can
	SEP 26 Vir		JUN 14 Leo
	NOV 14 Lib		AUG 1 Vir
1937 JAN 5 Scp		SEP 17 Lib
	MAR 13 Sag		NOV 1 Scp
	MAY 14 Scp		DEC 15 Sag
	AUG 8 Sag	1943 JAN 26 Cap
	SEP 30 Cap		MAR 8 Aqu
	NOV 11 Aqu		APR 17 Pic
	DEC 21 Pic		MAY 27 Ari
1938 JAN 30 Ari		JUL 7 Tau
	MAR 12 Tau		AUG 23 Gem
	APR 23 Gem	1944 MAR 28 Can
	JUN 7 Can		MAY 22 Leo
	JUL 22 Leo		JUL 12 Vir
	SEP 7 Vir		AUG 29 Lib
	OCT 25 Lib		OCT 13 Scp
	DEC 11 Scp		NOV 25 Sag
1939 JAN 29 Sag	1945 JAN 5 Cap
	MAR 21 Cap		FEB 14 Aqu
	MAY 25 Aqu		MAR 25 Pic
	JUL 21 Cap		MAY 2 Ari
	SEP 24 Aqu		JUN 11 Tau

	JUL	23	Gem	1951	JAN	22	Pic
	SEP	7	Can		MAR	1	Ari
	NOV	11	Leo		APR	10	Tau
	DEC	26	Can		MAY	21	Gem
1946	APR	22	Leo		JUL	3	Can
	JUN	20	Vir		AUG	18	Leo
	AUG	9	Lib		OCT	5	Vir
	SEP	24	Scp		NOV	24	Lib
	NOV	6	Sag	1952	JAN	20	Scp
	DEC	17	Cap		AUG	27	Sag
1947	JAN	25	Aqu		OCT	12	Cap
	MAR	4	Pic		NOV	21	Aqu
	APR	11	Ari		DEC	30	Pic
	MAY	21	Tau	1953	FEB	8	Ari
	JUL	1	Gem		MAR	20	Tau
	AUG	13	Can		MAY	1	Gem
	OCT	1	Leo		JUN	14	Can
	DEC	1	Vir		JUL	29	Leo
1948	FEB	12	Leo		SEP	14	Vir
	MAY	18	Vir		NOV	1	Lib
	JUL	17	Lib		DEC	20	Scp
	SEP	3	Scp	1954	FEB	9	Sag
	OCT	17	Sag		APR	12	Cap
	NOV	26	Cap		JUL	3	Sag
1949	JAN	4	Aqu		AUG	24	Cap
	FEB	11	Pic		OCT	21	Aqu
	MAR	21	Ari		DEC	4	Pic
	APR	30	Tau	1955	JAN	15	Ari
	JUN	10	Gem		FEB	26	Tau
	JUL	23	Can		APR	10	Gem
	SEP	7	Leo		MAY	26	Can
	OCT	27	Vir		JUL	11	Leo
	DEC	26	Lib		AUG	27	Vir
1950	MAR	28	Vir		OCT	13	Lib
	JUN	11	Lib		NOV	29	Scp
	AUG	10	Scp	1956	JAN	14	Sag
	SEP	25	Sag		FEB	28	Cap
	NOV	6	Cap		APR	14	Aqu
	DEC	15	Aqu		JUN	3	Pic

	DEC	6	Ari	MAR	12	Pic
1957	JAN	28	Tau	APR	19	Ari
	MAR	17	Gem	MAY	28	Tau
	MAY	4	Can	JUL	9	Gem
	JUN	21	Leo	AUG	22	Can
	AUG	8	Vir	OCT	11	Leo
	SEP	24	Lib	1963 JUN	3	Vir
	NOV	8	Scp	JUL	27	Lib
	DEC	23	Sag	SEP	12	Scp
1958	FEB	3	Cap	OCT	25	Sag
	MAR	17	Aqu	DEC	5	Cap
	APR	27	Pic	1964 JAN	13	Aqu
	JUN	7	Ari	FEB	20	Pic
	JUL	21	Tau	MAR	29	Ari
	SEP	21	Gem	MAY	7	Tau
	OCT	29	Tau	JUN	17	Gem
1959	FEB	10	Gem	JUL	30	Can
	APR	10	Can	SEP	15	Leo
	JUN	1	Leo	NOV	6	Vir
	JUL	20	Vir	1965 JUN	29	Lib
	SEP	5	Lib	AUG	20	Scp
	OCT	21	Scp	OCT	4	Sag
	DEC	3	Sag	NOV	14	Cap
1960	JAN	14	Cap	DEC	23	Aqu
	FEB	23	Aqu	1966 JAN	30	Pic
	APR	2	Pic	MAR	9	Ari
	MAY	11	Ari	APR	17	Tau
	JUN	20	Tau	MAY	28	Gem
	AUG	2	Gem	JUL	11	Can
	SEP	21	Can	AUG	25	Leo
1961	FEB	5	Gem	OCT	12	Vir
	FEB	7	Can	DEC	4	Lib
	MAY	6	Leo	1967 FEB	12	Scp
	JUN	28	Vir	MAR	31	Lib
	AUG	17	Lib	JUL	19	Scp
	OCT	1	Scp	SEP	10	Sag
	NOV	13	Sag	OCT	23	Cap
	DEC	24	Cap	DEC	1	Aqu
1962	FEB	1	Aqu	1968 JAN	9	Pic

	FEB	17	Ari		DEC	24	Tau
	MAR	27	Tau	1974	FEB	27	Gem
	MAY	8	Gem		APR	20	Can
	JUN	21	Can		JUN	9	Leo
	AUG	5	Leo		JUL	27	Vir
	SEP	21	Vir		SEP	12	Lib
	NOV	9	Lib		OCT	28	Scp
	DEC	29	Scp		DEC	10	Sag
1969	FEB	25	Sag	1975	JAN	21	Cap
	SEP	21	Cap		MAR	3	Aqu
	NOV	4	Aqu		APR	11	Pic
	DEC	15	Pic		MAY	21	Ari
1970	JAN	24	Ari		JUL	1	Tau
	MAR	7	Tau		AUG	14	Gem
	APR	18	Gem		OCT	17	Can
	JUN	2	Can		NOV	25	Gem
	JUL	18	Leo	1976	MAR	18	Can
	SEP	3	Vir		MAY	16	Leo
	OCT	20	Lib		JUL	6	Vir
	DEC	6	Scp		AUG	24	Lib
1971	JAN	23	Sag		OCT	8	Scp
	MAR	12	Cap		NOV	20	Sag
	MAY	3	Aqu	1977	JAN	1	Cap
	NOV	6	Pic		FEB	9	Aqu
	DEC	26	Ari		MAR	20	Pic
1972	FEB	10	Tau		APR	27	Ari
	MAR	27	Gem		JUN	6	Tau
	MAY	12	Can		JUL	17	Gem
	JUN	28	Leo		SEP	1	Can
	AUG	15	Vir		OCT	26	Leo
	SEP	30	Lib	1978	JAN	26	Can
	NOV	15	Scp		APR	10	Leo
	DEC	30	Sag		JUN	14	Vir
1973	FEB	12	Cap		AUG	4	Lib
	MAR	26	Aqu		SEP	19	Scp
	MAY	8	Pic		NOV	2	Sag
	JUN	20	Ari		DEC	12	Cap
	AUG	12	Tau	1979	JAN	20	Aqu
	OCT	29	Ari		FEB	27	Pic

	APR	7	Ari		MAR	15	Tau
	MAY	16	Tau		APR	26	Gem
	JUN	26	Gem		JUN	9	Can
	AUG	8	Can		JUL	25	Leo
	SEP	24	Leo		SEP	10	Vir
	NOV	19	Vir		OCT	27	Lib
1980	MAR	11	Leo		DEC	14	Scp
	MAY	4	Vir	1986	FEB	2	Sag
	JUL	10	Lib		MAR	28	Cap
	AUG	29	Scp		OCT	9	Aqu
	OCT	12	Sag		NOV	26	Pic
	NOV	22	Cap	1987	JAN	8	Ari
	DEC	30	Aqu		FEB	20	Tau
1981	FEB	6	Pic		APR	5	Gem
	MAR	17	Ari		MAY	21	Can
	APR	25	Tau		JUL	6	Leo
	JUN	5	Gem		AUG	22	Vir
	JUL	18	Can		OCT	8	Lib
	SEP	2	Leo		NOV	24	Scp
	OCT	21	Vir	1988	JAN	8	Sag
	DEC	16	Lib		FEB	22	Cap
1982	AUG	3	Scp		APR	6	Aqu
	SEP	20	Sag		MAY	22	Pic
	OCT	31	Cap		JUL	13	Ari
	DEC	10	Aqu		OCT	23	Pic
1983	JAN	17	Pic		NOV	1	Ari
	FEB	25	Ari	1989	JAN	19	Tau
	APR	5	Tau		MAR	11	Gem
	MAY	16	Gem		APR	29	Can
	JUN	29	Can		JUN	16	Leo
	AUG	13	Leo		AUG	3	Vir
	SEP	30	Vir		SEP	19	Lib
	NOV	18	Lib		NOV	4	Scp
1984	JAN	11	Scp		DEC	18	Sag
	AUG	17	Sag	1990	JAN	29	Cap
	OCT	5	Cap		MAR	11	Aqu
	NOV	15	Aqu		APR	20	Pic
	DEC	25	Pic		MAY	31	Ari
1985	FEB	2	Ari		JUL	12	Tau

	AUG	31	Gem		FEB	15	Pic
	DEC	14	Tau		MAR	24	Ari
1991	JAN	21	Gem		MAY	2	Tau
	APR	3	Can		JUN	12	Gem
	MAY	26	Leo		JUL	25	Can
	JUL	15	Vir		SEP	9	Leo
	SEP	1	Lib		OCT	30	Vir
	OCT	16	Scp	1997	JAN	3	Lib
	NOV	29	Sag		MAR	8	Vir
1992	JAN	9	Cap		JUN	19	Lib
	FEB	18	Aqu		AUG	14	Scp
	MAR	28	Pic		SEP	28	Sag
	MAY	5	Ari		NOV	9	Cap
	JUN	14	Tau		DEC	18	Aqu
	JUL	26	Gem	1998	JAN	25	Pic
	SEP	12	Can		MAR	4	Ari
1993	APR	27	Leo		APR	13	Tau
	JUN	23	Vir		MAY	24	Gem
	AUG	12	Lib		JUL	6	Can
	SEP	27	Scp		AUG	20	Leo
	NOV	9	Sag		OCT	7	Vir
	DEC	20	Cap		NOV	27	Lib
1994	JAN	28	Aqu	1999	JAN	26	Scp
	MAR	7	Pic		MAY	5	Lib
	APR	14	Ari		JUL	5	Scp
	MAY	23	Tau		SEP	2	Sag
	JUL	3	Gem		OCT	17	Cap
	AUG	16	Can		NOV	26	Aqu
	OCT	4	Leo	2000	JAN	4	Pic
	DEC	12	Vir		FEB	12	Ari
1995	JAN	22	Leo		MAR	23	Tau
	MAY	25	Vir		MAY	3	Gem
	JUL	21	Lib		JUN	16	Can
	SEP	7	Scp		AUG	1	Leo
	OCT	20	Sag		SEP	17	Vir
	NOV	30	Cap		NOV	4	Lib
1996	JAN	8	Aqu		DEC	23	Scp

1901	JAN	19	Cap		1930	JUN	26	Can
1902	FEB	6	Aqu		1931	JUL	17	Leo
1903	FEB	20	Pic		1932	AUG	11	Vir
1904	MAR	1	Ari		1933	SEP	10	Lib
	AUG	8	Tau		1934	OCT	11	Scp
	AUG	31	Ari		1935	NOV	9	Sag
1905	MAR	7	Tau		1936	DEC	2	Cap
	JUL	21	Gem		1937	DEC	20	Aqu
	DEC	4	Tau		1938	MAY	14	Pic
1906	MAR	9	Gem			JUL	30	Aqu
	JUL	30	Can			DEC	29	Pic
1907	AUG	18	Leo		1939	MAY	11	Ari
1908	SEP	12	Vir			OCT	30	Pic
1909	OCT	11	Lib			DEC	20	Ari
1910	NOV	11	Scp		1940	MAY	16	Tau
1911	DEC	10	Sag		1941	MAY	26	Gem
1913	JAN	2	Cap		1942	JUN	10	Can
1914	JAN	21	Aqu		1943	JUN	30	Leo
1915	FEB	4	Pic		1944	JUL	26	Vir
1916	FEB	12	Ari		1945	AUG	25	Lib
	JUN	26	Tau		1946	SEP	25	Scp
	OCT	26	Ari		1947	OCT	24	Sag
1917	FEB	12	Tau		1948	NOV	15	Cap
	JUN	29	Gem		1949	APR	12	Aqu
1918	JUL	13	Can			JUN	27	Cap
1919	AUG	2	Leo			NOV	30	Aqu
1920	AUG	27	Vir		1950	APR	15	Pic
1921	SEP	25	Lib			SEP	15	Aqu
1922	OCT	26	Scp			DEC	1	Pic
1923	NOV	24	Sag		1951	APR	21	Ari
1924	DEC	18	Cap		1952	APR	28	Tau
1926	JAN	6	Aqu		1953	MAY	9	Gem
1927	JAN	18	Pic		1954	MAY	24	Can
	JUN	6	Ari		1955	JUN	13	Leo
	SEP	11	Pic			NOV	17	Vir
1928	JAN	23	Ari		1956	JAN	18	Leo
	JUN	4	Tau			JUL	7	Vir
1929	JUN	12	Gem			DEC	13	Lib

1957	FEB	19	Vir	1973	FEB	23	Aqu
	AUG	7	Lib	1974	MAR	8	Pic
1958	JAN	13	Scp	1975	MAR	18	Ari
	MAR	20	Lib	1976	MAR	26	Tau
	SEP	7	Scp		AUG	23	Gem
1959	FEB	10	Sag		OCT	16	Tau
	APR	24	Scp	1977	APR	3	Gem
	OCT	5	Sag		AUG	20	Can
1960	MAR	1	Cap		DEC	30	Gem
	JUN	10	Sag	1978	APR	12	Can
	OCT	26	Cap		SEP	5	Leo
1961	MAR	15	Aqu	1979	FEB	28	Can
	AUG	12	Cap		APR	20	Leo
	NOV	4	Aqu		SEP	29	Vir
1962	MAR	25	Pic	1980	OCT	27	Lib
1963	APR	4	Ari	1981	Nov	27	Scp
1964	APR	12	Tau	1982	DEC	26	Sag
1965	APR	22	Gem	1984	JAN	19	Cap
	SEP	21	Can	1985	FEB	6	Aqu
	NOV	17	Gem	1986	FEB	20	Pic
1966	MAY	5	Can	1987	MAR	2	Ari
	SEP	27	Leo	1988	MAR	8	Tau
1967	JAN	16	Can		JUL	22	Gem
	MAY	23	Leo		NOV	30	Tau
	OCT	19	Vir	1989	MAR	11	Gem
1968	FEB	27	Leo		JUL	30	Can
	JUN	15	Vir	1990	AUG	18	Leo
	NOV	15	Lib	1991	SEP	12	Vir
1969	MAR	30	Vir	1992	OCT	10	Lib
	JUL	15	Lib	1993	NOV	10	Scp
	DEC	16	Scp	1994	DEC	9	Sag
1970	APR	30	Lib	1996	JAN	3	Cap
	AUG	15	Scp	1997	JAN	21	Aqu
1971	JAN	14	Sag	1998	FEB	4	Pic
	JUN	5	Scp	1999	FEB	13	Ari
	SEP	11	Sag		JUN	28	Tau
1972	FEB	6	Cap		OCT	23	Ari
	JUL	24	Sag	2000	FEB	14	Tau
	SEP	25	Cap		JUN	30	Gem

SATURN SIGN 1903–2000

1903	JAN	19	Aqu		1942	MAY	8	Gem
1905	APR	13	Pic		1944	JUN	20	Can
	AUG	17	Aqu		1946	AUG	2	Leo
1906	JAN	8	Pic		1948	SEP	19	Vir
1908	MAR	19	Ari		1949	APR	3	Leo
1910	MAY	17	Tau			MAY	29	Vir
	DEC	14	Ari		1950	NOV	20	Lib
1911	JAN	20	Tau		1951	MAR	7	Vir
1912	JUL	7	Gem			AUG	13	Lib
	NOV	30	Tau		1953	OCT	22	Scp
1913	MAR	26	Gem		1956	JAN	12	Sag
1914	AUG	24	Can			MAY	14	Scp
	DEC	7	Gem			OCT	10	Sag
1915	MAY	11	Can		1959	JAN	5	Cap
1916	OCT	17	Leo		1962	JAN	3	Aqu
	DEC	7	Can		1964	MAR	24	Pic
1917	JUN	24	Leo			SEP	16	Aqu
1919	AUG	12	Vir			DEC	16	Pic
1921	OCT	7	Lib		1967	MAR	3	Ari
1923	DEC	20	Scp		1969	APR	29	Tau
1924	APR	6	Lib		1971	JUN	18	Gem
	SEP	13	Scp		1972	JAN	10	Tau
1926	DEC	2	Sag			FEB	21	Gem
1929	MAR	15	Cap		1973	AUG	1	Can
	MAY	5	Sag		1974	JAN	7	Gem
	NOV	30	Cap			APR	18	Can
1932	FEB	24	Aqu		1975	SEP	17	Leo
	AUG	13	Cap		1976	JAN	14	Can
	NOV	20	Aqu			JUN	5	Leo
1935	FEB	14	Pic		1977	NOV	17	Vir
1937	APR	25	Ari		1978	JAN	5	Leo
	OCT	18	Pic			JUL	26	Vir
1938	JAN	14	Ari		1980	SEP	21	Lib
1939	JUL	6	Tau		1982	NOV	29	Scp
	SEP	22	Ari		1983	MAY	6	Lib
1940	MAR	20	Tau			AUG	24	Scp

1985	NOV	17	Sag	1994	JAN	28	Pic
1988	FEB	13	Cap	1996	APR	7	Ari
	JUN	10	Sag	1998	JUN	9	Tau
	NOV	12	Cap		OCT	25	Ari
1991	FEB	6	Aqu	1999	MAR	1	Tau
1993	MAY	21	Pic	2000	AUG	10	Gem
	JUN	30	Aqu		OCT	16	Tau

URANUS IN VIRGO BIRTH DATES:

November 1, 1961–January 10, 1962
August 10, 1962–September 28, 1968
May 20, 1969–June 24, 1969

URANUS IN LIBRA BIRTH DATES:

September 28, 1968–May 20, 1969
June 24, 1969–November 21, 1974
May 1–September 8, 1975

URANUS IN SCORPIO BIRTH DATES:

November 21, 1974–May 1, 1975
September 8, 1975–February 17, 1981
March 20–November 16, 1981

URANUS IN SAGITTARIUS BIRTH DATES:

February 17–March 20, 1981
November 16, 1981–February 15, 1988
May 27, 1988–December 2, 1988

URANUS IN CAPRICORN BIRTH DATES:

December 20, 1904–January 30, 1912
September 4–November 12, 1912
February 15–May 27, 1988
December 2, 1988–April 1, 1995
June 9, 1995–January 12, 1996

URANUS IN AQUARIUS BIRTH DATES:

January 30–September 4, 1912
November 12, 1912–April 1, 1919
August 16, 1919–January 22, 1920

URANUS IN PISCES BIRTH DATES:

April 1–August 16, 1919
January 22, 1920–March 31, 1927
November 4, 1927–January 13, 1928

LOOK UP YOUR NEPTUNE PLACEMENT by finding your birthday on the following lists:

NEPTUNE IN CANCER BIRTH DATES:

July 19–December 25, 1901
May 21, 1902–September 23, 1914
December 14, 1914–July 19, 1915
March 19–May 2, 1916

NEPTUNE IN LEO BIRTH DATES:

September 23–December 14, 1914
July 19, 1915–March 19, 1916
May 2, 1916–September 21, 1928
February 19, 1929–July 24, 1929

NEPTUNE IN VIRGO BIRTH DATES:

September 21, 1928–February 19, 1929
July 24, 1929–October 3, 1942
April 17–August 2, 1943

NEPTUNE IN LIBRA BIRTH DATES:

October 2, 1942–April 17, 1943
August 2, 1943–December 24, 1955
March 12–October 9, 1956
June 15–August 6, 1957

NEPTUNE IN SCORPIO BIRTH DATES:

August 6, 1957–January 4, 1970
May 3–November 6, 1970

NEPTUNE IN SAGITTARIUS BIRTH DATES:

January 4–May 3, 1970
November 6, 1970–January 19, 1984
June 23–November 21, 1984

NEPTUNE IN CAPRICORN BIRTH DATES:

January 19, 1984–June 23, 1984
November 21, 1984–January 29, 1998

FIND YOUR PLUTO PLACEMENT in the following list:

Pluto in Gemini—Late 1800s until May 28, 1914
Pluto in Cancer—May 28, 1914–June 16, 1939
Pluto in Leo—July 16, 1939–August 19, 1957
Pluto in Virgo—August 19, 1957–October 5, 1971
                April 17, 1972–July 30, 1972
Pluto in Libra—October 5, 1971–April 17, 1972
                July 30, 1972–August 28, 1984
Pluto in Scorpio—August 28, 1984–January 17, 1995
Pluto in Sagittarius–starting January 17, 1995

4

Find Your Power Planets

Certain planets in your horoscope can play especially important roles in determining your success and happiness. These are your personal power planets, which at times can even be more decisive in your life than the sun! Here is how to locate them and what they could mean to you.

Many factors determine how powerful a planet can be. First, there is the planet's sign. Each planet rules a special sign where it is most comfortably at home. But it also excels in another sign, called its "exaltation," where it functions more like a special guest.

Then consider the planet's position in your chart. Situated on the horizontal or vertical axes of the horoscope wheel, a planet can be the driving force of your chart, especially if it's at the top of your chart or on the ascendant (rising sign). It is also powerful when isolated from other planets. It then becomes a center of attention—your chart could "swing" on the happenings of that lone planet!

Sometimes the planet that rules a sign packs an extra wallop. For example, if there are three or more planets in one sign, then the planetary ruler of that sign assumes high priority, even if it is located elsewhere, because it "disposes" of (or masterminds) the energy in that heavily populated sign. The planet that rules your rising sign is very high status because it colors your outward identity. This planet can guide you to a successful career choice, one that reflects its sign and house placement. Yet other important planets to reckon with are the rulers of your sun and moon signs, which influence how your personality and emotions operate.

* * *

Check the chart in this chapter to find out how your planets rate!

A Planet in the Sign It Rules ("dignity")

Each sign is ruled by a planet, so naturally, any planet in your chart located in the sign it rules is sure to be one of the most important. There it is most at home and can work most effectively. Because you'll express the clear energy of the planet, astrologers call this placement the planet's "dignity" for it is here the planet shows off its best qualities. For example, the moon can express its nature most strongly through the watery sign of Cancer. So those with this placement will be strongly emotional, have all the lunar qualities of good memory, insight, psychic abilities, interest in nurturing. Venus expresses itself most easily in Taurus, the earthy, sensual side of Venus emerges or in Libra, where Venus is more abstract, aesthetic, concerned with the ideals of beauty.

When a Planet Is in Its Detriment

The sign opposite (six signs away) from the one it rules is a planet's detriment. Here it is considered to be at a disadvantage—the dreamy nature of the moon is not as easily expressed through the "here and now" matter-of-fact sign of Capricorn. Venus goes to extremes in Scorpio (the opposite of Taurus) and is self-centered in Aries (the opposite of Libra).

When a Planet Is Exalted

The qualities of a planet also function especially well in the sign that is called its exaltation—here it is able to express its highest purpose—the moon in Taurus promotes emotional steadiness and growth. The nurturing qualities of the moon can "bear fruit" in this fixed earth sign. Venus in Pisces expresses the sensitive, loving, giving, elevated side of the planet.

If Your Planet Is in Its Fall . . .

Opposite its exaltation is the sign of a planet's fall, often considered a disadvantage. Mars, which expresses its goal-directed energy most forcefully in Capricorn, could be diverted by emotional concerns in Cancer, its fall. Venus, which functions well in the accepting, unjudgmental sign of Pisces, is ill at ease in critical Virgo. But, cheer up if you have one or more planets in this situation—you'll have many opportunities to develop and expand that planet's energy in this lifetime.

Power Planet Chart:

Planet	Sign Ruled	Detriment	Exaltation	Fall
The Sun	Leo	Aquarius	Aries	Libra
The Moon	Cancer	Capricorn	Taurus	Scorpio
Mercury	Gemini/Virgo	Sagittarius	Virgo	Pisces
Venus	Taurus/Libra	Scorpio/Aries	Pisces	Virgo
Mars	Aries/Scorpio	Libra/Taurus	Capricorn	Cancer
Saturn	Capricorn/Aquarius	Cancer/Leo	Libra	Aries

Planet	Sign Ruled	Detriment	Exaltation	Fall
Jupiter	Sagittarius/ Pisces	Gemini/Virgo	Cancer	Capricorn
Uranus	Aquarius	Leo	Scorpio	Taurus
Neptune	Pisces	Virgo	Gemini	Sagittarius
Pluto	Scorpio	Taurus	Leo	Aquarius

A Powerful Sun: This gives you a desire to put your stamp on the world, to be "somebody." You'll have a forceful personality, love to be noticed, and need recognition for your work. You head for leadership positions, where you command the spotlight. Negatively, you can be quite self-centered and occasionally arrogant.

EXAMPLE: Rock star Mick Jagger, who has the sun and three planets in Leo with Leo rising, was bound to make his presence felt. Although his looks are not particularly impressive, he has dramatized himself to the hilt to make himself the "king" of any stage on which he performs.

A Powerful Moon: You have an expressive emotional nature, with sharp perceptions and an excellent memory. Your personality may be more reflective, changeable according to mood. Family life is especially important to you. You have a talent for intimacy—may prefer one-on-one relationships to a crowded social life.

EXAMPLE: Romantic singer Julio Iglésias, with a powerful moon in Cancer, its ruling sign, started out as a soccer player but made his fortune as a singer of tender, emotional ballads. Linda Ronstadt, whose sun sign is moon-ruled Cancer, yet her moon stands alone in Aquarius, is an interesting lunar type who favors ballads and love songs but with an unpredictable "Aquarian" individualistic twist; her musical mood shifts from country music, to rock, to mariachi, to classic ballads of the forties.

A Powerful Mercury: Your special gifts are an analytical mind and talent for communicating via the written or spoken word. Your thought processes work quickly, helping you to handle a variety of interests, several projects or careers efficiently.

EXAMPLE: Joan Collins, with five planets in Mercury-ruled Gemini and Virgo, has managed dual careers as an actress and a writer of best-selling gossipy novels, true to her Gemini sun sign nature.

A Powerful Venus: You excel in relationships and express yourself artistically with grace and charm. You may have highly developed senses, and could be prone to overindulge them. You love to surround yourself with beauty, present an image that helps you relate to others, have a beautiful smile.

EXAMPLE: Singer Willie Nelson, whose sun and Venus are in Venus-ruled Taurus, adopted hippie garb, which won him legions of free-thinking fans.

A Powerful Mars: This gives you a dynamic drive to achieve goals; a competitive spirit; vigorous energy; a direct, assertive, aggressive manner.

EXAMPLE: Rock star/entrepreneur Prince, with Mars in Aries, its ruling sign, pioneered his own hard-driving music genre and founded a successful state-of-the-art recording studio and film production center in Minneapolis, which could change the image of that conservative city.

A Powerful Jupiter: You have an optimistic personality with a joyous sense of humor, a love and rapport with animals and the outdoors, and athletic ability. You place much emphasis on faith and luck. You could be a big risk taker, a gambler, or you could embody Jupiter's philosophical, spiritual side.

EXAMPLE: Robert Redford, with Jupiter in Sagittarius standing alone at the top of his chart, has gambled successfully with acting, directing, and ski resort development, and has backed environmental concerns.

A Powerful Saturn: This emphasizes function, order, structure. You keep your eye on the bottom line. Saturn gives you discipline, a strong sense of family duty, of following the rules to the letter. You'll be concerned with things that last. You'll never let up on pursuing your goals and may become more successful as you grow older.

EXAMPLE: Actor Paul Newman, with conservative Saturn standing alone at the top of his chart, is a very serious actor who exercises great self-discipline in his work. Shunning Hollywood, he prefers quiet family life in Connecticut. His career has expanded into business ventures, and he has become even more popular as he has aged.

A Powerful Uranus: You possess brilliant insights, an unconventional approach, a touch of eccentricity, a charisma that appeals to the masses. You challenge the establishment with original but sometimes rebellious ideas. You have an unpredictable streak. You love to experiment and could be especially successful in fields that use electronic media.

EXAMPLE: Outrageous comedienne Phyllis Diller has a Cancer sun sign, but her offbeat charisma is revealed by Uranus in its ruler Aquarius, standing alone at the top of her chart, which emphasizes the unconventional, eccentric, zany side of Aquarius and her major career success on television (Uranus ruled).

A Powerful Neptune: This gives you creativity, especially in the world of illusion, glamour, film, and theater. You have a need to get "high" (and may choose drugs or alcohol to get there), but you could also satisfy this need by developing your spiritual and creative gifts to express the one-ness of life.

EXAMPLE: David Bowie, with magical Neptune on the ascendant, is a master of illusion, with a quick-change personality who has become a film star (Neptune ruled) as well as a singer.

A Powerful Pluto: You have personal magnetism, sex appeal, an inner power. You'll probe beneath the surface of life for deep meaning, and transform others in some way. You are intense and can be manipulative.

EXAMPLE: Michael Jackson, with Pluto in Virgo on the ascendant, has, since childhood, been able to sway the masses; he has also totally transformed his own physical appearance (ruled by his Pluto ascendant).

5

When to Make
Your Moves in 1992

It's no secret that some of the most powerful and famous people, from Julius Caesar to financier J. P. Morgan, from Ronald Reagan to Cher, have consulted astrologers before they made their moves. If it works for the rich and famous, why not learn how to put astrology to work for you?

You can get control of your life and set it on its most successful course by letting astrology help you coordinate your activities. For instance, if you know the dates that the tricky planet Mercury will be creating havoc with communications, you'll back up that vital fax with a duplicate by Express Mail, you'll read between the lines of contracts and put off closing that deal until you have double-checked all the information. When Venus is on your side, you'll revamp your image or ask someone special to dinner. A retrograde Mars period would not be the best time to launch an aggressive campaign.

To find out for yourself if there's truth to the saying "timing is everything," mark your own calendar for love, career moves, vacations, and important events, using the following information and the tables in this chapter and the one titled "Look Up Your Planets," as well as the moon sign listings under your daily forecast. Here are the happenings to note on your agenda:

- Dates of your astrological sun sign (high-energy period)
- The month previous (low-energy period)
- Dates of planets in your sun sign (see "Look Up Your Planets")
- Full and new moons (with special attention to those falling in your sun sign)
- Eclipses (mark off eclipse period)

- Moon in your sun sign every month as well as moon in opposite sign (listed in daily forecast)
- Mercury retrogrades
- Other retrograde periods

With your astrological agenda, you have a tool for making the most of your personal best days this year and taking advantage of the "down times" to relax, reevaluate, and reorganize.

YOUR PERSONAL POWER TIME

Every birthday starts a cycle of solar energy for you. You should feel a new surge of vitality as the powerful sun enters your sign. This is the time when predominant energies are most favorable to you. So go for it! Start new projects, make your big moves. You'll get the recognition you deserve now when everyone is attuned to your sun sign. Look in the tables in this book to see if other planets will be passing through your sun sign at this time. Venus (love, beauty), Mars (energy, drive), or Mercury (communication, mental sharpness) reinforce the sun and give an extra boost to your life in the areas they affect. Venus will rev up your social and love life, making you seem especially attractive. Mars gives you extra energy and drive. Mercury fuels your brain power and helps you communicate. Jupiter signals an especially lucky period of expansion.

There are two "down" times related to the sun. During the month before your birthday period, when you are winding up your annual cycle, you could be feeling especially vulnerable and depleted so get extra rest, watch your diet, don't overstress yourself. Use this time to gear up for a big "push" when the sun enters your sign.

Another "down" time is when the sun in the opposite sign (six months from your birthday)—and the prevailing energies are very different from yours. You may feel at odds with the world, and things might not come easily. You'll have to work harder for recognition, because people are not on your wavelength. However, this could be a good time to work on a team, in cooperation with others or behind the scenes.

How to Use the Moon's Phase and Sign

Working with the PHASES of the moon is as easy as looking up at the night sky. At the new moon, when both sun and moon are in the same sign, it's the best time to begin new ventures, especially the activities that are favored by that sign. You'll have powerful energies pulling you in the same direction. You'll be focused outward, toward action, doing. Postpone breaking off, terminating, deliberating, or reflecting, activities that require introspection and passive work.

Get your project under way during the first quarter, then go public at the full moon, a time of high intensity, when feelings come out into the open. This is your time to shine—to express yourself. Be aware however, that because pressures are being released, other people are also letting off steam and confrontations are possible. So try to avoid arguments. Traditionally, astrologers often advise against surgery at this time, which could produce heavier bleeding.

During the last quarter of the new moon, you'll be most controlled. This is a winding-down phase, a time to cut off unproductive relationships, do serious thinking, and inward-directed activities.

You'll feel some new and full moons more strongly than others, especially those new moons that fall in your sun sign and full moons in your opposite sign. Because that full moon happens at your low-energy time of year, it is likely to be an especially stressful time in a relationship, when any hidden problems or unexpressed emotions could surface.

1992 FULL AND NEW MOONS

	DATE:	SIGN:
NEW MOON	January 4	Capricorn*
FULL MOON	January 19	Cancer
NEW MOON	February 3	Aquarius
FULL MOON	February 18	Leo

	DATE:	SIGN:
NEW MOON	March 4	Pisces
FULL MOON	March 18	Virgo
NEW MOON	April 3	Aries
FULL MOON	April 17	Libra
NEW MOON	May 2	Taurus
FULL MOON	May 16	Scorpio
NEW MOON	June 1	Gemini
FULL MOON	June 15	Sagittarius*
NEW MOON	June 30	Cancer*
FULL MOON	July 14	Capricorn
NEW MOON	July 29	Leo
FULL MOON	August 13	Aquarius
NEW MOON	August 28	Virgo
FULL MOON	September 12	Pisces
NEW MOON	September 26	Libra
FULL MOON	October 11	Aries
NEW MOON	October 25	Scorpio
FULL MOON	November 10	Taurus
NEW MOON	November 24	Sagittarius
FULL MOON	December 9	Gemini*
NEW MOON	December 24	Capricorn*

* Take special note: there are eclipses at these times.

HOW TO HANDLE ECLIPSES

One of the most amazing phenomena in the cosmos, which many of us take for granted, is the spatial relationship between the sun and the moon. How many of us have ever noticed or marveled that, relative to our viewpoint here on earth (the physically largest source of energy), the sun, and the smallest, the moon, appear to be the same size! This is most evident to us at the time of the solar eclipse, when the moon is directly aligned with the sun and so nearly covers it that scientists use the moment of eclipse to study solar flares.

When the two most powerful forces in astrology—the sun and moon—are lined up, we're sure to feel the effects, both in world events and in our personal lives. So it might help us to learn how best to cope with the periods around eclipses, especially because there are five coming up in 1992.

Both solar and lunar eclipses are times when our natural rhythms are changed, depending on where the eclipse falls in your horoscope. If it falls on or close to your sign—Capricorn, Sagittarius, Cancer, and Gemini this year—you're going to have important changes in your life, perhaps a turning point. The other cardinal (Aries and Libra) and mutable (Pisces and Virgo) signs may experience this year's eclipse effects to a lesser degree.

Lunar eclipses happen at times when the earth is on a level plane with the sun and moon and moves between them at the time of the full moon, breaking the powerful monthly opposition cycle of these two forces. Normally the full moon is the time when emotions come to a head and are released. During an eclipse, however, this rhythmic process is temporarily short-circuited. The effect can be either confusion or clarity—as our subconscious energies that normally feel the "pull" of the opposing sun and moon are turned off. Freed from subconscious attachments, we might have objective insights that could help us change any destructive emotional patterns, such as addictions, which normally occur at this time. This momentary "turn-off" could help us turn our lives around. On the other hand, this break in the cycle could cause a bewildering disorientation that intensifies insecurities.

The solar eclipse occurs at the new moon, when the moon comes between the earth and the sun, blocking the sun's energies. This time the objective, conscious force in our life will be temporarily darkened, because the "pull" between the earth and sun is cut off by the moon. The subconscious lunar forces then dominate, putting us in a highly subjective state. Emotional truths can be revealed—or emotions can run wild, as our objectivity is cut off and hidden patterns surface. If your sun sign is affected, you may find yourself beginning a period of work on a deep inner level, you may have psychic experiences or a surfacing of deep emotional truths.

You'll start feeling the energies of an upcoming eclipse a few days after the previous new or full moon. The energy continues to intensify until the actual eclipse, then disperses for three or four days. So plan ahead at least a week or more before an eclipse and allow several days after, for the natural rhythms to return. Try not to make major moves during this period (it's not a great time to get married, change jobs, or buy a home).

ECLIPSES IN 1992

	DATE		SIGN
SOLAR ECLIPSE	January 4	in	Capricorn
LUNAR ECLIPSE	June 15	in	Sagittarius
SOLAR ECLIPSE	June 30	in	Cancer
LUNAR ECLIPSE	December 9	in	Gemini
SOLAR ECLIPSE	December 24	in	Capricorn

VOID OF COURSE MOON

Approximately every two days, just before the moon changes into another sign, is the period known as the "void of course," which refers to the time between the last contact or aspect a moon makes with another planet and the time when it changes signs. This is a kind of twilight zone—a time for inner activity such as meditation, spiritual work, sleep, reading—basically passive experiences. This time can last for a few minutes or for almost a day, so it is worth noting if you have many important activities to plan. If you do not have an astrological ephemeris, as the detailed book of planetary tables is called, you can find astrological calendars that show the void of course in your local metaphysical bookstore. The key for the void of course is to put major projects on hold— there will be lots of talk but little follow-through. Don't look for results now. You might, however, negatively, work on projects where you *don't* want action. If you want nothing to happen, choose the void of course moon.

Moon Sign Timing

For the daily emotional "weather" for your monthly high and low days and to synchronize your activities with the cycle and the sign of the moon, take note of the moon's SIGN under your daily forecast at the end of the book. Here are some of the activities favored and moods you are likely to encounter under each sign.

MOON IN ARIES

Get moving! The new moon in Aries is an ideal time to start new projects. Everyone is pushy, raring to go, rather impatient, and short-tempered. Leave details and follow-up for later. Competitive sports or martial arts are great ways to let off steam. Quiet types could use some assertiveness training, but it's a great day for dynamos!

MOON IN TAURUS

It's time to do solid, methodical tasks. This is the time to tackle follow-through or backup work. Lay the foundations for success. Make investments, buy real estate, do appraisals, do some hard bargaining. Enjoy creature comforts, music, a good dinner, sensual lovemaking.

MOON IN GEMINI

Talk means action today. Telephone, write letters, fax! Make new contacts, stay in touch with steady customers. You can handle lots of tasks at once. A great day for mental activity of any kind. Don't try to pin people down—they too are feeling restless. Keep it light. Flirtations and socializing are good. Watch gossip—and don't give away secrets.

MOON IN CANCER

This is a moody, sensitive, emotional time. People respond to personal attention, mothering. Stay at home, have a family dinner, call your mother. Nostalgia, memories, psychic powers are heightened. You'll want to hang on to people and things (don't clean out your closets now). You could have some shrewd insights into what others really need and want now. Pay attention to your dreams, intuition, gut reactions.

MOON IN LEO

Everybody is in a much more confident, warm, generous mood. It's a good day to ask for a raise, show what you can do, dress like a star. People will respond to flattery, enjoy a bit of drama and theater. You may be extravagant, treat yourself royally, and show off a bit (but don't break the bank!). Be careful that you don't promise more than you can deliver!

MOON IN VIRGO

Do solid down-to-earth work. Review your budget. Make repairs. Be an efficiency expert. *Not* a day to ask for a raise. Have a health checkup. Revamp your diet. Buy vitamins or health food. Take care of details, piled-up chores. Reorganize your work and life so they run more smoothly and efficiently. Save money. Be prepared for others to be in a critical, fault-finding mood.

MOON IN LIBRA

Attend to legal matters. Negotiate contracts. Arbitrate. Do things with your favorite partner. Socialize. Be romantic. Buy a special gift, a beautiful object. Decorate yourself or your surroundings. Buy new clothes. Throw a party. Have an elegant, romantic evening. Smooth over any ruffled feathers. Avoid confrontations, stick to civilized discussions.

MOON IN SCORPIO

This is a day to do things with passion. You'll have excellent concentration and focus. Try not to get too intense emotionally, however, and avoid sharp exchanges with loved ones. Others may tend to go to extremes, get jealous, overreact. Great for troubleshooting, problem-solving, research, scientific work—and making love. Pay attention to psychic vibes.

MOON IN SAGITTARIUS

A great time for travel. Have philosophical discussions. Set long-range career goals. Work out, do sports, or buy athletic equipment. Others will be feeling upbeat, exuberant, and adventurous. Risk taking is high—you may feel like taking a gamble, betting on the horses. Teaching, writing, and spiritual activities also get the green light. Relax outdoors. Take care of animals.

MOON IN CAPRICORN

You can accomplish a lot today, so get on the ball! Issues concerning your basic responsibilities, duties, family, and parents could crop up. You'll be expected to deliver on promises now. Weed out the dead wood from your life. Get a dental checkup. The moon passing over Neptune and Uranus will illuminate your dreams and imagination—and could stir up some fantasies. Write down those creative ideas and listen to your intuition.

MOON IN AQUARIUS

A great day for doing things with groups—clubs, meetings, outings, politics, parties. Campaign for your candidate. Work for a worthy cause. Deal with larger issues that affect humanity: the environment, metaphysical questions. Buy a computer or electronic gadget. Watch TV. Wear something outrageous. Try something you've never done before. Present an original idea. Don't stick to a rigid schedule—go with the flow. Take a class in meditation, mind control, yoga.

MOON IN PISCES

This can be a very creative day, so let your imagination work overtime. Film, theater, music, ballet could inspire you. Spend some time alone, resting and reflecting, reading or writing poetry. Daydreams can be profitable. Help those less fortunate or lend a listening ear to someone who may be feeling blue. Don't overindulge in self-pity or escapism, however—people are especially vulnerable to substance abuse now. Turn your thoughts to romance and someone special.

When the Planets Go Backward

All the planets except for the sun and moon have times when they seem to move backward—or retrograde—in the sky from our point of view on earth. At these times, planets do not work as they usually do, leading us to "take a break" from that planet's energies in our life and do some work on an inner level.

MERCURY RETROGRADE

Mercury goes retrograde most often and its effects can be especially irritating. When it reaches a short distance ahead of the sun three times a year, it seems to move backward from our point of view. Astrologers often compare retrograde motion to the optical illusion that occurs when we ride on a train that passes another train traveling at a different speed—the second train appears to be moving in reverse.

What this means to you is that the Mercury-ruled areas of your life—analytical thought processes, communications, scheduling, and such—are subject to all kinds of snafus. Be prepared. People will change their minds, renege on commitments. Communications equipment can break down. Schedules must be changed on short notice. People are late for appointments or don't show up at all. Traffic is terrible. Major purchases malfunction, don't work out, or get delivered in the wrong color. Letters don't arrive or are delivered to the wrong address. Co-workers will make errors that have to be corrected later. Contracts don't work out or must be renegotiated.

Since most of us can't put our lives on "hold" for nine weeks every year, we should learn to tame the trickster and make it work for us. The key is in the prefix "re." This is the time to go back over things in your life—REflect on what you've done during the previous months. Look for deeper insights, spot errors you've missed, take time to review and reevaluate what has happened. This time is very good for inner spiritual work and meditation. REst and REward yourself—it's a good time to take a vacation, especially if you revisit a favorite place. REorganize your work and finish up projects that have been hanging around. Clean out your desk and closets. If you must sign contracts or agreements, do so with a contingency clause that lets you reevaluate the terms later.

Postpone major purchases or commitments. Don't get married. Try not to rely on other people keeping appointments, contracts, or agreements to the letter—have several alternatives. Double-check and read between the lines. Don't buy anything connected with communications or transportation (if you must, be sure to cover yourself). Mercury retrograding through your sun sign will intensify its effect on your life.

If Mercury was retrograde when you were born, you may be one of the lucky people who don't suffer the frustrations of this period. If so, your mind probably works in a very intuitive, insightful way.

The sign Mercury is retrograding through can give you an idea of what's in store—as well as the sun signs that will be especially challenged. This year, it's the fire signs—so look before you leap, and don't make promises you can't keep.

MERCURY RETROGRADE PERIODS IN 1992

March 17–April 9 in Aries
July 20–August 13 in Leo
November 11–December 1 in Sagittarius

MARS RETROGRADE

Mars retrograde times are fascinating periods when drive, arrogance, aggressive maneuvers, and fast action are sure to trip you up. If there is ever a time when passive, reactive, peaceful action will get you farther ahead, this is it! People who are normally that way will make surprising gains, whereas the go-getters will be stalled or become losers. So watch the so-called wimps for some surprising moves! If you have planned to go full speed ahead on anything, first check out Mars. If it's retrograde, put your plans on the back burner. Flight COULD get you farther than fight, now!

Fortunately Mars only turns retrograde every 2½ years;

however, we will be hit this December, just in time for the holidays! Try to avoid buying mechanical gifts—they often malfunction. This is a time to take extra care of your health—your energy may be low. So, even though you may be raring to go after the Mercury retrograde ends on December 1, be patient a while longer.

Those who aggressively initiate at this time will be at a disadvantage (you could, of course, profit from this if your competition launches a new venture). Let others fire first! Arrogance is a particular danger now. Avoid it! And never underestimate the underdog at this time. Remember the last game of the 1990 World Series? A stunning surprise upset by the underdog Cincinnati Reds over the cocksure Oakland Athletics occurred on the very day Mars turned retrograde. So don't bet on a "sure thing" during a Mars retrograde, and keep your eye on the dark horse! Fortunately this period occurs after this year's Presidential elections, so it should not adversely affect the candidates as it did Mars-ruled Michael Dukakis' campaign during the Mars retrograde that preceded the 1988 Presidential elections!

Rather than bottle up anger or aggressive feelings during this time, try to find nondestructive ways to let off steam. Physical exercise is a good idea, particularly low-risk, noncompetitive exercise such as cross-country skiing, swimming, jogging, or bike riding.

Mars-ruled signs of Scorpio and Aries, normally quite strong-willed and forceful, may seem unusually slow-moving and reflective now. Aries may seem especially out of character in a more introspective mode. Since Mars will be transiting the emotionally sensitive sign of Cancer this year, watch for any tendency to take things too personally, especially family disputes or well-meaning criticism.

Mars turns retrograde November 28 and remains so through February 16, 1993. Cancers and Capricorns will experience this passage most acutely.

VENUS RETROGRADE

Fortunately, there is no Venus retrograde in 1992. You will have to deal with it next year, however. A Venus retrograde can cause trouble in relationships, causing you to be extravagant and impractical. Not a good time to redecorate—you'll hate the color of the walls later—to try a new hairstyle, or to fall in love. But if you wish to make amends in an already troubled relationship, make peaceful overtures then.

WHEN OTHER PLANETS RETROGRADE

Planets retrograding at the same time indicate a period of readjustment on many levels. Luckily this will be happening during the summer months of 1992; it's an excellent idea to take time off for a vacation! During this July, five planets will be retrograde: Mercury, which we've discussed, will have the most dramatic effects. So double-check travel plans, reservations, and maps. Plan several alternatives in case of foul-ups, and be patient with delays.

The other, slower-moving planets, stay retrograde for months at a time—Saturn, Neptune, Uranus, and Pluto. Saturn is retrograde almost five months in Aquarius (May 28–October 16), a time when you may feel more like hanging out at the beach than getting things done. It's an uphill battle with self-discipline at this time. In Capricorn, Neptune retrograde (April 20–September 27) promotes a dreamy escapism from reality, whereas Uranus retrograde (April 21–September 22) may mean setbacks in areas where there have been sudden changes and a general lack of originality and inspiration. Think of this as an adjustment period. Pluto retrograde in Scorpio (February 24–July 30) is not a good time for extreme military action or dramatic transformations. This is a better time to work on establishing proportion, balance.

When the planets start moving forward again, there's a shift in the atmosphere. Activities connected with each planet start moving ahead, plans that were stalled get rolling. Make a special note of those days on your calendar and proceed accordingly.

WILL THIS BE YOUR LUCKY YEAR?

Look to Jupiter for the lucky times of your life. When Jupiter is passing through your sun sign, you're due for a period of expansion as you begin a new twelve-year cycle. This is the time to expose yourself to new things, take risks, get higher education, travel, meet new people. This is true to a lesser degree for those born in sun signs of the same element (earth, air, fire, water signs). Jupiter retrogrades in Virgo until April 30, however, so postpone risk-taking ventures until that date. Virgo and other earth signs (Taurus, Capricorn) should have many new opportunities coming their way for the rest of the summer. When Jupiter enters Libra, October 10, this air sign (plus Aquarius and Gemini) should get set for beneficial rays through the remainder of 1992.

WHO WILL BE TIGHTENING THEIR BELTS?

Saturn moving through your sun sign signals a period of self-discipline—the very opposite of a Jupiter period! This year Aquarians will have to buckle down and put nose to the grindstone. With your ruler, Uranus, helping out in no-nonsense Capricorn, this can be a time when you'll achieve much on a practical level, giving those far-out ideas a solid foundation. Saturn periods aren't easy, but there is some consolation in that the work you do now will have lasting results. Leo, the opposite sign of Aquarius, will also feel Saturn's restrictions. We'll be seeing more of the hard-working side of Leo and less of his flamboyant show-biz side this year.

The Merger of the 1990s— Uranus and Neptune

No discussion of when to make your moves would be complete without dealing with this year's major planetary happening, the alignment of Uranus and Neptune in Capricorn. This alignment will be exact (and have the most dramatic effects) next year—but the forces have been in effect since April 1991, and will continue until December 1995. They're sure to be affecting the overall focus of your life and determining the prevailing trends of the 1990s.

Alignments of the slow-moving outer planets (Uranus, Neptune, and Pluto) are rare, but when they do occur, there is a global change in consciousness that alters the course of history. The last time was a Pluto-Uranus merger in the radical 1960s (in Virgo) and in the last century, the same conjunction in Aries preceded the Civil War. Those of you born from September 1964–September 1968, at the time of the 1960s alignment, will be especially energized on a personal and collective level by the happenings of the 1990s.

Uranus (revolution, social reform, sudden changes, electricity, high tech) and Neptune (imagination, creativity, dissolution, escapism, film, drugs, oil!), two mysterious planets, together in Capricorn (tradition, structure, organizations, corporations, status) suggest both spiritual and sociological revolutions. Possibilities include the dissolving of established structures—anything with an "ism" attached, including rigid fundamentalist systems of belief. On a positive note, this could be a time of creative renaissance—revolutionary medicines, imaginative spiritual high-tech ventures, the blending of spiritual and social concerns, the expanded use of electronic media such as global satellite entertainment networks, revolutionary changes in energy use, which could positively affect oil-producing countries—this is another potential face of a decade when these two creative planetary forces, working in tandem, bring us together in new ways.

Look for more futuristic, imaginative structures in the creative arts, imaginative yet practical inventions, a structured space-age look in fashions reminiscent of the 1960s, a more creative and expanded use of computers. In Capricorn, the sign of traditions and institutions, the establishment as we know it is due for sweeping changes. Take note of these changes on a personal level (especially if you have planets in Capricorn or Capricorn rising) to plan how you can maximize your role in the drama of the decade.

6

How to Pick
the Big Day

You may have wondered what a difference a day could make when planning a party, timing your big event, signing a lease or contract. Twenty-four little hours can make a big difference, most astrologers would agree. You can give your event the luckiest send-off possible by choosing the time according to the techniques of electional astrology, which astrologers use to find the optimum time for a specific action.

When you set a date for an event, whether it's something as routine as a business meeting or as momentous as a wedding, you are giving that event a "birthday." Therefore, that moment has a horoscope, with the planets and aspects to be interpreted just like the horoscope of a person. Astrologers, who believe that each moment reveals potential for success or failure, have developed a technique called electional astrology for finding the best time for a given event.

Electional astrology is routinely practiced in the Far East, where the governments of India, Sri Lanka, Thailand, and Nepal regularly consult astrologers before setting important dates. Closer to home, Thomas Jefferson is thought to have set the signing of the Declaration of Independence by consulting astrological tables. The governor of California in 1967, Ronald Reagan, is believed to have timed his 12:16 A.M. inauguration by the stars and is known to have relied on astrological advice to time his later Presidential schedule. Tycoon J. P. Morgan and opera legend Enrico Caruso were among those who moved on the advice of astrologer Evangeline Adams. The most successful English monarch, Elizabeth I, had her personal court astrologer, John Dee, time her coronation for the most auspicious aspects of her horoscope.

Though the techniques for electional astrology are often quite complex for a neophyte astrologer, there are some basic guidelines that can be very helpful in planning your schedule. When choosing the right time for a special event such as a marriage, the launching of a product, starting a business, or signing an important document, you should realize that it is not always possible to find the "perfect" time, one that meets all the possible criteria for success. However, you can try to avoid the major problem times within the parameters of your schedule.

Here are a few general rules for choosing the right day for your event. First, consider the fast-moving planets, the moon and Mercury. A waxing moon is considered better for action than a waning moon. Avoid the period every two days known as the void of course moon (this is the time period between the last aspect of the moon and its entrance into a new sign). If you cannot find an astrological calendar that lists the void of course, try for a time period within the first ten hours after the moon changes signs, which are most often "safe" from the void of course. Moon sign changes are noted for Eastern Standard Time in the daily forecast section of this book. Also avoid the time period near an eclipse (this is known as the "shadow of the eclipse"—if possible, allow two weeks before the eclipse and a week after for good measure!).

The other major "no-no" is the Mercury retrograde period (explained in Chapter 5 "When to Make Your Moves in 1992"), which is a three-week time period. The best Mercury is directly AFTER the retrograde.

Since we will be referring to the element of signs, here is a handy reference list. In general, harmonious combinations are:

EARTH SIGNS (Taurus, Virgo, Capricorn) with WATER SIGNS (Cancer, Scorpio, Pisces)
AIR SIGNS (Gemini, Libra, Aquarius) with FIRE SIGNS (Aries, Leo, Sagittarius)
Bear these combinations in mind when you consider the relationship of any two planets on a given day.

When planning your date, you should also consider the nature of the event. If you're signing a contract, going for a job interview, giving a speech—anything where your ability to communicate in the written or spoken word is critical—pay attention to the sign of Mercury. It would be most helpful if Mercury was in an air sign, with the moon harmoniously placed in a fire or air sign.

Mars-related events are the aggressive moves in your life, daring competitive sports and launching new products. Make sure Mars is in direct motion, and preferably in a fire or earth sign such as Aries or Capricorn. However, make certain that Mars is not challenged by Saturn at this time, which can put a damper on your plans. Try to have Saturn in either the same or a complimentary element as Mars, if possible, but not in the same sign or six signs away.

When beginning any venture, time it for the period following a new moon, preferably if the moon is in a fire sign.

A strong Venus in the same sign or element as the sun or moon will enhance artistic projects. Venus also adds sparkle and beauty to parties and social affairs. Plan your party when the moon is in Libra, for an elegant social event. Moon in Cancer or Taurus is good for family gatherings. Moon in Leo or Sagittarius is great for a theatrical production—when you want to make a big splash. Jupiter in harmony with the moon will put everyone in a upbeat mood.

Retrograde periods of Mercury and Saturn are good for getaways, vacations, rest, and relaxation. Try to make your reservations before the retrograde period begins, however. The moon in adventure-loving Sagittarius or communicative Gemini is an excellent time for travel, meeting new people, getting a change of scene. (Avoid the moon in homebound Taurus and Cancer.)

HOW TO SET THE BEST WEDDING DATES

First set your time parameters, giving yourself ample leeway and avoiding Mercury retrograde periods (time it for after a retrograde if possible). Then consider each of the following prerequisites, trying to accomplish as many as possible:

1. First choose the sun sign of your wedding. It is helpful if this is in the same sun sign or element as your birth sign or that of your mate. Some signs, such as Venus-ruled Libra or Taurus are considered naturally favorable. June weddings, most often in Gemini (the "dual" sign of the "twins"), emphasize strong communications and would be best if Mercury is in an air or fire sign.
2. The moon sign should be in harmony with the sun sign in either an earth/water or air/fire element combination. It is also very helpful to have Venus and Jupiter in harmonious elements. Your best bet is a waxing moon, preferably the quarter before the full moon.
3. The ascendant or rising sign sets up the happenings of the marriage and also reveals the attitudes of both partners. Fixed signs (Taurus, Scorpio, Aquarius, Leo) are stable, enduring, steady. These are most preferable, so check the rising sign tables in this book. Active cardinal signs (Aries, Cancer, Capricorn, Libra) could signify striving or competition, rather than a nurturing atmosphere. Mutable signs (Gemini, Virgo, Sagittarius, Pisces) could bring restlessness, instability, infidelity. Try not to have the disruptive planet Uranus six signs away from the ascendant, which could indicate break-offs. Therefore be very careful of marriages with Cancer rising this year.

Helpful Tables in This Book

Mercury Retrograde Periods as well as New Moons, Full Moons, and Eclipses—"When to Make Your Moves in 1992"
Daily Moon Sign Changes—"Daily Forecasts"
Rising Sign Tables
Planetary Movements—"Look Up Your Planets"

A CHECKLIST FOR SCHEDULING BY THE STARS

Moon sign is _____
Moon phase is _____
Sun sign is _____
   (Are they in harmony?)

Is the date in an eclipse period?

Is Mercury retrograde?

Mars and Saturn signs for beginning a project, sports events _____

(check if harmonious—should not be six signs apart or close together in the same sign)

For social events:

Moon sign _____

Venus sign _____

Jupiter sign _____

For weddings:

Sun sign _____

Sun signs of bride and groom _____

Moon sign _____

Venus _____

Jupiter _____

7

Understanding
Your Horoscope Chart

When you first see your chart you'll probably be bewildered by the page filled with mysterious symbols placed on a circle, which is divided into twelve sectors. It looks like another language—and not an easy one to read, at first. But as you get acquainted with your chart, you'll see how it makes common, cosmic sense.

What you are looking at is a picture of a moment in time as seen from a particular place on earth. The earth is the center of the chart, surrounded by the zodiac portion of the sky, divided into wedge-shaped segments. This is simply a graphic depiction of the energies happening at a given moment at a certain place.

Anything that happens can have a horoscope—a meeting, a person, a marriage—anything that can be pinned down to a time and a place. There are horoscopes for countries, cities, businesses and events as well as people.

Each wedge-shaped segment of the chart is called a "house" and deals with a specific area of life. The house reflects the character of two signs. First, the sign that rules the house, which has a natural affinity for it. You might think of this as the house's owner. The planet that rules this sign is also naturally at home in this house. The other important sign is the one that is passing over the house at the moment the chart is cast, which colors the house individually; this sign is what makes the house uniquely "yours" because it is passing over at your moment in time.

The houses rotate counterclockwise from the left center horizontal spoke (that would be the number 9 on a clock), which is the first house or ascendant. The signs were moving clockwise around the chart at the time they were "frozen" in place on the chart.

The houses progress around the chart, starting with the birth of the self in the first chart and evolving through the different areas of life, as the self becomes mature and finally "dissolves" in the twelfth house. It is somewhat like a "Hero's Journey"—a progression of growth and maturity. Here is what each house will tell you about your development.

THE FIRST HOUSE
natural place of Aries and Mars

How you assert yourself—what others see first.

This is the house of "firsts"—the first gasp of independence, the first impression you make, how you initiate matters, the image you choose to project. This is where you advertise yourself. Planets that fall here will intensify how you come across to others. Often the first house will project an entirely different type of personality than the sun sign. For instance a Capricorn with Leo in the first house will come across as much more flamboyant than the average Capricorn. The sign passing over this house is known as your ascendant or rising sign.

THE SECOND HOUSE
home of Taurus and Venus

How you experience the material world, what you value.

Here is your contact with the material world—your attitudes about money, possessions, finances, whatever belongs to you—what you own. Your earning and spending capacity. On a deeper level, this house reveals your sense of self-worth, the inner values that draw wealth in various forms.

THE THIRD HOUSE
home of Gemini and Mercury

How well you communicate with others—are you understood?

This house shows how you reach out to others nearby and interact with the immediate environment. Here is how your thinking process works, how you communicate, if you are misunderstood. It shows your first relationships, experiences with brothers and sisters, how you deal with people close to you, such as your neighbors or pals. It's where you take short trips, write letters, or use the telephone. It shows how your mind works in terms of left-brain logical and analytical functions.

THE FOURTH HOUSE
natural place of Cancer and the Moon

How you are nurtured and made to feel secure.

At the bottom of the chart, the fourth house, like the home, shows the foundation of life, the psychological underpinnings. Here is where you have the deepest confrontations with whom you are, how you make yourself feel secure. It shows your early home environment and the circumstances of the end of your life—your final "home"—as well as the place you call home now. Astrologers look here for information about the parental nurturers in your life.

THE FIFTH HOUSE
home of Leo and the Sun

How you express yourself creatively—your idea of play.

The Leo house is where creative potential develops. Here you express yourself and procreate (children), in the sense that children are outgrowths of your creative ability. But this house most represents your inner childlike self who delights in play. Assuming inner security has been established by the time you reach this house, you are now free to have fun, romance, love affairs, and to GIVE of yourself. This is also the place astrologers look for playful love affairs and brief romantic encounters (rather than long-term commitments).

THE SIXTH HOUSE
home of Virgo and Mercury

How you function in daily life.

The sixth house has been called the "repair and maintenance" department. Here is the shop where you get

101

things done, how you look after others and fulfill responsibilities, such as taking care of pets. Here is your daily survival, your "job" (as opposed to your career, which is the domain of the tenth house), your diet, health, and fitness regimens. This house shows how you take care of your body and maintenance systems so you can perform efficiently in the world.

THE SEVENTH HOUSE
natural place of Libra and Venus

How you form a partnership.

Here is how you relate to others, your close, intimate one-on-one relationships. Your attitudes toward partners and those with whom you enter commitments, contracts, or agreements are here. Open hostilities, lawsuits, divorces as well as marriages happen here. If the first house is the "I"—the seventh or opposite house is the "Not-I"—the complementary partner you attract by the way you come across. If you are having trouble with partnerships, consider what you are attracting by the energies of your first and seventh houses.

THE EIGHTH HOUSE
home of Scorpio and Pluto (also Mars)

How you merge with something greater than yourself.

This is one of the most mysterious and powerful houses, where your energy transforms itself from "I" to "we." As you give up power and control, you unite with what is larger than yourself—two kinds of energies merge and become something greater—and lead to a regeneration of the self. Here are your attitudes toward sex, shared resources, taxes (you share with the government). Because this house involves what belongs to others, you face issues of control and power struggles, or undergo a deep psychological transformation as you bond with another. Here you transcend yourself with the occult, dreams, drugs, or psychic experiences that reflect the collective unconscious.

THE NINTH HOUSE
home of Sagittarius and Jupiter

How you search for wisdom and higher knowledge, your belief system.

As the third house represents the "Lower Mind," its opposite on the wheel, the ninth house, is the "Higher Mind," the abstract, intuitive, spiritual mind that asks "big" questions like why are we here. The ninth house shows what you believe in. After the third house explored what was close at hand, the ninth stretches out to explore more exotic territory, either by traveling, broadening mentally with higher education or stretching spiritually with religious activity. Here is where you write a book or extensive thesis, where you pontificate, philosophize, or preach.

THE TENTH HOUSE
natural place of Capricorn and Saturn

Your public image and how you handle authority.

This house is located directly overhead at the "high noon" position. This is the most "visible" house in the chart, the one where the world sees you. It deals with your public image, your career (but not your routine "job"), your reputation. Here is where you go public, take on responsibilities (as opposed to the fourth house, where you stay home). This will affect the career you choose and your "public relations." This house is also associated with the father figure or whoever else was the authority figure in your life.

THE ELEVENTH HOUSE
home of Aquarius and Uranus

Your support system, how you relate to society, your goals.

Here you extend yourself to a group, a goal, a belief system. This house is where you define what you really want, what kinds of friends you have, your political affiliations, what kind of groups you identify with as an equal. Here is where you could become a socially-conscious humanitarian—or a party-going social butterfly, where you look to others to stimulate you, where you discover your kinship to the rest of humanity. The sign on this house can help you understand what you gain and lose from friendships.

THE TWELFTH HOUSE
home of Pisces and Neptune

How you become selfless.

Here is where the boundaries between yourself and others are blurred. In your trip around the zodiac, you've gone from the "I" of self-assertion in the first house to the final house symbolizing the dissolution that happens before a rebirth, a place where the accumulated experiences are processed in the unconscious. Spiritually oriented astrologers look to this house for your past lives and karma. Places where we go to be alone and do spiritual or reparatory work belong here, such as retreats, religious institutions, hospitals. Here is also where we withdraw from society—or are forced to withdraw because of antisocial activity. Self-less giving through charitable acts is part of this house. In your daily life, the twelfth house reveals your deepest intimacies, your best-kept secrets—especially those you hide from yourself, repressed deep in the unconscious. It is where we surrender a sense of a separate self to a deep feeling of wholeness, such as selfless service in religion or any activity that involves merging with the greater whole. Many famous athletes have important planets in the twelfth house, which enable them to "go with the flow" of the game, to rise above competition and find an inner, almost mystical, strength that transcends their limits. Madonna, the rock star, has a strong twelfth-house emphasis in her horoscope and reflects this house's religious, psychological, and sexual concerns.

WHO'S HOME IN YOUR HOUSES?

Houses are stronger or weaker depending on how many planets are inhabiting them. If there are many planets in a given house, it follows that the activities of that house will be especially important in your life. If the planet that rules the house is also located there, this too adds power to the house.

ASTROLOGY'S SIGN LANGUAGE

Beginners are often baffled by the strange-looking symbols all over their charts. Actually, these symbols are universally recognized and make life easier for the astrologer, because they enable any astrologer of any nationality—from Indian to Russian to American—to read your chart with ease.

This international symbolic language is written in mysterious-looking hieroglyphics called "glyphs"—those are the odd-looking characters, which are actually sort of a cosmic shorthand, representing planets, signs, and aspects. Each character contains the code to its meaning, so once you learn the "code," it's full of clues to the sign, the planet, or relationship between the planets.

The glyphs for the planets are stylized representations of three basic cosmic symbols—the circle for the eternal spirit, the semicircle for the soul, and the cross for matter. The exception to this rule is Pluto, which can be represented either by a glyph that combines the preceding symbols or one that is a stylized version of the letters PL. The relative size and placement of the elements divulge the planet's meaning. For instance, the symbol for Neptune, which is often stylized into a trident, is actually the upturned semicircle of the soul penetrated by matter, revealing this planet's dynamics of bringing cosmic energy into material form and dissolving material form into cosmic energy, the union of the material with the divine.

The more recent discoveries of the asteroids and Chiron are often included on computer charts. These are also exceptions to the rule and have specific glyphs based on their individual personalities rather than the basic cosmic symbols.

Glyphs for the signs go back to ancient times, some as far as ancient Egypt or Chaldea. Some forms are abstractions of the animal symbol of the sign, such as a bull's head for Taurus and a ram's horns for Aries. The roman numeral for two hints at the Gemini twins; similarly the two curved lines joined at the center for Pisces fish. The Libra scales, Sagittarius arrow, and Aquarius waves are keys to the sign's meaning. Scorpio and Virgo's variation on the M shape hint at male and female genitalia. Cancer and Capricorn require you to stretch your imagination a bit more. Cancer's horizontal 69 figure could remind you of a crab's claws or female breasts. Capricorn's V shape, ending in a looped flourish, could be the horns and tail of the sea goat.

The preceding two kinds of glyphs are shown on most astrological charts. However, there are also symbols to describe the aspects or relationships between planets. These are shown by geometric forms, the most important of which are:

- The triangle for a "trine" (120-degree angle)
- A circle with a vertical line for a conjunction, or two planets in near-exact alignment
- Two vertically slanted circles for an opposition (180 degrees)
- A square for 90 degrees
- A six-pointed "asterisk" for a sextile (60 degrees)
- A horizontal K shape for a quincunx (150 degrees)

8

The Ultimate Compatibility Chart

"I've got your number!" is the old saying when you've finally figured out what makes someone tick. But, in astrology, this cliché takes on new meaning—getting someone's astrological number in relation to your sign can give you terrific clues, not only to *how* you'll relate to each other, but *why!*

Use this chart to get the "number" of those close to you and then read the explanation in this chapter. I've called it the "ultimate compatibility chart" because you can use it not only to compare sun signs, but to relate *any* two planets within your own horoscope chart or to compare your planets with those of another chart.

Use it to help you understand the dynamics between you and the people you interact with. You might find it the key to getting along better with your boss and co-workers. Or discover what the real dynamics are with your difficult relatives and your best friends.

What this chart *won't* do is tell you that there are signs you can't get along with. There are no two totally incompatible signs—there are many happy marriages between signs that succeed because of the stimulation and "chemistry" their differences provide. To understand your astrological connection with another person, you need to identify the spatial relationship between signs. The sign "next door" is something like your next-door neighbor, who loans you his lawn mower or feeds your cats—or disputes your property boundaries. Signs distant from yours also have attitudes based on their "neighborhood."

A sign by definition is a specific territory, a division of an energy belt called the zodiac, which circles the earth. Each division is distinguished by an element (earth, air, fire, water), a quality or modality (cardinal, fixed, mutable), and a polarity or "charge" (positive/negative). No two signs have the same combination. These variables alternate around the zodiac belt in an established order: first fire, next earth, air, and water. The qualities alternate first with cardinal (active), then fixed (growth), and last mutable (change) signs. It follows that the positive and negative signs also alternate, like the charge of a battery. As the energy flow progresses around the zodiac, starting with Aries, the signs become more complex, less self-oriented. So the place in line around the "belt" becomes a factor, too.

Since the zodiac is a circle, the signs also relate to each other according to the angle of the distance between them. Between signs of the same polarity (masculine/feminine, positive/negative, yin/yang), which are numbers 0, 2, and 4, energy flows most easily (with one exception: the sign opposite yours—number 6). Between signs of different polarity, which are numbered 1, 3, 5, you'll experience tension or challenge (and possibly a very sexy "charge!") Here's how it works out . . .

THE ULTIMATE COMPATIBILITY CHART

	AR	TA	GE	CAN	LEO	VIR	LIB	SC	SAG	CAP	AQ	PIS
Aries	0	1	2	3	4	5	6	5	4	3	2	1
Taurus	1	0	1	2	3	4	5	6	5	4	3	2
Gemini	2	1	0	1	2	3	4	5	6	5	4	3
Cancer	3	2	1	0	1	2	3	4	5	6	5	4
Leo	4	3	2	1	0	1	2	3	4	5	6	5
Virgo	5	4	3	2	1	0	1	2	3	4	5	6
Libra	6	5	4	3	2	1	0	1	2	3	4	5
Scorpio	5	6	5	4	3	2	1	0	1	2	3	4
Sagittarius	4	5	6	5	4	3	2	1	0	1	2	3
Capricorn	3	4	5	6	5	4	3	2	1	0	1	2
Aquarius	2	3	4	5	6	5	4	3	2	1	0	1
Pisces	1	2	3	4	5	6	5	4	3	2	1	0

Find your sign in the vertical list. Then read across the row until you come to the column under the sign of your partner, mate, lover, boss, and so on. Then read the description of the number in this chapter.

Your "0" Relationships

"0" relationships are with those of your own sign, so naturally you'll have much in common. This could be the soul mate you've been looking for—one who understands and sympathizes with you like no other sign can! One who understands your need for space, yet knows how and when to be "there" for you. There are many examples of long-term partnerships between sun sign twins—Roy Rogers and Dale Evans (both Scorpio), Abigail and John Adams (Scorpio), George and Barbara Bush (Gemini), Bob and Delores Hope (both Gemini). Working relationships fare especially well with sun signs in common, though you may have to delegate unwanted tasks to others. In a public lifestyle or one where there is much separation or stimulation, your similarities can hold you together—there is the feeling of "you and me against the world." The problem is when there is too much of a good thing with no stimulation or challenge—or when there is no "chemistry," which can often happen between signs that share so much—the same element, quality, and polarity. The solution is to bring plenty of outside excitement into your lives!

Your "1" Relationships

These signs are your next-door neighbors on the zodiac wheel. Your relationship is based on evolution—you've evolved out of the previous sign carrying energies that have been accumulating and developing through the zodiac cycle. The sign following yours is where your energy is headed, the next step. In a way, it's like sitting at a dinner table and passing the plate from left to right. You receive certain qualities from the previous sign and pass on those, plus your own, to the next.

This is also like a sibling relationship where the sign coming before yours is like a protective older brother or sister, who's "been there," and the next sign is your eager younger sibling. Every sign also has a compensating factor for its predecessor—this sign embodies lessons you should have learned (and which could trip you up if you've forgotten them).

But although both are in the same "family," sibling signs actually have little in common, because you have different basic values (elements), ways of operating (qualities), and types of energy (polarity). You probably won't feel sparks of chemistry or the deep rapport of a soul mate unless other planets in your horoscopes provide this bond. Instead, the emphasis is on pals, best friends, working partners, who are enhanced by the sibling sign position.

The sign ahead can inspire you—they're where you are heading, but you may be afraid to take the first brave step. For example, to Pisces, Aries embodies dynamic, forceful, self-oriented will—whereas Pisces is the formless, selfless, imaginative state where Aries originated. So Aries energizes Pisces, gets Pisces moving. The sign behind backs you up, supports you. This relationship often makes one of the most lasting and contented unions—several famous examples are the Duke and Duchess of Windsor (Cancer/Gemini), Paul Newman and Joanne Woodward (Aquarius/Pisces), and Jerry Hall/Mick Jagger (Cancer/Leo).

To reveal how you'll relate to your zodiac "sibling," here's how energy evolves through the twelve signs:

Aries, the first sign of the zodiac, is "born" from Pisces, the last. In Pisces, individual energy has dissolved into universal energy—to be reasserted again in Aries. Aries is the new "baby"—Pisces is the pre-birth gestation, full of spiritual energy. Pisces reminds self-oriented Aries that there is more to life than "me." Pisces teaches Aries compassion, and consciousness of others, whereas Aries infuses Pisces with new energy and gets Pisces to assert itself.

Taurus is the baby taking the first steps into the material world, feeling its way with the senses. Taurus stabilizes Aries, gives this sign direction and purpose, asks where all that energy and drive is going. Taurus also imposes boundaries and limits to Aries—pulls it down to earth and stubbornly insists "you can't have it your way all the time," or "what are you really getting done?" or "what will it cost?"

Gemini teaches Taurus (who is often stuck on its own turf) to communicate, to socialize, to reach out to others, paving the way for the first emotional water sign, Cancer, where feelings are top priority, so the energy becomes nurturing, self-protective. Cancer adds the dimension of caring to Gemini (who would rather not deal with emotions at all).

The nurturing qualities of Cancer burst forth in Leo. Leo's confidence and self-expression come out of the security Cancer provides. Leo, who needs this kind of caring to shine, can be quite insecure and demanding if good mothering has not been received. And that becomes a hallmark of the Cancer/Leo relationship: ideally, Cancer nurtures Leo (in a not-so-ideal relationship, Cancer's fearfulness holds Leo back) and Leo in turn brings this vulnerable sign out into public life. Virgo is concerned with making things work, with helping, and says, "Leo, this is all very impressive, but is it useful? Will it work? Here's how to improve it." Virgo edits Leo creativity (which Leo might resent, but which makes for a better end result). Leo's confidence rubs off on shyer Virgos.

Like Virgo, Libra is also concerned with measuring up. While Virgo is concerned with the practical, Libra is in love with beauty. When Virgo asks: What good is something beautiful if it doesn't work? Libra answers: Beauty is its own justification. Virgo stimulates and grounds Libra. Libra takes Virgo further into aesthetics.

Scorpio plunges into deep emotional territory that Libra might prefer not to enter. However, the balance of Libra is first necessary for Scorpio to reach its most positive, decisive expression. Scorpio's intensity challenges Libra to look deeper, not to be content with superficial beauty.

Sagittarius evolves from Scorpio's deeper understanding and projects this to higher levels. Sagittarius brings optimism, uplifting ideals and humor to counter Scorpio negativity. Sagittarius also gains direction from the following sign, Capricorn, who brings structure and order to Sagittarius, which can help achieve its aspirations.

Capricorn is inspired by Sagittarius, but this bottomline earth sign is concerned with getting concrete results. Aquarius, its neighbor, brings in higher principles, consideration for the elements of surprise, inventiveness, unpredictability. There is always a higher purpose with Aquarius.

Pisces, the final sign in the cycle, is the most sensitive to outside input (and as a result can be self-sacrificing or self-pitying) and shares a universal with Aquarius. However, Aquarius reminds Pisces of detachment, involvement with a group, and the need to keep perspective. Aries, which has no patience for self-pity, will dry out this watery sign with optimism and drive. Pisces, which represents the amorphous prenatal world, often brings the spiritual dimension into Aries life, which becomes an important part of their relationship.

Your "2" Relationships

With your "2" signs, you share the same electrical charge, so energy flows freely between you. You also are considered to have compatibility though different elements. For example, air and fire work well together—air makes fire burn brighter. But too much of either element can suffocate or blow out the flame. Earth and water signs can either make flowers—as the earth "contains" the water—or mud flats or a wasteland.

The "2's" line up as follows:

Combination A. The earth signs (Taurus, Virgo, Capricorn) with water signs (Cancer, Scorpio, Pisces).

These are usually very fertile nurturing combinations, each providing the emotional and material security the other sign needs to reach full potential. Problems arise when the earth sign's material orientation and "here-and-nowness" stifles the more cosmic water sign's creativity.

Combination B. The air signs (Gemini, Libra, Aquarius) with fire signs (Aries, Leo, Sagittarius).

112

These are very stimulating, energetic combinations. Both kinds of signs are positive, outgoing, active, and this usually describes their relationship as well. The problem with excess here is that the more objective, detached air sign's preference for reason over enthusiasm could cool the fire sign's ardor. The fire sign's enthusiastic but often egocentric and unreasonable approach could in turn exasperate reasoning, relationship-oriented air signs.

Your "3" Relationships

If you recognize that stress in a relationship often stimulates growth, and that sexual tension can be heightened by a challenge, you can succeed with a "3" relationship. These relationships between signs of a similar quality have lots of erotic energy, challenging sparks, and passion. Some of these thrive on difficulty. You can make peace with this sign, but the person probably won't be easy to be with. However, these will also be your least boring partners!

"3's" share the same modality; you're both either cardinal, fixed, or mutable signs. So you'll understand how the other operates, though you won't necessarily share the same basic values or type of energy. One of the things that often happens with this relationship is that you continually confront each other—here is a sign that is just as restless, just as stubborn, or just as driven as you are! This isn't going to be the partner who gives you security, who settles down, or backs you up. Will you compete, join forces, or forge an equal partnership?

Mutable signs, which are the most changeable, understand each other's restlessness and low tolerance for boredom. This is a couple that can easily fragment, however, going off in different directions. This union often falls apart under stress but challenges you mutables to make order out of chaos; in other words, get your act together.

Cardinal couples with equal drive and energy often are characterized by goal-driven intensity—they never sit still. Fixed signs can be the most stable partners or, negatively, they can wrestle for control, war over territory, or have a stubborn Mexican standoff.

Positively, this is one of the sexiest aspects—these two signs challenge each other, bring about growth. Here are some of the issues likely to arise between each "3" pair-up:

ARIES–CANCER

Aries is forced by Cancer to consider the consequences of actions, particularly those that threaten security and hurt feelings. However, introspection cramps Aries style—this sign wants perfect freedom to act as they please and has no patience for self-pity or self-protectiveness. Although Cancer admires Aries' courage, the interaction will have to confront the conflict between the Aries outward-directed desire to have their own way and Cancer's inward-turning drive to create safety and security.

CANCER–LIBRA

Cancer is most satisfied by symbiotic, intimate, emotionally dependent relationships. So when you meet someone you like who is very independent, you feel hurt, rejected and throw up a defensive shell or get moody and depressed. Unfortunately, you risk this happening with Libra, a romantic, but rather emotionally cool sign. Libras want an equal partner, tends to judge their partner on a detached idealistic level, by their looks, style, ideas, conversation. Libra recognizes that the best partnerships are between equals, but the issue here is what do you have to share? Libra won't be able to escape emotions through social activities or intellectual analysis here.

LIBRA–CAPRICORN

Both of you love the good life, but you may have conflicting ideas about how to get it. Capricorn is a very disciplined, goal-directed, ordered worker who requires concrete results. Libra is more about style, abstract principles, and can be quite self-indulgent. Libran indulgence versus Capricorn discipline could be the cruncher here. Another bone to pick would be differing ideas about what's fair and just. Capricorn often believes that the "ends justify the means." Libra upholds fairness over bottom-line concerns.

CAPRICORN–ARIES

Earth wants solidity, fire wants freedom. Both are survivors who love to win. But Capricorn works for status and material rewards—Aries works for glory, heroism, for the joy of being first. Capricorn wants to stay in control. Aries wants freedom. In a positive way, Aries must grow up with Capricorn, but gives this tradition-oriented sign a new young lease on life.

TAURUS–LEO

Leo has an insatiable appetite for admiration, Taurus for pleasure. Taurus sensuality can make Leo feel like a star. Leo's romantic gestures appeal to Taurus on a grand scale. Taurus will have to learn courtship and flattery to keep Leo happy—bring on the champagne and caviar! Leo will have to learn not to tease the bull, especially by withholding affection—and to enjoy simple meat-and-potatoes kinds of pleasures as well. Money can be an important issue here: Leo likes to spend royally, Taurus likes to accumulate.

SCORPIO–LEO

Scorpio wants adventure in the psychic underworld, Leo wants to stay in the throne room. Scorpio challenges Leo to experience life intensely, which can bring out the best in Leo. Leo burns away Scorpio negativity—with low tolerance for dark moods. Scorpio is content to work behind the scenes, giving Leo center stage. But Leo must never mistake a quiet Scorpio for a gentle pussycat. There will be plenty of action behind the scenes. Settle issues of control without playing power games.

SCORPIO–AQUARIUS

Aquarius' love of freedom and Scorpio's possessiveness could clash here. Scorpio wants to own you—Aquarius wants to remain friends. This is one unpredictable sign Scorpio can't figure out but has fun trying. Aquarius' flair for group dynamics could bring Scorpio out. However, too many outside interests could put a damper on this combination.

TAURUS–AQUARIUS

Taurus lives in the touchable realm of the earth, Aquarius in the electric, invisible realm of air, which can't be fenced in. It's anyone's guess if Taurus can ground Aquarius or if Aquarius can uplift Taurus. Taurus' talent as a realist could be the anchor this free spirit needs. Aquarian originality opens new territory to Taurus.

GEMINI–VIRGO

Nerves can be stimulated or frayed when these Mercury-ruled signs sound off. Both have much to say to each other—from different points of view. Gemini deals in abstractions, Virgo in down-to-earth facts. Common interests could keep this pair focused on each other.

VIRGO–SAGITTARIUS

Safety versus risk could be the hallmark of this relationship. Virgo plays it safe and cautious, Sagittarius operates on faith and enthusiasm. You're two natural teachers who have different philosophies and have much to learn from each other. When Virgo picks things apart or gets bogged down in details, Sag urges them to look for the TRUTH—the big picture. Sag's lack of organization or follow-through will either drive Virgo crazy or provide a job. Virgo pins Sagittarius down with facts, deflating overblown promises and sales pitches.

SAGITTARIUS–PISCES

There should be many philosophical and spiritual discussions and debates here. When Sagittarius says I'm right, Pisces says everything's relative. We're all right and wrong, so what? Sagittarius is about elevating the self and Pisces is about merging the self, losing the self. On a less cosmic level, these too high-flying signs may never get down to earth. Pisces' supersensitivity is easily wounded by Sagittarius' moments of truth. But Sag can help sell those creative Piscean ideas; that is, if you don't wander off in different directions.

PISCES–GEMINI

Gemini is always trying to understand, abstract, rationalize. Pisces wants to merge and flow, find a soul mate, go beyond the mind. Pisces' moods get on Gemini's nerves. Gemini runs away from emotional mergers, which really matter to Pisces. Yet Pisces' glamour can intrigue Gemini and Gemini's lightness and wit help Pisces laugh away the blues.

Your "4" Relationships

These are considered the easiest relationships possible, the most compatible partners. You share the same element and the same polarity, but sometimes there is too much of a good thing. These tend to lack the dynamism and sexy sparks of the "3" and "5" relationships. They can be too comfortable as you adjust very easily to each other. But what can you teach each other? If it's too easy, you might look for excitement elsewhere.

Relationships between the three earth signs (Taurus, Virgo, Capricorn) are mutually profitable, both professionally and personally. You won't find the other sign tampering with your financial security, frittering away hard-earned funds, or flirting with danger. You could fulfill your dreams of a comfortable life together. Too much comfort could leave you yawning, however—you need someone to shake you up once in a while.

Fire signs (Aries, Leo, Sagittarius) can ignite each other, but watch out for temper and jealousy. You both demand exclusive attention, are happiest when your ego is stroked and you feel like number one, so you may have to curb any tendency to flirt. Because you tend to be big risk takers and free spenders, you may have to delegate the financial caretaking carefully or find an expert adviser.

Water signs (Cancer, Scorpio, Pisces) have found partners who aren't afraid of emotional depths or heights. These are the ones who can understand and sympathize with your moods. This could be your soul mate who gives you the emotional security you need. When moods collide, however, you could find it difficult to get each other out of deep water.

Air signs (Gemini, Libra, Aquarius) communicate well together. There is no heavy emotionalism or messy ego or possessiveness to deal with. You both respect the need for freedom and personal space and can make your own rules for an open, equal partnership. Staying in touch is the problem here. You could be so involved in your own pursuits that you let romance fly by or are never there for each other. Be sure to cultivate things in common because, unless there are many shared interests, it is easy to float away.

Your "5" Relationships

This is the relationship that challenges your sign the most. You have to stretch yourself to make this work. You are totally different in basic values (element), way of acting (quality), kind of energy (polarity) and, unlike your next-door signs that also have those differences, you don't have the closeness of being next in line. Instead of being beside you, the other sign is off on the other side of the zodiac.

On the other hand, this very separateness can have an erotic quality, the attraction of the unknown (and unattainable). This is someone you'll never quite figure out.

And this sign also has many threatening traits—if you get into this relationship, there will be risks, you won't quite know what to expect. The "5" relationship is the proverbial square peg and round hole. Even though the stress of making this relationship work can be great, so can the stimulation and creativity that result from trying to find out what makes each other tick.

When positive and negative signs come together, lights go on, as you discover methods in dealing with situations and different ways of viewing the world, which can move you out of the doldrums. Here is how your sign relates to its "5" partners.

ARIES: SCORPIO/VIRGO

Scorpio, who tends to be secretive and manipulative, embodies everything that is foreign to Aries. Aries is clearcut, openly demanding. If an Aries attacks, it will be swift and open. Scorpio will wait for the time when an opponent is most vulnerable—years, if necessary—to deal the lethal blow. Aries burns out much sooner. Yet your very strong differences only make the conquest more exciting.

Virgo thinks the way to solve problems is to get organized, think things through—steamrolling Aries wants fast action, quick results. Both Scorpio and Virgo will challenge Aries to go against the grain—be careful, organized, persevere, delve deeply, look at the long haul. Aries will have to tone down impulsiveness with these signs.

TAURUS: LIBRA/SAGITTARIUS

Libra, also Venus ruled, is involved with the abstract, idealistic side of the planet, whereas Taurus is involved with the sensual, materialistic, self-indulgent side. Libra challenges Taurus to abstract, to get into the mind as well as the body. Taurus will bring Libra down to earth and provide stability for this sign.

Sagittarius challenges Taurus to expand its territory. Taurus is the most rooted of signs, and can be immobile—Sagittarius is the happy wanderer. Taurus moves outside its turf with Sagittarius, who challenges it intellectually, spiritually, and physically.

GEMINI: SCORPIO/CAPRICORN

Here, playful, verbal, mental Gemini is confronted by the failure to probe, the failure to deal with passion, deep real emotional stuff with Scorpio. Contact with Scorpio often precipitates a crisis in Gemini's life as this sign realizes there is something powerful it's been missing. Scorpio challenges Gemini to delve deeply and make commitments rather than deals.

Capricorn makes Gemini develop discipline, set goals, and do practical bottom-line things the sign is not prepared to do. Capricorn has no tolerance for fragmented efforts and forces Gemini to focus and produce.

CANCER: SAGITTARIUS/AQUARIUS

Fearful, frugal Cancer must take risks to make a relationship work with Sagittarius, who loves to gamble, has faith in the Universe. Everyone's buddy, Aquarius makes Cancer give love with an open hand, placing less emphasis on personal security, property.

Cancer must give up possessiveness with both these signs, who actually enjoy the kind of insecurity that Cancer most fears. In these relationships, Cancer's expectations of what a relationship should be have to change. It gets no protection from either sign and its favorite sympathy-winning techniques (playing "poor little me," whining, clinging, or complaining) only alienate these signs further. In the process of coping with these distant signs, however, Cancer can eventually become more independent and truly secure within itself.

LEO: CAPRICORN/PISCES

Capricorn demands that Leo deliver on promises. With this down-to-earth sign, Leo can't coast for long on looks and star power. Capricorn wants results, pushes Leo to produce, and casts a cold eye on shows of ego and sees through bluffs. Conversely, both enjoy many of the same things, such as a high-profile lifestyle, if for different reasons.

Pisces is on another planet from solar Leo—the Neptunian embodies all that is not-self. This is a sign that devalues the ego. Pisces teaches Leo to be unselfish, to exercise compassion and empathy, to walk in others' shoes. Leo has to give up arrogance and false pride for a lasting relationship with Pisces.

VIRGO: AQUARIUS/ARIES

Aquarius sheds light on Virgo's problem with getting bogged down in details. Interaction with Aquarius expands Virgo, prepares this sign for the unpredictable, the sudden, the unexpected. Aquarius gets Virgo to broaden scope—to risk experimenting. Aries gives Virgo positive energy and gets Virgo away from self-criticism and out into the world.

LIBRA: PISCES/TAURUS

Looking for a decision-maker—Libra won't find it in Pisces! Pisces and Libra both share an artistic nature, but executed in a different way. Libra can't project its need for direction onto Pisces. Libra says, "What should I do?" Pisces says, "I know how you feel. It's tough not knowing what to do." Pisces challenges Libra to go within, to understand where others are coming from rather than expecting them to conform to an abstract ideal.

Taurus brings Libra into the practical material world and gives this sign grounding, but Taurus will also insist on material value. Taurus will ask, "How much does it cost?" Libra says, "I don't care, it's so pretty." Libra would rather not worry about function and operations, which become Taurus' task. Libra will either desperately need Taurus' practicality or find it a drag.

SCORPIO: ARIES/GEMINI

Listen for the clanking of iron shields as Mars-ruled Aries and Scorpio get together. Both of you thrive on challenge and find it in each other. The issue here: who's the conquerer when neither will give in or give up? You'll have to respect each other's courage and bravery, and enjoy the sparks, like the archetypal Aries/Scorpio couple, Spencer Tracy and Katharine Hepburn.

Gemini is the sign you can never pin down or possess—and this is super-fascinating for Scorpio. Their quicksilver wit and ability to juggle many people and things are talents not found in the Scorpio repertoire. Scorpios never stop trying to fathom the power of Gemini—just when they've almost got them pegged, Gemini's on to something or someone else! As long as you don't expect devotion, you won't be disappointed.

SAGITTARIUS: TAURUS/CANCER

This is a dialogue between the rooted and the rootless. Both Taurus and Cancer are the most home-loving signs of the zodiac, while Sagittarius is the eternal wanderer—mentally, physically, or both. Will they be content to keep the home fires burning for Sagittarius? Another sticky point: both signs are very careful with money. However, these two financially savvy signs could help Sagittarius achieve miracles instead of talking about them. Sag will have to learn patience with Taurus, who will inevitably try to tie Sag down. Cancer could dampen Sag's spirits with self-pity if they feel neglected in any way. Sag will have to learn sensitivity to feelings. If Sag can give up the position as teacher and become a student, these relationships might last.

CAPRICORN: GEMINI/LEO

Both of these signs are social charmers who need organization, which is Capricorn's forte. They can help Capricorn get a desired position with Gemini's deft charm or Leo's warmth and poise. The trade-off is that Capricorn will have to learn to take life less seriously, be as devoted to the partnership as to work. Otherwise these two signs will look for amusement elsewhere. Gemini should inspire Capricorn to diversify, communicate, and spread wings socially. Leo adds confidence, authority, status. They'll appreciate Capricorn's adding structure to their lives.

AQUARIUS: CANCER/VIRGO

Aquarius, the most freedom-loving sign, here encounters two different dimensions, both of which tend to bring this sign back to the realities of operating on a day-to-day level (Virgo) and honoring emotional attachments, the level of feeling (Cancer). Cancer is the home-loving sign who values security, family, emotional connections—an area often dismissed by Aquarians. Virgo is about organization, critical judgment, efficiency—which enhance Aquarius accomplishments.

PISCES: LEO/LIBRA

With Leo, Pisces learns to find and project itself. Leo enjoys Pisces talent and often profits by it. In return Leo gives this often-insecure sign confidence. With Leo, Pisces can't hide any longer, must come out from the depths—but Leo will not sympathize or indulge Pisces' blue moods or self-pity. Pisces has to give up negativity with Leo.

Libra's instinct is to separate and analyze. Pisces instinct is to merge. The more Pisces goes into emotions, the more Libra becomes cool and detached. But Pisces can gain objectivity from this relationship, which insists on seeing both sides of any matter equally. Libra can provide the balance that keeps Pisces out of the depths.

Your "6" Relationships

"6" relationships are with your opposite sign in the zodiac. This sign is your complement, your other half who manifests qualities that you think you don't have. There are many marriages between "opposite numbers," because one sign expresses what the other suppresses.

Because most lasting relationships are between equals, the attraction to your "opposite number" could backfire. What happens if you're an easygoing Aquarius married to a star-quality Leo and you decide it's time to show off your natural charisma on center stage? Or a disorganized Pisces with an efficient Virgo who goes on a clean-up, shape-up program and out-organizes the Virgo? No longer does the opposite partner have exclusive rights to certain talents or attitudes. If they can make adjustments to the new you, fine. Otherwise, someone could be out of a job.

It's an excellent idea to ask yourself, if you are attracting your opposite number in love or other relationships, what these signs are acting out for you. It could be a clue to what you need to develop. Sometimes, after the initial chemistry dies down, and two opposite signs actually begin living together, you'll be irritated by the same qualities that at first attracted you. That's because they reveal the part you are afraid of within yourself—the part you haven't really claimed for yourself, and you resent them from taking it over. Here's how it works out with opposite numbers: The more you learn to express "both sides of the same coin," the better chance your relationship with a "6" will have.

ARIES–LIBRA

Aries brings out Libra's placating, accommodating talents. And at first, Libra is happy to play the charmer in exchange for Aries' decisiveness. Aries revels in the chance to take charge and to be so openly needed. But in close quarters, Aries seems too pushy, too bossy. And when Libra decides to make its own decisions, Aries had better learn to charm.

VIRGO–PISCES

In Pisces, Virgo finds someone who apparently needs their services badly. Virgo in turn is attracted to Pisces because this sign can deal with the tricky side of life that can't be organized or made to run on schedule. Sensitive Pisces seems to need Virgo's clarity, orderliness, and practicality to keep together and in line. You can see how easy it is for this to become a bargain between the helper and the apparently helpless. When Pisces gets organized and Virgo gets in touch with their own irrational side, these two could form a more solid relationship.

TAURUS–SCORPIO

This is one of the most powerful attractions, which is often found in marriages and long-term relationships. Some of these couples manage to balance out their differences nicely; others are just too stubborn to give up or give in. The uncomplicated, earthy, sensual Taurus likes safety, comfort, and pleasurable physical things. Scorpio, who enjoys the challenge and dangers of intense feelings (and could live in a monk's cell) is often attracted to danger and risk. Scorpio wants a deep, powerful merger. Taurus likes to stay above ground, enjoying innocent pleasures. Both are possessive and jealous, with a need to control their own territory. Scorpio marvels at the uncomplicated basic drives of Taurus—couldn't they get into trouble together? Taurus enjoys teasing Scorpio with promises of innocent pleasure, but learns that Scorpios sting when teased. Settle issues of control early on—and never underestimate each other's strength.

GEMINI–SAGITTARIUS

Gemini is the eager student of the world; Sagittarius is the perfect guide, only too happy to teach, enlighten, and expound. This is a very stimulating combination. Sagittarius enjoys telling others what to believe, however, and Gemini can't be bossed. Gemini also turns off fiery confrontations and absolute declarations of truth, and may deflate Sagittarius with barbs of wit. On a positive note, this could be a wonderful combination both socially and professionally. Romantically it works best if they can be both student and teacher to each other.

CANCER–CAPRICORN

Both of these signs have strong defense mechanisms. Cancer's is a protective shell, Capricorn's is a cold stony wall. In a relationship, both of these defenses play off one other. Cancer shows weakness (complains, whines) as a means of getting protection, which dovetails nicely with Capricorn's need to play the authoritarian parental father figure (even if female) who takes responsibility for the vulnerable child (Cancer). But if Capricorn shows vulnerability, such as a fear of not being "right," Cancer panics, becomes insecure, and erects a self-protective shell. On the other hand, if Capricorn takes over Cancer's life, this active cardinal sign gets crabby. Learning to "parent" each other and reinforce strong traditional values could be the key to happiness here.

LEO–AQUARIUS

Here we have two stubborn fixed signs with opposite points of view. Leo is "me-oriented" and does not like to share. Aquarius is "them-oriented" and identifies with others. The Leo charisma comes from projecting the self—others are there for applause. Aquarius shines as the symbol of spokesperson of a group, which reflects self-importance. Leo stands apart, onstage; Aquarius stands with the crowd. Leo is not about to become one of the Aquarius crowd (especially if the crowd includes Aquarius' ex-lovers). Aquarius will not confine interests to Leo (become a Leo fan). If Leo can learn to share and Aquarius can give one-on-one attention, this could balance out.

9

Keeping Your
Lover Faithful

According to the last U.S. census report, marriage and committed relationships are on the upswing. But with women entering and staying in the workplace, generally leading more independent lives, and mingling with available men, extramarital affairs are also on the rise! Although the danger of sexually transmitted diseases has discouraged promiscuity, the actual statistics on marital success are not encouraging—almost four out of ten marriages fail before the fourth anniversary, according to a 1990 survey by Adweek's *Marketing Week*.

With so many temptations to stray, one of the biggest concerns in any long-term relationship is keeping your love life exciting and fulfilling—and your mate from wandering. Even though there is no "golden rule" for fidelity, astrology can help you to assess your lover's needs for freedom versus closeness and balance them with your own, for a more fulfilling and committed partnership.

To understand your partner's potential for fidelity, it's important to discover what an ideal relationship means to him or her—for some people, the major emphasis is on a safe, secure home; for others it's a soul mate; for still others, it's stimulating companionship. One of the easiest ways to get insights into your partner's expectations and turn-ons is by using their astrological element. Signs are grouped by four elements—fire, earth, air, and water; each element has certain characteristics that can give you valuable clues to your partner's basic romantic character.

THE FIRE SIGNS (Aries, Leo, Sagittarius)

Fire signs are the Don Juans of the zodiac who like the excitement of "playing with fire" but rarely consider the consequences of possibly being burned. Great romantics, they tend to fall head over heels in love—and while the fantasy lasts, it's a blazing passion. When disappointed, however, fire signs can burn out fast and fall out of love easily, which often happens when the responsibilities and realities of life close in. Fire sign women enjoy the excitement of a life outside the home and are rarely content with a wife/mother role. In love, they often have idealistic fantasies that are difficult for mates to sustain. They tend to "see what they want to see" and become very disillusioned when their lover's human frailties become obvious. Nevertheless, it is possible to have a lasting relationship—and not get burned—with these passionate lovers.

The Aries Lover—To keep your Aries mate red-hot, be sure to maintain your energy level. This is one sign that shows little sympathy for aches, pains, and physical complaints. Curb any tendency toward self-pity—whining is one sure Aries turn-off (water signs take note). This is an open, direct sign—don't expect your lover to probe your innermost needs. Intense psychological discussions that would thrill a Cancer or Scorpio only make Aries restless. Aries is not the stay-at-home type; this sign is sure to have plenty of activities going on at once. Share them (or they'll find someone else who will)!

Always be a bit of a challenge to your Aries mate—this sign loves the chase almost as much as the conquest. So don't be too easy or accommodating—let them feel a sense of accomplishment when they've won your heart.

Stay up-to-date in your interests and appearance. You can wear the latest style off the fashion-show runway with an Aries, especially if it's bright red. Aries is a pioneer, an adventurer, always ahead of the pack. Play up your frontier spirit. Present the image of the two of you as an unbeatable team, one that can conquer the world, and you'll keep this courageous sign at your side.

Since they tend to idealize their lovers, Aries is especially disillusioned when their mates flirt. Be sure they always feel like number one in your life.

The Leo Lover—Whether the Leo is a sunny upbeat partner or reveals catlike claws could depend on how you handle the royal Leo pride. A relationship is for TWO people—a fact that ego-centered Leo can forget. You must gently remind them. Be well-groomed and dressed, someone they're proud to show off.

Leo thinks big—so don't you be petty or miserly—and likes to live like a king. Remember special occasions with a beautifully wrapped gift or flowers. Make an extra effort to treat them royally. Keep a sense of fun and playfulness and loudly applaud Leo's creative efforts. React, respond, be a good audience! If Leo's ignored, this sign will seek a more appreciative audience—fast! Cheating Leos are almost always looking for an ego boost.

Be generous with compliments. You can't possibly overdo here. Always accentuate the positive. Make them feel important by asking for advice and consulting them often. Leo enjoys a charming, sociable companion, but be sure to make them the center of attention in your life.

The Sagittarius Lover—Be a mental and spiritual traveling companion. Sagittarius is a footloose adventurer whose ideas know no boundaries—so don't try to fence them in! Sagittarians resent restrictions of any kind. For a long-lasting relationship, be sure you are in harmony with Sagittarius' ideals and spiritual beliefs. They like to feel that their life is constantly being elevated, taken to a higher level. Since down-to-earth matters often get put aside in the Sagittarian's scheme of things, get finances under control (money matters upset more relationships with Sagittarians than any other problem), but try to avoid being the stern disciplinarian in this relationship (find a good accountant).

Sagittarius is not generally a homebody (unless there are several homes). Be ready and willing to take off on the spur of the moment, or they'll go without you. Sports, outdoor activities, and physical fitness are important—stay in shape with some of Sagittarian Jane Fonda's tapes. Dress with flair and style—it helps if you look especially good in sportswear. Sagittarian men like beautiful legs, so play up yours. And this is one of the great animal lovers so try and get along with the dog, cat, or horse.

THE EARTH SIGNS (Taurus, Virgo, Capricorn)

Earth signs tend to think long and hard before leaving a solid relationship. These signs naturally revere home life. However, if there is something lacking sensually in the relationship, or if outside activities seem too important to their mate, they can be shaken up and swept away by a very unlikely and surprisingly impractical affair. Earth sign infidelities are the stuff of scandals. In the 1950s, cool Virgo actress Ingrid Bergman stunned the nation by leaving her solid marriage for a volcanically passionate liaison with an Italian director. But your earthy lover will stay faithful if you focus on building a solid foundation; don't stint on affection, and emphasize the cozy comforts of home.

The Taurus Lover—Taurus is an extremely sensual, affectionate, nurturing lover, but can be quite possessive. Taurus likes to "own" you. Don't hold back with them or play power games. If you need more space in the relationship, be sure to set clear boundaries, letting them know exactly where they stand. When ambiguity in a relationship makes Taurus uneasy, they may go searching for someone more solid and substantial. A Taurus romance works best where the limits are clearly spelled out.

Taurus needs physical demonstrations of affection—don't hold back on hugs. Together, you should create an atmosphere of comfort, good food, and beautiful surroundings. In fact, Taurus is often seduced by surface physical beauty alone. Their five senses are highly susceptible so find ways to appeal to all of them! Your home should be a restful haven from the outside world. Get a great sound system, some comfortable furniture to sink into, and keep the refrigerator stocked with treats. Most Taureans would rather entertain on their own turf than gad about town, so it helps if you're a good host or hostess.

Taurus likes a calm, contented, committed relationship. This is not a sign to trifle with. Don't flirt or tease if you want to please. Don't rock the boat or try to make this sign jealous. Instead, create a steady, secure environment with lots of shared pleasures.

The Virgo Lover—Virgo may seem cool and conservative on the surface, but underneath you'll find a sensual romantic. Think of Raquel Welch, Sophia Loren, Jacqueline Bisset, Garbo! It's amazing how seductive this practical sign can be!

They are idealists, however, looking for someone who meets their high standards. If you've measured up, they'll do anything to serve and please you. Virgos love to feel needed, so give them a job to do in your life. They are great fixer-uppers. Take their criticism as a form of love and caring, of noticing what you do. Bring them out socially—they are often very shy. Calm their nerves with good food, a healthy environment, trips to the country.

Mental stimulation is a turn-on to this Mercury-ruled sign. An intellectual discussion could lead to romantic action, so stay on your toes and keep well-informed. This sign often mixes business with pleasure so it helps if you share the same professional interests—you'll get to see more of your busy mate. With Virgo, the couple who works as well as plays together, stays together.

The Capricorn Lover—These people are ambitious—even if they are the stay-at-home-partner in your relationship. They will be extremely active, have a strong sense of responsibility to their partner, and take commitments seriously. However, they might look elsewhere if the relationship becomes too dutiful. They also need romance, fun, lightness, humor, adventure!

Generation gaps are not unusual in Capricorn romances, where the older Capricorn partner works hard all through life and seeks pleasurable rewards with a young partner, or the young Capricorn gets a taste of luxury and instant status from an older lover. This is one sign that grows more interested in romance as they age! Younger Capricorns often tend to put business way ahead of pleasure.

Capricorn is impressed by those who entertain well, have "class," and can advance their status in life. Keep improving yourself and cultivate important people. Stay on the conservative side. Extravagant or frivolous loves don't last—Capricorn keeps an eye on the bottom line. Even the wildest Capricorns, such as Elvis Presley, Rod Stewart, or David Bowie, show a conservative streak in their personal lives. It's also important to demonstrate a strong sense of loyalty to your family, especially older members. This reassures Capricorn, who'll be happy to grow old along with you!

THE AIR SIGNS (Gemini, Libra, Aquarius)

Air sign lovers usually think their actions are justified and can rationalize any affair away, but they are least likely to get involved in an outside relationship if they communicate well with their partner. If they feel that their wings are clipped by commitment or if heavy emotional dramas weigh them down, they could fly away. They often tend to have accidental affairs, which happen on the spur of the moment, rather than deliberately planned and executed conquests. Sometimes relationships with friends become intimate sexually, because these are already people with whom they communicate. But they are unlikely to stray too far from the nest if they are given plenty of space and a stimulating atmosphere.

The Gemini Lover—Keeping Gemini faithful is like walking a tightrope. This sign needs stability and a strong home base to accomplish their goals. But they also require a great deal of personal freedom.

A great role model is Barbara Bush, a Gemini married to another Gemini. This is a sign that loves to communicate! Sit down and talk things over. Don't interfere: be interested in your partner's doings, but have a life of your own and ideas to contribute. Since this is a gadabout social sign, don't insist on quiet nights at home when your Gemini is in a party mood.

Gemini needs plenty of rope but a steady hand. Focus on common goals and abstract ideals. Gemini likes to share—be a twin soul, do things together. Keep up on their latest interests. Stay in touch mentally and physically, use both your mind and your hands to communicate.

Variety is the spice of life to this flirtatious sign. Guard against jealousy—it is rarely justified. Provide a stimulating sex life—this is a very experimental sign—to keep them interested. Be a bit unpredictable. Don't let love-making become a routine. Most of all, sharing lots of laughs together can make Gemini take your relationship very seriously.

The Libra Lover—Libra enjoys life with a mate and needs the harmony of a steady relationship. Outside affairs can throw them off balance. However, members of this sign are natural charmers who love to surround themselves with admirers, and this can cause a very possessive partner to feel insecure. Most of the time, Librans, who love to be the belle of the ball, are only testing their allure with harmless flirtations and will rarely follow through, unless they are not getting enough attention or there is an unattractive atmosphere at home.

Mental compatibility is what keeps Libra in tune. Unfortunately this sign, like Taurus, often falls for physical beauty or someone who provides an elegant lifestyle, rather than someone who shares their ideals and activities, the kind of sharing that will keep you together in the long run.

Do not underestimate Libra's need for beauty and harmony. To keep them happy, avoid scenes. Opt for calm, impersonal discussion of problems (or a well-reasoned debate) over an elegant dinner. Pay attention to the niceties of life. Send little gifts like Valentines and don't forget birthdays and anniversaries. Play up the romance to the hilt—with all the lovely gestures and trimmings—but tone down intensity and emotional drama (Aries, Scorpio take note). Libra needs to be surrounded by a physically tasteful atmosphere—elegant, well-designed furnishings, calm colors, good manners, and good grooming at all times.

The Aquarius Lover—Aquarius is one of the most independent, least domestic signs. Finding time alone with this sign may be one of your greatest challenges. They are everybody's buddy, usually surrounded by people they collect, some of whom may be old lovers who are now "just friends." However, it is unlikely that old passions will be rekindled if you become Aquarius' number-one best friend as well as lover, and if you get actively involved in other important aspects of Aquarius' life, such as the political or charitable causes they believe in.

Aquarius needs a supportive backup person who encourages them, but is not overly possessive when their natural charisma attracts admirers by the dozen. Take a leaf from Joanne Woodward, whose marriage to perennial Aquarius heartthrob Paul Newman has lasted more than 30 years! Encourage them to develop their original ideas. Don't rain on their parade if they decided suddenly to market their spaghetti sauce and donate the proceeds to their favorite charity, or drive racing cars. Share their goals, be their fan, or you'll never see them otherwise.

You may be called on to give them grounding where needed. Aquarius needs someone who can keep track of their projects. But always remember, it's basic friendship—with the tolerance and common ideals that implies—that will hold you together.

THE WATER SIGNS (Cancer, Scorpio, Pisces)

The fidelity of these emotional signs is often determined by how secure they feel in a relationship. Always consider their feelings (this might be difficult for air and fire signs) because when their feelings are hurt or they are made to feel insecure, water signs head for consolation, solace, or escape elsewhere. Emotional manipulation and power trips are other negative manifestations of insecurity that could make water signs difficult to live with. But when they do feel secure and supported, they reveal their talent for true intimacy and make romantic, tender, and loving mates.

The Cancer Lover—This is probably the water sign that requires the most TLC. Cancers tend to be very private people who may take some time to open up. They are extremely self-protective and will rarely tell you what is truly bothering them. They operate indirectly, like the movements of the crab. You may have to divine their problem by following subtle clues. Draw them out gently and try to voice any criticisms in the most tactful, supportive way possible.

Family ties are especially strong for Cancer. They will rarely break a strong family bond. Create an intimate family atmosphere, with emphasis on food and family get-togethers. You can get valuable clues to Cancer appeal from their mothers and their early family situation. If their early life was unhappy, it is even more important that they feel they have found a close family with you.

Encouraging their creativity can counter Cancer's moodiness, which is also a sure sign of emotional insecurity. Find ways to distract them from negative moods. Calm them with a good meal or a trip to the seashore. Cancers are usually quite nostalgic and attached to the past. So be careful not to throw out their old treasures or photos.

The Scorpio Lover—Scorpios are often deceptively cool and remote on the outside, but don't be fooled: this sign always has a hidden agenda and feels very intensely about most things. The disguise is necessary because Scorpio does not trust easily; but when they do, they are devoted and loyal, will stick with you through the toughest times. You can lean on this very intense and focused sign. The secret is in first establishing that basic trust through mutual honesty and respect.

Mars-ruled Scorpio is fascinated by power and control in all its forms. They don't like to compromise—it's all or nothing. Therefore they don't trust or respect anything that comes too easily. Be a bit of a challenge, keep them guessing. Maintain your own personal identity, in spite of Scorpio's desire to probe your innermost secrets.

Sex is especially important to this sign, which will demand fidelity from you (though they may not plan to deliver it themselves), so communication on this level is critical. Explore Scorpio's fantasies together. Scorpio is a detective—watch your own flirtations—don't play with fire. This is a jealous and vengeful sign, so you'll live to regret it. Scorpio's rarely flirt for the fun of it themselves. There is usually a strong motive behind their actions.

Scorpio has a fascination with the dark, mysterious side of life. If unhappy, they are capable of carrying on a secret affair. So try to emphasize the positive, constructive side of life with them. Don't fret if they need time alone to sort out problems. They may also prefer time alone with you to socializing with others, so plan romantic getaways together to a private beach or a secluded wilderness spot.

The Pisces Lover—To keep a Pisces hooked, don't hold the string too tight! This is a sensitive, creative sign that may appear to need someone to manage their lives or point the direction out of their Neptunian fog; but if you fall into that role, expect your Pisces to rebel against any strong-arm tactics. Pisces is more susceptible to a play for sympathy than a play for power. They are suckers for a sob story, the most empathetic sign of the zodiac. More than one Pisces has been seduced and held by someone who plays the underdog role.

They are great fantasists, and extremely creative lovers, so use your imagination to add drama and spice to your times together. You can let your fantasies run wild with this sign—and they'll go you one better! They enjoy variety in lovemaking, so try never to let it become routine.

Long-term relationships work best if you can bring Pisces down to earth and, at the same time, encourage their creative fantasies. Deter them from escapism into alcohol or substance abuse by helping them to get counseling, if needed. Pisces will stay with the lover who gives positive energy, self-confidence, and a safe harbor as well as one who is their soul mate.

10

What Your Rising Sign Can Tell You About Your Luckiest Career Choice

Luck is often defined as being in the right place at the right time; that is, a place where you'll be noticed and where you'll make the best possible first impression. Both of these factors are strongly influenced by your rising sign, or ascendant, the sign coming over the horizon at the time you were born.

Your rising sign announces your presence in the world. It's your personal advertisement, casting an overlay or mask on your sun sign, which can make you appear like another sign entirely. Some people's sun signs are so difficult to guess because they have a rising sign with a much stronger public face—it is only after you get to know them that the personality of the sun shines through.

Rising signs change every two hours with the earth's rotation. Those born early in the morning, when the sun was on the horizon, will project the image of the sun sign most strongly. These people are often called a "double Cancer" or a "double Capricorn," because the two strong components of the sun and ascendant reinforce each other. There is usually no problem guessing their sun sign!

In your horoscope chart, the other signs follow the rising sign in sequence, rotating counterclockwise. The rising sign rules your first sector, or "house," which governs your physical impression—and also influences the way you choose to present yourself—your taste and style, as well as your preferred physical environment.

The tenth house around the horoscope circle governs the area of life where you are most visible to the public, where you get noticed and recognized. And this is also used as an indicator of your career, which reflects what you want to become in the public eye and the position you want to achieve in the world. By understanding this area of your chart you have an effective guide to choosing the position that's best for you.

Look up your rising sign in the chart in this book then read the following descriptions for an idea of the type of career criteria most fortunate for you and the way you come across to influential people—such as your job interviewer. These descriptions are based on the most likely mid-heaven position for each rising sign—yours may vary according to the time and latitude you were born. (Check the preceding and following rising signs, if your description doesn't seem to fit.)

ARIES RISING

Lucky Career Tips: You have a strong need to "make it" in spite of difficulties or disappointments. You'll do it the hard way, if necessary. The business world is a natural for you, and you're a born entrepreneur who can take all the "lumps" on the way to the top. Your career choice should be in a highly regarded prestige field. You might also win medals and stripes in the military. Select a job that rewards hard work and dedication, which offers you the chance to work toward executive responsibility. It'll be sure to pay off especially if you start the business yourself. You could take the proverbial shoestring and make a fortune.

Interview Personality: You'll be the most aggressive version of your sun sign. You'll come across as a go-getter, headed for the fast track, dynamic, energetic, aggressive. Billy Graham and Bette Midler show the sparkle and fire of this ascendant. But you can also be somewhat combative, so try to be more diplomatic or head for an area where your feistiness will be appreciated.

TAURUS RISING

Lucky Career Tips: You'll succeed by being an "original." You luckiest career is one in which you can stand out, break out of the mold. Highly creative professional work is fine, but by playing it safe, you could miss the boat. You'll also work well in an unusual group. Head for a futuristic area in the sciences, particularly electronics. You have excellent staying power, good concentration, and an analytical mind. The key is to cultivate and capitalize on the unusual—you may have a very distinctive voice—like Greta Garbo—and could talk your way to success via the electronic media.

Interview Personality: There is nothing lightweight about you. You come across as powerful, steady, thorough, not easily dismissed. You may have a very unusual and memorable voice, great concentration, and stamina.

GEMINI RISING

Lucky Career Tips: Make the most of your ability to sense and communicate the mood of the masses. Though you may not openly seek the spotlight, your strong imagination and vision could put you on center stage. You need a creative career that offers you variety and creative challenges (or you may tend to job-hop). You're a gadabout, so watch a tendency to scatter your energies. You may not be suited to a corporate job or anything too confining. Jobs that use your visionary talents are worth waiting for. Look in the more free-flowing imaginative areas of business, in publishing, literature, the creative or spiritual arts.

Interview Personality: You're a social, articulate, witty personality, a quick thinker and a quick study. You also could come across as nervous, undirected, too scattered, a jack-of-all-trades. Play up your analytical mind, your ability to communicate well and to adapt to different people and environments.

CANCER RISING

Lucky Career Tips: You're competitive and quite assertive in your career. You enjoy having goals to reach or promotions to win. Physical activity is also important: there are many athletes and dancers with this placement. John Travolta in *Saturday Night Fever* is a typical success story. But be careful of jobs that require too much physical risk! Some of you are attracted and challenged by danger. Find stimulation through pioneering career maneuvers. You'd be great at starting up your own business.

Interview Personality: You may come across as shy, sweet, sensitive, and caring. You'll be able to convince others that you are nurturing, protective, the "mother of the world." But you are also very astute business-wise, with a sharp sense of what will sell.

LEO RISING

When you feel worthwhile in your job, you have a remarkably stable career. You can stick firmly to a game plan. Some of you will strongly uphold your beliefs in public, sometimes against great odds, like Martin Luther or Jane Fonda. Many religious figures have this placement. You may work your way to the top slowly. But you may have great success at Venus-ruled occupations in the beauty, exercise, fashion, or art world. Or consider other Taurus-influenced careers of finance (like J. P. Morgan), agriculture, or mining.

Interview Personality: You project a regal air of authority, which instills confidence in your abilities. You come across as someone who can take charge. You are very poised in the spotlight and know how to present yourself to play up your special star quality, such as Ava Gardner or ballerina Cynthia Gregory and Marilyn Monroe. You attract attention, and tend to take center stage. In business you can be the epitome of executive style.

VIRGO RISING

Lucky Career Tips: Mental stimulation is a key for you. You have a talent for originating ideas, communicating with others, and will probably gravitate to people-oriented jobs where you are constantly dealing with many different personalities. You have the ability to juggle many tasks, details, and contacts, yet stay emotionally detached. Some of you may have two or more professions or a variety of clients.

*   *   *

Interview Personality: Your intelligence and analytical ability come across. You seem well-organized, with a no-nonsense air of knowing what you're doing. You're a hard worker who gets on with it. You're not one to slack off. Your manner may be a bit aloof, critical of others who don't share your sense of mastery of your craft, of doing it to perfection.

LIBRA RISING

Lucky Career Tips: You need to care deeply about your career and are most successful in areas that appeal to human needs, such as providing a home, child care, or serving your country. For example, entertainers such as Sally Field have been most successful in roles in which they play parents, nurturers, or patriots. Sally Struthers' success in "All in the Family" is another case in point. Food, architecture, the hotel business are several possibilities. You work especially well in a family business or as part of a supportive team, and your career may surge ahead after you've found the right partner. This is important because you may feel especially anxious and indecisive at times.

Interview Personality: You come across as charming, attractive, well-dressed, diplomatic. Your first impression is one of social ease, harmony. You enjoy working with others and it shows.

SCORPIO RISING

Lucky Career Tips: You need a career that allows you to assume authority. If you can't be the boss, many of you choose to work alone rather than as a team player. This is one of the most dramatic career positions, a natural for the public eye. Jacqueline Kennedy Onassis, Diana Ross, Joan Crawford, and Katharine Hepburn personify the type of command and control found with this placement— you usually aren't in the position of taking orders. You have great personal flair—a standout look, not one of the crowd. Your job should allow you to exercise creative ability, self-expression and provide a form of recognition.

Interview Personality: You come on strong, with a touch of mystery, even if you don't say a word. Intense, charismatic, you'll make your presence felt with a penetrating gaze. Be careful not to come on too strong. You might consider toning down your intensity, tempering it with a touch of humor.

SAGITTARIUS RISING

Lucky Career Tips: Intellectual and communications fields are natural for you. You excel at analytical problem-solving tasks and long to contribute something of lasting value to humanity. You often make excellent teachers or gravitate to fields where you can convey an example. Many of you choose careers in health care or professional sports. Publishing, as an editor or writer spreading the truth, appeals to many, like Candice Bergen, who has had careers as a writer, journalist, and TV actress (playing a journalist). Since you are extremely flexible, you may have several different careers in your lifetime. You often have strong civic interests outside your career.

Interview Personality: Good-humored and enthusiastic, you are an excellent salesperson. You present an upbeat, athletic, energetic image. Your sense of humor wins fans, but some of you may have to work on developing tact and diplomacy.

CAPRICORN RISING

Lucky Career Tips: Since Libra rules your career sector, you could be especially successful in fields that promote justice and fairness, such as the legal profession, or in a position where you are called upon to mediate or judge. You might also shine in any Venusian profession, such as fashion, the arts, or the promotion, sale, or creation of beautiful things—or work that deals with relationships, such as the single-girls' mentor, Helen Gurley Brown, editor of *Cosmopolitan* magazine. You work especially well in partnership with another. It is doubly important that your working environment be tasteful and harmonious. You have a talent for appealing to popular tastes and lifestyles.

Interview Personality: You come across as a serious, conservative, disciplined worker. But you could also choose the traditional flair of Fred Astaire. Not a frivolous type, you aim to be taken seriously, which could be intimidating. You'll easily adapt to present the classiest impression appropriate to your business.

AQUARIUS RISING

Lucky Career Tips: Your ideal job is one where you can wield power and transform other lives in some way, especially if you can enhance individual rights or promote freedom. You may head for a career in research, investigation, or probing psychological depths. In business, you are attracted to powerful positions and can be quite manipulative, focusing all your efforts on reaching the top. You may have extremes of success/failure during the course of your working life, depending on the political and cultural orientation of your time. But you also have a marvelous ability to bounce back from setbacks. You could be happiest working free lance—or alone, rather than in a regimented environment.

Interview Personality: Like daredevil Evil Knievel you're charismatic and individualistic—you know how to get attention, sometimes in a startling way that shakes everyone up. You'll dress to please yourself—never mind the dress codes. Be sure to find a business that appreciates your eccentric side, one with a cause or principles you believe in.

PISCES RISING

Lucky Career Tips: Growth, plus freedom of choice should be your career criteria. You have high goals and the faith to achieve them. You project enthusiasm for any products and ideas you sell, elevating them to the highest level. You also have a great gift for inspiring others. You are determined to be the best you can be, like ice-skater

Rising Signs—A.M. Births

	1 AM	2 AM	3 AM	4 AM	5 AM	6 AM	7 AM	8 AM	9 AM	10 AM	11 AM	12 NOON
Jan 1	Lib	Sc	Sc	Sc	Sag	Sag	Cap	Cap	Aq	Aq	Pis	Ar
Jan 9	Lib	Sc	Sc	Sag	Sag	Sag	Cap	Cap	Aq	Pis	Ar	Tau
Jan 17	Sc	Sc	Sc	Sag	Sag	Cap	Cap	Aq	Aq	Pis	Ar	Tau
Jan 25	Sc	Sc	Sag	Sag	Sag	Cap	Cap	Aq	Pis	Ar	Tau	Gem
Feb 2	Sc	Sc	Sag	Sag	Cap	Cap	Aq	Pis	Pis	Ar	Tau	Gem
Feb 10	Sc	Sag	Sag	Sag	Cap	Cap	Aq	Pis	Ar	Tau	Tau	Gem
Feb 18	Sc	Sag	Sag	Cap	Cap	Aq	Pis	Pis	Ar	Tau	Gem	Gem
Feb 26	Sag	Sag	Sag	Cap	Aq	Aq	Pis	Ar	Tau	Tau	Gem	Gem
Mar 6	Sag	Sag	Cap	Cap	Aq	Pis	Pis	Ar	Tau	Gem	Gem	Cap
Mar 14	Sag	Cap	Cap	Aq	Aq	Pis	Ar	Tau	Tau	Gem	Gem	Can
Mar 22	Sag	Cap	Cap	Aq	Pis	Ar	Ar	Tau	Gem	Gem	Can	Can
Mar 30	Cap	Cap	Aq	Pis	Pis	Ar	Tau	Tau	Gem	Can	Can	Can
Apr 7	Cap	Cap	Aq	Pis	Ar	Ar	Tau	Gem	Gem	Can	Can	Leo
Apr 14	Cap	Aq	Aq	Pis	Ar	Tau	Tau	Gem	Gem	Can	Can	Leo
Apr 22	Cap	Aq	Pis	Ar	Ar	Tau	Gem	Gem	Gem	Can	Leo	Leo
Apr 30	Aq	Aq	Pis	Ar	Tau	Tau	Gem	Can	Can	Can	Leo	Leo
May 8	Aq	Pis	Ar	Ar	Tau	Gem	Gem	Can	Can	Leo	Leo	Leo
May 16	Aq	Pis	Ar	Tau	Gem	Gem	Can	Can	Can	Leo	Leo	Vir
May 24	Pis	Ar	Ar	Tau	Gem	Gem	Can	Can	Leo	Leo	Leo	Vir
June 1	Pis	Ar	Tau	Gem	Gem	Can	Can	Can	Leo	Leo	Vir	Vir
June 9	Ar	Ar	Tau	Gem	Gem	Can	Can	Leo	Leo	Leo	Vir	Vir
June 17	Ar	Tau	Gem	Gem	Can	Can	Can	Leo	Leo	Vir	Vir	Vir
June 25	Tau	Tau	Gem	Gem	Can	Can	Leo	Leo	Leo	Vir	Vir	Lib
July 3	Tau	Gem	Gem	Can	Can	Can	Leo	Leo	Vir	Vir	Vir	Lib
July 11	Tau	Gem	Gem	Can	Can	Leo	Leo	Leo	Vir	Vir	Lib	Lib
July 18	Gem	Gem	Can	Can	Can	Leo	Leo	Vir	Vir	Vir	Lib	Lib
July 26	Gem	Gem	Can	Can	Leo	Leo	Vir	Vir	Vir	Lib	Lib	Lib
Aug 3	Gem	Can	Can	Can	Leo	Leo	Vir	Vir	Lib	Lib	Lib	Sc
Aug 11	Gem	Can	Can	Leo	Leo	Leo	Vir	Vir	Lib	Lib	Lib	Sc
Aug 18	Can	Can	Can	Leo	Leo	Vir	Vir	Vir	Lib	Lib	Sc	Sc
Aug 27	Can	Can	Leo	Leo	Leo	Vir	Vir	Lib	Lib	Lib	Sc	Sc
Sept 4	Can	Can	Leo	Leo	Leo	Vir	Vir	Vir	Lib	Lib	Sc	Sc
Sept 12	Can	Leo	Leo	Leo	Vir	Vir	Lib	Lib	Lib	Sc	Sc	Sag
Sept 30	Leo	Leo	Leo	Vir	Vir	Vir	Lib	Lib	Sc	Sc	Sc	Sag
Sept 28	Leo	Leo	Leo	Vir	Vir	Lib	Lib	Lib	Sc	Sc	Sag	Sag
Oct 6	Leo	Leo	Vir	Vir	Vir	Lib	Lib	Sc	Sc	Sc	Sag	Sag
Oct 14	Leo	Vir	Vir	Vir	Lib	Lib	Lib	Sc	Sc	Sag	Sag	Cap
Oct 22	Leo	Vir	Vir	Lib	Lib	Lib	Sc	Sc	Sc	Sag	Sag	Cap
Oct 30	Vir	Vir	Vir	Lib	Lib	Sc	Sc	Sc	Sag	Sag	Cap	Cap
Nov 7	Vir	Vir	Lib	Lib	Lib	Sc	Sc	Sc	Sag	Sag	Cap	Cap
Nov 15	Vir	Vir	Lib	Lib	Sc	Sc	Sc	Sc	Sag	Sag	Cap	Aq
Nov 23	Vir	Lib	Lib	Lib·	Sc	Sc	Sag	Sag	Sag	Cap	Cap	Aq
Dec 1	Vir	Lib	Lib	Sc	Sc	Sc	Sag	Sag	Cap	Cap	Aq	Aq
Dec 9	Lib	Lib	Ltb	Sc	Sc	Sag	Sag	Sag	Cap	Cap	Aq	Pis
Dec 18	Lib	Lib	Sc	Sc	Sc	Sag	Sag	Cap	Cap	Aq	Aq	Pis
Dec 28	Lib	Lib	Sc	Sc	Sag	Sag	Sag	Cap	Aq	Aq	Pis	Ar

Rising Signs—P.M. Births

	1 PM	2 PM	3 PM	4 PM	5 PM	6 PM	7 PM	8 PM	9 PM	10 PM	11 PM	12 MIDNIGHT
Jan 1	Tau	Gem	Gem	Can	Can	Can	Leo	Leo	Vir	Vir	Vir	Lib
Jan 9	Tau	Gem	Gem	Can	Can	Leo	Leo	Leo	Vir	Vir	Vir	Lib
Jan 17	Gem	Gem	Can	Can	Can	Leo	Leo	Vir	Vir	Vir	Lib	Lib
Jan 25	Gem	Gem	Can	Can	Leo	Leo	Leo	Vir	Vir	Lib	Lib	Lib
Feb 2	Gem	Can	Can	Can	Leo	Leo	Vir	Vir	Vir	Lib	Lib	Sc
Feb 10	Gem	Can	Can	Leo	Leo	Leo	Vir	Vir	Lib	Lib	Lib	Sc
Feb 18	Can	Can	Can	Leo	Leo	Vir	Vir	Vir	Lib	Lib	Sc	Sc
Feb 26	Can	Can	Leo	Leo	Leo	Vir	Vir	Lib	Lib	Lib	Sc	Sc
Mar 6	Can	Leo	Leo	Leo	Vir	Vir	Vir	Lib	Lib	Sc	Sc	Sc
Mar 14	Can	Leo	Leo	Vir	Vir	Vir	Lib	Lib	Lib	Sc	Sc	Sag
Mar 22	Leo	Leo	Leo	Vir	Vir	Lib	Lib	Lib	Sc	Sc	Sc	Sag
Mar 30	Leo	Leo	Vir	Vir	Vir	Lib	Lib	Sc	Sc	Sc	Sag	Sag
Apr 7	Leo	Leo	Vir	Vir	Lib	Lib	Lib	Sc	Sc	Sc	Sag	Sag
Apr 14	Leo	Vir	Vir	Vir	Lib	Lib	Sc	Sc	Sc	Sag	Sag	Cap
Apr 22	Leo	Vir	Vir	Lib	Lib	Lib	Sc	Sc	Sc	Sag	Sag	Cap
Apr 30	Vir	Vir	Vir	Lib	Lib	Sc	Sc	Sc	Sag	Sag	Cap	Cap
May 8	Vir	Vir	Lib	Lib	Lib	Sc	Sc	Sag	Sag	Sag	Cap	Cap
May 16	Vir	Vir	Lib	Lib	Sc	Sc	Sc	Sag	Sag	Cap	Cap	Aq
May 24	Vir	Lib	Lib	Lib	Sc	Sc	Sag	Sag	Sag	Cap	Cap	Aq
June 1	Vir	Lib	Lib	Sc	Sc	Sc	Sag	Sag	Cap	Cap	Aq	Aq
June 9	Lib	Lib	Lib	Sc	Sc	Sag	Sag	Sag	Cap	Cap	Aq	Pis
June 17	Lib	Lib	Sc	Sc	Sc	Sag	Sag	Cap	Cap	Aq	Aq	Pis
June 25	Lib	Lib	Sc	Sc	Sag	Sag	Sag	Cap	Cap	Aq	Pis	Ar
July 3	Lib	Sc	Sc	Sc	Sag	Sag	Cap	Cap	Aq	Aq	Pis	Ar
July 11	Lib	Sc	Sc	Sag	Sag	Sag	Cap	Cap	Aq	Pis	Ar	Tau
July 18	Sc	Sc	Sc	Sag	Sag	Cap	Cap	Aq	Aq	Pis	Ar	Tau
July 26	Sc	Sc	Sag	Sag	Sag	Cap	Cap	Aq	Pis	Ar	Tau	Tau
Aug 3	Sc	Sc	Sag	Sag	Cap	Cap	Aq	Aq	Pis	Ar	Tau	Gem
Aug 11	Sc	Sag	Sag	Sag	Cap	Cap	Aq	Pis	Ar	Tau	Tau	Gem
Aug 18	Sc	Sag	Sag	Cap	Cap	Aq	Pis	Pis	Ar	Tau	Gem	Gem
Aug 27	Sag	Sag	Sag	Cap	Cap	Aq	Pis	Ar	Tau	Tau	Gem	Gem
Sept 4	Sag	Sag	Cap	Cap	Aq	Pis	Pis	Ar	Tau	Gem	Gem	Can
Sept 12	Sag	Sag	Cap	Aq	Aq	Pis	Ar	Tau	Tau	Gem	Gem	Can
Sept 20	Sag	Cap	Cap	Aq	Pis	Pis	Ar	Tau	Gem	Gem	Can	Can
Sept 28	Cap	Cap	Aq	Aq	Pis	Ar	Tau	Tau	Gem	Gem	Can	Can
Oct 6	Cap	Cap	Aq	Pis	Ar	Ar	Tau	Gem	Gem	Can	Can	Leo
Oct 14	Cap	Aq	Aq	Pis	Ar	Tau	Gem	Gem	Can	Can	Leo	Leo
Oct 22	Cap	Aq	Pis	Ar	Ar	Tau	Gem	Gem	Can	Can	Leo	Leo
Oct 30	Aq	Aq	Pis	Ar	Tau	Tau	Gem	Can	Can	Can	Leo	Leo
Nov 7	Aq	Aq	Pis	Ar	Tau	Tau	Gem	Can	Can	Can	Leo	Leo
Nov 15	Aq	Pis	Ar	Tau	Gem	Gem	Can	Can	Can	Leo	Leo	Vir
Nov 23	Pis	Ar	Ar	Tau	Gem	Gem	Can	Can	Leo	Leo	Leo	Vir
Dec 1	Pis	Ar	Tau	Gem	Gem	Can	Can	Can	Leo	Leo	Vir	Vir
Dec 9	Ar	Tau	Tau	Gem	Gem	Can	Can	Leo	Leo	Leo	Vir	Vir
Dec 18	Ar	Tau	Gem	Gem	Can	Can	Can	Leo	Leo	Vir	Vir	Vir
Dec 28	Tau	Tau	Gem	Gem	Can	Can	Leo	Leo	Vir	Vir	Vir	Lib

Dorothy Hamill or baseball's Pete Rose, and you'll get the higher education necessary to do so. You tend to attract notice, have a strong theatrical quality—you may be attracted to politics, religion, education, or drama. You're always aiming for something higher, need a career that provides plenty of room to advance—and you tend to move ahead in bursts rather than a slow, steady climb.

Interview Personality: You'll express the most artistic, theatrical, and imaginative side of your sun sign. Like Phil Donohue, you'll come across as empathetic, a good listener who is able to cue in to where others are coming from—a valuable interview asset. You may be quite dramatic in the way you present yourself, as a "character" like baseball's Yogi Berra or author Norman Mailer.

11

The Stars of Aquarius

Have you ever noticed how often celebrities fit the archetype of their sun sign? Could Madonna be anything but a dazzling Leo golden girl? How about Diana Ross as the prototype of a dynamic Aries woman. You can easily find the Taurus musical talent and strong focus in Barbra Streisand, the Cancer sensitivity in Tom Cruise and Geraldo Rivera, the Aquarian charisma in the "mustache trio" of Burt Reynolds, Tom Selleck, and Clark Gable.

You can also compare other planets with the celebrity members of your sign using the "Look Up Your Planets" chapter. It's fun to find out how much you have in common—as well as the significant differences. You may be able to see how other planetary placements have colored their personalities and public image. It's an interesting way to sharpen your skills in astrology and apply what you have learned so far.

The following list contains the stars' birthdays and years wherever possible. Take the birthday of someone who fascinates you and do your own astrological study! Look up Venus and Mars to learn about their tastes and romantic preferences, Pluto and the outer planets for their audience appeal, Jupiter for their luck, and Saturn their trials. (If you're curious about celebrities of other sun signs, you'll find many celebrity birthdays listed in the annual edition of the *World Almanac*, which is available in the reference section of your local library or bookstore.)

Lorenzo Lamas (1/20/58)
Patricia Neal (1/20/26)
Federico Fellini (1/20/20)
Placido Domingo (1/21/41)
Jill Eikenberry (1/21/47)

Telly Savalas (1/21/24)
Geena Davis (1/21/57)
Wolfman Jack (1/21/39)
Bill Bixby (1/22/34)
Chita Rivera (1/23/33)
Jeanne Moreau (1/23/28)
Mary Lou Retton (1/24/68)
Dean Jones (1/25/35)
Paul Newman (1/26/25)
Eartha Kitt (1/26/28)
Wayne Gretsky (1/26)
Mimi Rogers (1/27)
William Randolph Hearst (1/27/1863)
Alan Alda (1/28/36)
Mikhail Baryshnikov (1/28/48)
Barbi Benton (1/28/50)
Tom Selleck (1/29/45)
Oprah Winfrey (1/29/54)
Ann Jillian (1/29/51)
John Forsythe (1/29/18)
Vanessa Redgrave (1/30/37)
Dorothy Malone (1/30/25)
Johnny Rotten (1/31/56)
Princess Stephanie of Monaco (2/1/65)
Clark Gable (2/1/01)
Lisa Marie Presley (2/1/68)
Farrah Fawcett (2/2/47)
Tom Smothers (2/2/37)
Morgan Fairchild (2/3/49)
David Brenner (2/4/45)
Lisa Eichhorn (2/4/52)
Charlotte Rampling (2/5/46)
Barbara Hershey (2/5/48)
Molly Ringwald (2/6/68)
Zsa Zsa Gabor (2/6/15)
Tom Brokaw (2/6/40)
James Dean (2/8/31)
Nick Nolte (2/8/40)
Lana Turner (2/8/20)
Ted Koppel (2/8/40)
Roger Mudd (2/9/28)
Mia Farrow (2/9/45)
Robert Wagner (2/10/30)

Roberta Flack (2/10/40)
Eva Gabor (2/11/21)
Burt Reynolds (2/11/36)
General Manuel Noriega (2/11/40)
Arsenio Hall (2/12/57)
Jane Seymour (2/15/51)
John McInroe (2/16/59)
Cybill Shepherd (2/18/50)
Lou Diamond Phillips (2/17/62)
Vanna White (2/19/57)
Matt Dillon (2/18/64)
Yoko Ono (2/18/33)
John Travolta (2/18/54)
Margaux Hemingway (2/19/55)
Prince Andrew of England (2/19/60)
Lee Marvin (2/19/24)

12

Aquarius Self-Discovery

The Aquarius Man

You're a charismatic heartthrob who is always tantalizingly out of reach. But your contradictions make you even more fascinating. Your magnetism, contrasted with your distance and detachment invites others to project their fantasies upon you (and makes you an excellent candidate for public life). Hollywood has had a stable of Aquarian stars who embodied the American ideal of virility—Clark Gable, Paul Newman, Burt Reynolds, Tom Selleck, and John Forsythe, to name a few. Because you manage to be simultaneously remote and accessible, no one really knows the "real you." The embodiment of this mysterious Aquarian persona is former President Ronald Reagan. As an actor who reached the highest office in the land, he fulfilled our public image of a President, yet few who worked with him felt truly close to him. You're the man we vote for, even though we are not quite sure what you stand for or what you are really like.

Often you use your position in the spotlight to accomplish humanitarian goals. It is the rare Aquarian celebrity who does not promote a favorite charity or worthy cause. Sometimes you combine self-promotion with altruistic motives—another interesting Aquarian contradiction— where you get as much publicity as your cause. A perfect example is Paul Newman's successful line of salad dressing, popcorn, and lemonade with his picture on the label and the proceeds awarded to a charity. Your ideas are sometimes so far ahead of their time that others may call them crazy—but they're crazy like a fox. You have the knack of extending whatever you do to reach the broadest audience, so listen to those flashes of inspiration— and take them to the limit for fame and fortune.

The Aquarius Husband

Free-thinking Mr. Aquarius is downright old-fashioned about marriage. He guards his private life carefully and usually will not wander unless his wife is the domineering or manipulative type. In that case, he will leave her on the doorstep like Rhett Butler, and detach emotionally.

He needs a woman who is "one of the great broads," as Paul Newman describes his wife, which can be a very tall order to fill with this contradictory man. A combination of saint, sister, and seductress! An Aquarian's wife must be her man's best friend; she must be unpossessive enough to grant him plenty of space, and never succumb to moods. She should have interests of her own, yet be supportive of him and share his causes. And, of course, be loyal and faithful. However, she must also be able to tolerate sharing life with a slew of his buddies and with consuming outside interests. He can fully accept, and even prefer, a woman with a life of her own. But her career should relate to (or complement) his or they will rarely see one other.

The Aquarius Woman

The Aquarius woman is a fascinating challenge! You appear friendly, open, flirtatious, and sometimes a bit wild. But let anyone try to dominate or confine you and you'll quickly flash your sharp wit, insightful mind, and powerful will. You can be unsinkable, not caring about public opinion when you are standing up for what you believe in, and trying to create a better world for everyone. In fact, no matter how you present yourself, as a conservative corporate type or a flamboyant eccentric, you need to feel that you are championing something greater than personal goals.

You are always, in some way, an original. Aquarians can be as outrageous and avante garde as Yoko Ono or Princess Stephanie of Monaco, as zany as Zsa Zsa Gabor or as forthright as Oprah Winfrey, but they are unique and unpredictable. In the extreme, you love surprise for its own sake and enjoy shocking your audience.

Sometimes you become so involved with your cause that you neglect personal relationships, but you'll usually find a way to include friends and family in your many outside activities. Many Aquarian mothers think nothing of bringing their children into their workplace. Sometimes this works out very well; the exposure to different situations broadens the outlook of everyone involved. But there is a down side: sometimes your entire life is lived in public and there are no intimate moments left for those who want to be close to you (some Aquarians actually fear being left alone).

The Aquarian woman's single-mindedness is a two-edged sword. When you feel you know what is best for everyone, you push ahead, don't hear the word *can't*. However, you are often at your best when most detached, remaining open to opposing ideas and providing much-needed insight and perspective, finding innovative ways to bend the rules to benefit everyone. You are fascinated by what makes people tick, and many of this sign make excellent psychologists and social workers. Regardless of your field, your primary interest is in influencing others rather exploiting them.

The Aquarius Wife

An Aquarian wife usually looks for a liberated liaison and invents her own matrimonial rules. She can be loyal and faithful, but not always homebound. Or she'll bring her interests right into the living room, which becomes an office, meeting room, or classroom. Sometimes she focuses on outer goals, at the expense of inner life, leaving no time for intimacy. Aquarius finds routine of any kind too confining and can invent some ingenious ways of taking care of chores or delegating them. Some Aquarians have large extended families that help share the domestic dilemmas.

Marriage to her is a friendly pact, where a "liberated"

husband does his share of the housework. In turn, she'll take over a sizable slice of the financial burden. The Aquarius woman may sing, "diamonds are a girl's best friend," but she's not averse to buying them for herself! Her ideal husband will be proud of her accomplishments and encourage her outside interests. She'll return the favor by giving him a life of delightful surprises and steady devotion.

13

The Aquarius Family

The Aquarius Parent

Aquarians often maintain that they are not natural stay-at-home parents. But who says a parent has to stay at home? Like everything else you do, you'll make your own rules. Aquarian mothers keep their outside interests going full steam with the aid of the telephone, the computer, the fax machine. Aquarians bring their children with them, including them in their workplace (it was surely Aquarian mothers who first persuaded companies to provide day care for children of employees). Aquarian film stars are known to have trailers on location for their children and even find them small roles to play. And it was an Aquarian who wrote the book titled *Having It All*. You believe it is good for children to be exposed to a wide range of experiences, developing social consciousness along the way. You may often leave your children in the care of others, but you feel that this develops independence. If an emotionally dependent child becomes a special challenge to you, your emotional detachment will help you find an innovative solution, perhaps an extended family situation, a joint sharing with other mothers, or sessions with a child psychologist. Because Aquarians especially appreciate the uniqueness of each human being, you are well-equipped to help your children develop independence and creativity by allowing them the freedom to experiment and find out what is truly right for themselves.

The Aquarius Stepparent

Because you enjoy having an extended family and sharing your life with others, you should be a very successful stepparent. Many Aquarian qualities make you well-suited to this often-delicate position: your lack of possessiveness toward your mate will allow him or her to spend guilt-free time with his children. And "gregarious Aquarius" will gladly open your home to activities that include the whole family. You'll come up with some unusual and interesting things to do together. Your objectivity serves you well as a trusted adviser and pal, one who won't shock easily or pass judgment. You'll encourage the youngster who is exceptional or unusual to develop his or her talents. And you'll help shy insecure children learn how to get along in groups or express their feelings in a creative way.

The Aquarius Grandparent

Aquarians who have always been ahead of the crowd may find the world catching up in their grandparent years, when their unique qualities are finally appreciated. Young of mind as well as heart, you can astonish and "turn on" the younger generations. You're interested and well-informed about all that's new—you probably have your own PC and are a whiz at video games. Not one to lounge around in a rocking chair, you'll take a yoga class, teach meditation, or get involved in local politics—or at least have some vociferous opinions about the state of the world. You're the person rebellious youngsters confide in when they want to try something new, something Mother and Dad might not approve of. Shock-proof Aquarian grandparents not only offer objective advice, they are living inspiration to grandchildren to invent their own lives!

14

Your Aquarius Healthwatch

Typical Aquarians are the health faddists of the zodiac, often trying every diet fad and health food trend that flares up. You probably know all about liquid fasts, vegetarianism, wheat-grass juice, spirulina, psychic healing, and exotic Chinese herbs. The more traditional among you have probably consulted a variety of experts within the medical community. Your experimental nature could have varying results, as you use yourself as a guinea pig.

Like other air signs, you are vulnerable to airborne viruses and allergies. Pay special attention to the air quality wherever you spend most of your time. If you constantly feel run down, an undetected allergy could be to blame. It is also important to build up your immune system with a healthy diet. A humidifier and an ionizer could make a big difference, especially if you spend time in closed quarters. Those of you who work with computers or in a high-tech electronic environment might also benefit from an ionizer, which charges the air with health-promoting ions, and an antiradiation screen. Ergonomic computer chairs are another wise investment for Aquarians who spend much time at their desks.

Aquarius naturally rules the lower leg, ankles, Achilles tendon, and certain functions of the circulatory system. Many of you suffer poor circulation and leg cramps, a particular problem for those with a more sedentary lifestyle. Regular aerobic exercise can improve circulation, but be sure to protect your ankles with the proper footgear and extra support if necessary, because you are vulnerable to strains and sprains.

Boredom, predictability, getting caught in a rigid routine where you have to follow other people's rules can produce great stress for independent Aquarians. Even though you are a "people person" who needs social contacts, possessive one-to-one relationships make you feel trapped. Finding meaningful work and relationships that allow you breathing space yet provide mental stimulation is a major task for Aquarius.

Because you can usually remain quite objective, you are not as affected by emotional turmoil as others. You can remain aloof and analytical, drawing your own conclusions and stubbornly sticking by them despite opposition from others. But at the same time, you can be accused of being an oddball, which causes much stress from being misinterpreted and misunderstood.

Look to your air element for the best antidote to stress. You need fresh air and plenty of exercise. You may find routine exercise boring, however, so you have to find something interesting to do consistently or alternate several sports or routines. Aquarians do best with an individually tailored program that can be varied and constantly changed to incorporate new techniques. New Age exercises that combine body/mind approaches work well, as does yoga. Consider a collection of exercise videos, where you can vary routines and work out whenever you please. Gyms with the latest high-tech exercise equipment also draw body-conscious Aquarians who can be found on treadmills, Stairmasters, and weight machines. A caution to the beginner: Don't be a know it all: get expert advice before using sophisticated machinery so you can adapt it to your own special needs.

Healthy Aquarius Vacation Spots

Aquarius getaways should have an interesting, unusual twist. You may decide to take many small vacations rather than one long one. You are attracted to places of current interest, or to New Age power spots such as Sedona, Arizona, or Taos, New Mexico, where there is an avant-garde community of colorful individualists. Your best vacations promise a certain spiritual enlightenment or educational value. Steer clear of boring traditional resorts. A resort that features a special health or diet approach, an undiscovered island, a futuristic environment—the latest, newest resort in the Caribbean are better ideas. You love to have a spontaneous element to your vacation, some unpredictable adventure—perhaps you'll get up and take off at a moment's notice. Some Aquarius-favored destinations to consider: the romantic inns of Quebec, the powerful energy vortexes of Arizona, a hideaway in tiny Lichtenstein, midnight sunbathing in Sweden, hiking in an Oregon forest.

15

Aquarius Astro-Outlook for 1992

You are now empowered to put some brakes and dampers on the unproductive events and situations in your life. Also, during 1992, your Aquarian vision and foresight operate in a much more practical way than usual, and you may literally feather your retirement nest.

You are still coping with past mistakes, however, most of which are the result of impatience, wanting total change instead of adaptability and adjustment.

Working in your favor this year is greater financial stability and many opportunities for savings and investments, with sheer good luck often operating in these matters.

In your career, you'll be able to turn current trends to your advantage. The climate is right for turning your ideas, aspirations, and hopes into realities.

During the closing week of February and throughout most of March, you have unbeatable drive and excellent motivation; don't let these go to waste. Push your earning power higher during April.

Watch social expenses around the middle of June, and don't take chances with your job as June draws to a close. At the same time, guard against overdoing during the last few days of June and the first days of July.

Your love life does well between late May and mid-September, and you can seize greater control of it in August.

You are given rare opportunities to replenish your economic larder during the October–December interval.

December can bring problems wherever there is too much rushing around. Try not to overburden yourself with volunteer work, or permit public life to make inroads on your primary private relationships. Love may require protection around December 9. You may also spend too much just before the holiday. Because holiday traditions can be eclipsed this year, don't risk your physical and mental health by attempting to give these traditions too much consideration.

16

Eighteen Months of Day-by-Day Predictions:

JULY 1991

Monday, July 1 (Moon in Aquarius to Pisces 12:51 p.m.) A perfect beginning for a month with your lunar cycle high revealing promising paths in life. You make your own decisions and can persuade many to your point of view. Your flair for personal independence is catching. Another Aquarius comes to center stage while Libra has marvelous advice. You can trust your intuitions. Your lucky number is 4.

Tuesday, July 2 (Moon in Pisces) You are ultra generous and may have to be more cautious with perennial borrowers. The motivation of others in their money dealings may not be clear at the moment. You can feel the rising cost of living in entertainment, needs of school children, and when paying medical and dental bills. Provide for your own needs first. Hot combination numbers: 6 and 3.

Wednesday, July 3 (Moon in Pisces to Aries 10:34 p.m.) In order to keep you happy and to entertain you, another is willing to spend heavily. You suddenly could learn of a source of extra funds. This is also a good day to acquire antique jewelry or other items that will increase in value as time passes. Pisces knows the answers. Lucky lottery numbers: 3, 21, 17, 35, 13, 29.

Thursday, July 4 (Moon in Aries) What you do socially must include your beloved. Leo and Aries have key roles. Spend the day close to home, appreciating your neighborhood and inviting kindred spirits into the backyard or patio. Gifts, enjoyable conversation, tradi-

161

tional picnic foods are represented. A slow, leisurely day is right for you. Count on number 1.

Friday, July 5 (Moon in Aries)   You lean toward seasonal interests, sports, and hobbies. No matter where you are, the wider and more open spaces can be calling to you. Each gender wants to do his or her own thing. You will be aware of how chauvinistic the male can be. At parties or just family get-togethers, segregate the males from the females, and they'll be happier. Hot combination numbers: 3 and 5.

Saturday, July 6 (Moon in Aries to Taurus 4:51 a.m.)   Influential people are represented along with Taurus and Scorpio. Go straight to the point in any discussions; no meandering around like a hoop skirt. A confrontation isn't the worst thing that can happen; it may help you sort and sift in the back of your mind and ultimately gain. Lucky lottery numbers: 14, 23, 32, 41, 5, 19.

Sunday, July 7 (Moon in Taurus)   Ignore opposition and try to avoid giving youngsters the feeling that you don't quite trust them. Others will resist any efforts by you to possess them. Family, home, property, community, and ownership matters are in strong focus. Don't permit your efforts to do the right thing encroach on the reaction of others. Trust Leo.

Monday, July 8 (Moon in Taurus to Gemini 7:42 a.m.)   The generation gap can't be denied. Dramatic showdowns can take place in home and community. You are rather restless and would love to move about not too far from home but without relatives on your trail. Moods are going to change rapidly. Building blocks aren't reliable; so stick to the present. Your lucky number is 2.

Tuesday, July 9 (Moon in Gemini)   A perfect day for home entertainment, opening your doors to relatives and friends. A family reunion, a picnic in your backyard, and lots of fond remembering will make you happy. Taurus and Virgo are in this scenario, along with many kind, generous, loving types. A good day for celebrating special family days that might fall this month. Hot combination numbers: 4 and 7.

Wednesday, July 10 (Moon in Gemini to Cancer 8:03 a.m.) A memorable lovemaking day, with passion rising along with special consideration for your loved one. Perfect for stealing away from the grind for perfection in love. Affections, approval, appreciation, creativity, and versatility are petals on this beautiful flower. Good days for buying precious and semiprecious stones. Lucky lottery numbers: 15, 10, 33, 42, 6, 44.

Thursday, July 11 (Moon in Cancer) A total solar eclipse can pressure water sports. Not a good day for foisting changes upon yourself or others. Virus-bred ailments are represented; colds and sore throats at this unlikely time must be taken seriously. Be cautious about what you drink. There is high accident-producing potential where crowds swim, surf, and boat. Trust number 8.

Friday, July 12 (Moon in Cancer to Leo 7:35 a.m.) Use caution on the job, especially around anything explosive. Stay out of heavily polluted areas. Otherwise, the day permits catching up on jobs that have been neglected earlier in the month. Keep your weather eye on dependents, pets, or anybody or anything for which you are responsible. Your lucky number is 1.

Saturday, July 13 (Moon in Leo) More than routine caution should be taken in and around the water and beaches. Marital, legal, contractural matters are in focus and progress can be chalked up in them. Abide stringently by promises made earlier and don't be stingy with compliments that another may need for survival. Leo and another Aquarius are in the script. Lucky lottery numbers: 3, 12, 19, 13, 47, 21.

Sunday, July 14 (Moon in Leo to Virgo 8:12 a.m.) You could feel strongly drawn to a stimulating conversationalist. Your search for kindred spirits may be rewarded. Invite a stranger, who comes to your door, into your parlor, if the password is something related to charitable and humanitarian endeavors. Gemini and Libra will have the explanations. Household budgets may have you wondering.

Monday, July 15 (Moon in Virgo) There may be limits in the mind of your mate on just how far your flair for originality and personal freedom can go. Virgo and

Taurus come center stage. The need to give lasting commitments is strongly apparent today. A divorced couple may try to unload too much on you. Agreement on a family decision isn't forthcoming now. Your lucky number is 9.

Tuesday, July 16 (Moon in Virgo to Libra 11:34 a.m.) The goodwill you spread earlier in the month can be rewarded. Your future takes on greater promise and brightness. Dress to the hilt today and let the world see you ready for action. You could be strongly attracted to a well-traveled newcomer. Changes are taken in stride. Sagittarius is diplomatic; Aries somewhat angry. Your lucky number is 2.

Wednesday, July 17 (Moon in Libra) A mutual ideal can remind you and your mate of the glories of your past together. Creative talents and skills refuse to be denied. Isn't it time you brought some of your work out from under wraps and let an authority judge it? A wonderful day for traveling to a place of historic interest. You enjoy all the learning processes. Lucky lottery numbers: 13, 4, 22, 31, 17, 40.

Thursday, July 18 (Moon in Libra to Scorpio 6:41 p.m.) Libra and another Aquarius will make this scene. You are involved with tourists, trips, sightseeing, and showing youngsters something of their land. Looking ahead is much more productive than looking back. Dreams, aspirations, and hopes for the future are served. You are ultra considerate of a person who is having a difficult time and this is like money in the bank. Hot combination numbers: 6 and 5.

Friday, July 19 (Moon in Scorpio) Career promise is growing. Something you read or see today can help you advance. A near stranger can give you valuable information that you can use to increase your income. Conversation flows freely. Somebody in authority will show a fortuitous interest in your work. Scorpio and Capricorn are present. Your lucky number is 8.

Saturday, July 20 (Moon in Scorpio) A bit of maneuvering can improve your financial situation. Even when this means giving Paul half of what Peter expected. You can assure your family of a higher social and economic status if they cooperate with your new toehold on an economic bandwagon moving up the hill. Taurus and Cancer are on your wave length. Lucky lottery numbers: 1, 20, 28, 37, 14, 46.

Sunday, July 21 (Moon in Scorpio to Sagittarius 5:17 a.m.) It would be easy to say the wrong thing under prevailing aspects. There are some worrywarts about talking to sappers of your energy. You may feel out of place. It's the kind of Sunday when you might consider changing your church membership. Others will resent any show of independence on your part. Discuss the matter with Pisces.

Monday, July 22 (Moon in Sagittarius) Any new relationship that you begin today is apt to be a strange one. Avoid people you may tend to pity more than like. Planning a party, festival, lawn fete with a committee won't make much headway. That proverbial light at the end of the tunnel becomes apparent. Sagittarius may not want to take a "no" answer. Your lucky number is 7.

Tuesday, July 23 (Moon in Sagittarius to Capricorn 5:56 p.m.) Your marriage can be jazzed up. A jaded affair can show signs of ending. Change is the order of the day and it touches all close emotional relationships. Parties attract and you may be able to relax a little but everything is overpriced. Membership and participation matters require a lot of give and take, plenty of tolerance. Hot combination numbers: 9 and 4.

Wednesday, July 24 (Moon in Capricorn) You may be puzzled by what you are told or read. There are mysteries at the end of the line, when the project is finished and when the month winds down. Talk to a supervisor to make sure your conclusions are shared. Capricorn and another Aquarius are in the picture. No matter how difficult or impossible a young person behaves, don't throw him or her out. Lucky lottery numbers: 24, 2, 20, 48, 5, 11.

Thursday, July 25 (Moon in Capricorn) You can claim certain honors and take the lead in closing out a project. Privacy offers greater potential for genuine effort than work done amid many distracting personalities. A Virgo can pick up the slack. More and more you can feel that you are coming out from under a cloud of opposition, resentment. Your lucky number is 4.

Friday, July 26 (Moon in Capricorn to Aquarius 6:49 a.m.)   Today's full moon illuminates highly personalized interests. In this lunar cycle high, you can light that proverbial stick of dynamite under the laggards and slothful who may be holding up your parade. Trust Taurus and Capricorn in any pinch but confide only in another Aquarius. Stake your claims, aim high, demand, command, announce. Hot combination numbers: 6 and 1.

Saturday, July 27 (Moon in Aquarius)   Money matters are speeded up again. You can take charge and steer your personal spacecraft in your own preferred direction. You can charm the opposition and win many points that you never could win earlier. The worm is turning; everything in career, business, financial is changing. Lucky lottery numbers: 17, 8, 27, 44, 35, 26.

Sunday, July 28 (Moon in Aquarius to Pisces 6:35 p.m.)   Give your free time to kindred spirits and avoid those whose ideas are diametrically opposed to your own. Good luck attends you in new contracts, agreements, and promises. You have unbeatable drive in learning all about money, stocks, investments generally. An Aries and a Sagittarius are helpful. Get the drop on the week ahead by making a few phone calls.

Monday, July 29 (Moon in Pisces)   Something you intended to discard has value and can be refurbished. A special project can be funded by you and friends in an unusual social way. Pisces comes to your assistance. You are generous and give gladly of your time, patience, stamina, and money. Correcting local and household situations is well within your scope. Count on number 5.

Tuesday, July 30 (Moon in Pisces)   A strange financial offer can come your way. There's also the possibility of a beggar or somebody to whom you made a loan in the past. You could purchase an expensive imported item and then wonder what led you into this mistake. Judgment may be off the beam. Avoid a know-all who loves to persuade others. Your lucky number is 7.

166

Wednesday, July 31 (Moon in Pisces to Aries 4:21 a.m.) You settle down and get a good picture of the past. There are fine trends for summarizing the month of July and using some part of it as a springboard to a better August. Local deterioration can be depressing. Nobody is spending enough money on the appearance and safety of the community. Lucky lottery numbers: 31, 9, 18, 27, 45, 3.

AUGUST 1991

Thursday, August 1 (Moon in Aries) Explore your own neighborhood and those adjoining. Walking, biking, and motorcycling are represented. Do not overlook new pleasures you can extract from old-fashioned pursuits—picnics, potluck dinners, backyard cookouts. Remember birthdays and other anniversaries of siblings, making a note so that you won't overlook when they occur. Your lucky number is 8.

Friday, August 2 (Moon in Aries to Taurus 11:32 a.m.) Arrange your day so that you can crowd in several kinds of shopping on the one excursion. Beach and water activities are represented. Aries and Scorpio have important roles. Press junior members of your household into assisting with yard and lawn chores. The familiar warms your heart. Your lucky number is 1.

Saturday, August 3 (Moon in Taurus) Personal contact rather than phone calls will do the trick. You want to be close to your immediate family and any projects that include all of you are favored. Keep all promises that are made to youngsters. There are chores that have to be done today and they can become repugnant when you want to play and relax. Lucky lottery numbers: 12, 3, 21, 48, 39, 31.

Sunday, August 4 (Moon in Taurus to Gemini 3:55 p.m.) Trust the views of Taurus. Messages arrive and may interfere with the day's plans. A member of your household may seem edgy and irritable and fight being included in overall plans. You are more sentimental than the traffic will bear and can feel disenchanted at the reception you receive. Rise above imaginary hurts.

167

Monday, August 5 (Moon in Gemini)   You feel romantic, adventurous, and ready for love. Turn your lover's attention back to those halcyon days right after you met. Enjoyment is pure, unquestioned, and social situations find you sparkling. Gemini has a dominant role. Love is medicinal and also seems to expand your sense of freedom and versatility. Play number 9 to win.

Tuesday, August 6 (Moon in Gemini to Cancer 5:47 p.m.)   Special closeness to loved ones can be achieved more easily. It's a day for gifts, entertainment, display of treasures. Few crimes are as bad as forgetting to tell your adored one of your need, desire, and admiration. Libra and another Aquarius figure importantly. Be generous, think big. Take a chance on number 2.

Wednesday, August 7 (Moon in Cancer)   Employment, special enterprises, and services you perform for others are in focus. You have the interest and attention of somebody who can advance your personal ambitions. Beach and water activities are favored. In sentiment and romance, situations pull you down to earth. Lucky lottery numbers: 4, 31, 22, 13, 7, 25.

Thursday, August 8 (Moon in Cancer to Leo 6:10 p.m.)   Delays touch savings, investments, banking, and tax matters. You can push health and work improvements, find the kind of pet you have been wanting for some time, and gain from practical and stable attitudes in household and community affairs. A Cancer and a Pisces make major contributions. Keep a lower profile in business. Hot combination numbers: 6 and 1.

Friday, August 9 (Moon in Leo)   A strong sense of unity is represented. Marital, legal, conventional, contractural matters get strong support. You can make your mark in compromises and reconciliations. Sign important documents. Search for lost papers, other legal materials. Resolve to put important documents in safe deposit box. Your lucky number is 8.

Saturday, August 10 (Moon in Leo to Virgo 6:35 p.m.)   The new moon illuminates ways of making your marriage more dynamic, exciting, up-to-date. There is enlightenment in getting along with others. You have enormous drive in security and financial improvement.

Luck touches you when you share fairly and demonstrate generosity. In-laws can make wonderful guests under these aspects. Lucky lottery numbers: 10, 19, 49, 28, 37, 1.

Sunday, August 11 (Moon in Virgo)   Evaluate present circumstances with an eye to making changes at this time. Ask questions of yourself. Should you change doctor? Dentist? Broker? Are investments paying off? What does your mate really think of your outside activities, hobbies, studies? Are too many keys to your home, office, garage in the hands of others? Virgo rises to challenges.

Monday, August 12 (Moon in Virgo to Libra 8:52 p.m.)   A surge of self-confidence and family strengths helps you tackle hard work that can improve comfort, light and cheer within house. Capricorn and Taurus come front and center. Painting, paperhanging, all the homely decorating tasks are demanding attention, and you feel good about tackling them now. Hot combination numbers: 7 and 3.

Tuesday, August 13 (Moon in Libra)   You extend your thinking and begin to perceive beyond the norm. What others most likely are thinking about you comes into more exact focus. Some fabulous romantic fantasies are possible and these could involve a coworker you hardly know. Libra and Gemini have much to contribute. The yen to see people who have moved away is strong. Your lucky number is 9.

Wednesday, August 14 (Moon in Libra)   Self-realization is linked to your popularity and outgoing ways. You can turn some former critic into a great supporter. Personality assets are more dramatically demonstrated. Newcomers and people from far away make this scene, along with Sagittarius and Pisces. Abide by usual preventive-medicine routines. Lucky lottery numbers: 2, 14, 20, 38, 47, 16.

Thursday, August 15 (Moon in Libra to Scorpio 2:34 a.m.)   Career possibilities can be pushed successfully. Look rich, royal, and like somebody able to make a big contribution rather than a supplicant. It's not what your boss can do for you but what you can do for his product.

Scorpio and Taurus come front and center. You are known by your attitude. Hot combination numbers: 4 and 8.

Friday, August 16 (Moon in Scorpio)   Is it time to switch to a new career? To secure more training? To recognize that this is a new electronic ballgame and that facts have to be faced? There can be big gains from securing work that permits you to express yourself more. Hot combination numbers: 6 and 1.

Saturday, August 17 (Moon in Scorpio to Sagittarius 12:11 p.m.)   The social side of your career shouldn't be neglected. When higher-ups discuss promotions and new department heads, they all must have an image of you in the back of their minds. Enthusiasm and optimism pay handsome dividends. Persuade coworkers to drop by this evening for potluck, ice tea, and cookies. Lucky lottery numbers: 17, 8, 26, 43, 35, 44.

Sunday, August 18 (Moon in Sagittarius)   Sagittarius teaches tact and diplomacy, while Gemini beckons you to a spontaneous adventure. Invite interesting, off-beat types in for luncheon and let the talk flow freely. Go along with the suggestions of happy-go-lucky, cheerful, optimistic types. You can learn much today about being truly carefree. Others find you witty.

Monday, August 19 (Moon in Sagittarius)   It's people you want around you today. Parties, entertainments, spontaneous get-togethers, beach and water activities are all in focus. Aries and Leo will make your day. The realization that you love many people tends to increase your sense of security. Liking yourself is a big assist in true living. Your lucky number is 5.

Tuesday, August 20 (Moon in Sagittarius to Capricorn 12:35 a.m.)   There are special opportunities for reconciliations and for coping with any possible impasse in a marriage or business partnership. Readying things before big changes is part of this script. Capricorn and a Cancer understand your bothersome hangups. People who have had to leave their own countries can be looking to you for genuine help. Your lucky number is 7.

Wednesday, August 21 (Moon in Capricorn)   You may find yourself compulsively and secretly enamored by

170

somebody you have no right to think about in this way. Don't feel guilty; this happens. Longings may not be able to escape your heart. There are mysterious forces at work, much going on behind the scenes, a sense of abandonment, banishment, exile. Lucky lottery numbers: 18, 45, 36, 21, 9, 30.

Thursday, August 22 (Moon in Capricorn to Aquarius 1:27 p.m.) Love is protective of marriage. In your high lunar cycle, you are self-assured, able to throw your weight around in a nice quiet way, and able to express your almost sacred liberalism and strong love of tolerance. Another Aquarius and a Libra can bring things to a happy finale. Approval comes to you in a strange way. Your lucky number is 2.

Friday, August 23 (Moon in Aquarius) You guard your personal flanks well. You don't want your hard-won freedom and independence to be limited in any way. Friends mean much more to you than business success or fortune. You love being part of the busy group, all bent on humanitarian and charitable endeavor. The day sees you encouraging the masses. Count on number 4.

Saturday, August 24 (Moon in Aquarius) You could stumble upon excellent investment advice. The events of the day can give you increased personal and family security. You feel right with the world as you move about, enjoying the season and the opportunities for operating in the midstream of life. Pisces has good advice. Virgo is protective. Lucky lottery numbers: 15, 6, 24, 11, 40, 34.

Sunday, August 25 (Moon in Aquarius to Pisces 12:52 a.m.) There are no free lunches; so resist the promises and get-rich-quick schemes offered to you. You may notice how cost of living is inching up in the entertainment, luxury, and transportation fields. Still, you can become annoyed when Madame Moneybags starts complaining. You could read some unfriendly resentment in the faces of service personnel. Gemini has the explanations.

Monday, August 26 (Moon in Pisces) You can uncover some surprising bargains in out-of-the-way places and along rural roads. A Taurus or Scorpio can advise on the sources of additional capital. There can be some genuine consideration of the mail order business and

171

cottage industries. Talk about small businesses can fascinate you. Hot combination numbers: 3 and 4.

Tuesday, August 27 (Moon in Pisces to Aries 10:01 a.m.) Contact business leaders in your own community for advice on possible assistance you can give, on ways in which you can play an important role socially or politically. The yen to stand out, to make a real contribution to society is strong and right in line with your Aquarian personality. Hot combination numbers: 5 and 9.

Wednesday, August 28 (Moon in Aries) Aries enters the picture. You can strike out on your own and see how green that grass is on the other side of the wall. Hobbies, studies, and areas where you can concentrate, things immediate and pressing are in focus. You want to break with old rules and rise above past limitations. Lucky lottery numbers: 28, 7, 16, 25, 34, 43.

Thursday, August 29 (Moon in Aries to Taurus) There is a need to stick to what has to be finished this month. The day moves along swiftly. There can be interference that slows some jobs up. Conflicts between home and job can develop. Hobbies and studies may be neglected. Aries and Sagittarius are front and center. Getting the whole unadulterated truth is difficult. Hot combination numbers: 9 and 6.

Friday, August 30 (Moon in Taurus) You can have the feeling that love and lovers are ultra possessive. Family members do not agree on household matters. Budgets are being ignored. A practical attitude toward household deterioration and security is required. In conversation, loved ones leave things up in the air. You may have questions about the way they are spending time. Your lucky number is 2.

Saturday, August 31 (Moon in Taurus to Gemini 10:03 a.m.) You may have to pull back from a possible confrontation with a loved one on the matter of household chores, responsibilities, and family togetherness. Taurus and Virgo have definite ideas. A community problem on which there is much disagreement can seem more burdensome than ever. Lucky lottery numbers: 4, 31, 22, 40, 14, 39.

Sunday, September 1 (Moon in Gemini)   You're ultra creative, imaginative, flexible, and inventive. Upcoming fall plans can be put together. Commitments can be honored in good fashion. Acceptance, approval, and gratitude can cross over into a more passionate feeling. Discussions with children will pay off. Aries and Gemini have important roles. An in-law can prove helpful.

Monday, September 2 (Moon in Gemini)   Romantic interludes and overtures demand their part of the day. Suddenly you could realize that somebody outwardly critical of you may secretly desire special closeness. A child can say something worth thinking about. Another Aquarius can steer you in the right direction. Love is medicinal this evening. Play number 7 to win.

Tuesday, September 3 (Moon in Gemini to Cancer 1:20 a.m.)   Work must be done, not dogged. You can encounter sloth in the market places of life. Take your questions to a Cancer or Capricorn. It's no good exhorting others to do what you should be doing yourself. Performing services for ungrateful types can be disheartening. Not a good day for hiring or expecting too much from the group. Hot combination numbers: 9 and 3.

Wednesday, September 4 (Moon in Cancer)   How can you inject a sense of adventure in your job? Anything repetitive will thwart and anger you. Boring conversations with long-winded coworkers should be avoided if possible. The urge to do something different, to change your scene can cause great restlessness. Even so, the effort you put into what has to be done will pay handsome dividends. Lucky lottery numbers: 4, 11, 20, 38, 13, 2.

Thursday, September 5 (Moon in Cancer to Leo 3:13 a.m.)   Compromise and conciliate. Unite closely with coworkers and others. Marital and legal interests can be advanced. Consult, cooperate, and consider carefully. Leo and another Aquarius are in the picture. Ideas that you have long nurtured can demonstrate new growth. Improve your public image. Your lucky number is 4.

Friday, September 6 (Moon in Leo)   Share, give, be generous and admire. You are popular because you are enthusiastic and jovial and you tend to look on the positive side of things. Sagittarius is helpful. Iron out any old differences with a loved one that still seem to signify. Through love and marriage you gain greater prestige and a sense of higher status. Hot combination numbers: 6 and 7.

Saturday, September 7 (Moon in Leo to Virgo 4:35 a.m.) You can close one door and open another. Improvements and corrections have free rein and easy sledding. Virgo takes charge and can be trusted. A keen sense of how you can make your loved ones more secure in this changing world is with you. What you figure out today, you can implement tomorrow. New alliances can be considered. Lucky lottery numbers: 17, 26, 44, 7, 35, 8.

Sunday, September 8 (Moon in Virgo) Today's new moon illuminates security matters and changes others may be foisting upon you. Aries comes to your rescue. Restrictions are lifting and what you delayed earlier in the month or year can go forward now. Trust old romance and long-existing friendships over pushy newcomers. The feeling that you are going to be happier is strong.

Monday, September 9 (Moon in Virgo to Libra 6:52 a.m.) Excellent aspects for a delayed summer vacation, also a budget trip. Fine trends where you are checking up on what you have going for yourself at a distance from home. You learn through observation. Old experiences are dusted off and can bring an up-to-date bonus. Gemini asks the right questions. Hot combination numbers: 5 and 1.

Tuesday, September 10 (Moon in Libra) Travel, sightseeing, conferences, interviews, and self-realization are accented. There is a gala atmosphere, a festival environment. The happier you are today, the more popular you will be. The more others will accept your ideas. Your powers of conviction are first rate. You look ahead and get the lay of the land. Play number 7 to win.

Wednesday, September 11 (Moon in Libra to Scorpio 11:43 a.m.) Innovations, amendments, improvements are speeded up. You do well when you keep on the go and see many people. Don't let any one person buttonhole you too long. Your mind is active, jumping from interest to interest. A lighthearted and buoyant attitude works wonders for you. Libra figures prominently. Lucky lottery numbers: 27, 11, 18, 36, 45, 39.

Thursday, September 12 (Moon in Scorpio) Push career, professional, economic and social status. Confide in Pisces and Scorpio. The opposite sex has interesting questions to ask, but may lack audacity if the environment lacks privacy. In love, romance, and a marital relationship, you can count on marvelous awareness. You can change a weak no into a strong yes. Hot combination numbers: 2 and 5.

Friday, September 13 (Moon in Scorpio to Sagittarius 8:15 p.m.) Marital and legal plans come out of the shadows. There is an air of superstition now. Know what the kids have on their program today. Make sure your reputation isn't suffering because of the company you keep. Leo and Sagittarius have key roles. The type of education available in your community must be questioned. Your lucky number is 4.

Saturday, September 14 (Moon in Sagittarius) Some conflicts involving career and group socializing can develop. Church, club, community can all make demands upon your time. Charitable and humanitarian endeavors are in focus. You want to get the most for your money and the time you give to projects. Aries and Cancer have important parts to play. Lucky lottery numbers: 29, 6, 15, 33, 42, 14.

Sunday, September 15 (Moon in Sagittarius) You can hear the call of the out-of-doors today and want to spend time moving about your own community, seeing people, noticing changes, and deciding on what you can do to improve things. You are reaching out for approval and understanding. Gemini will have a lot to say. You are outgoing, cheerful, informed, and enjoy socializing on the grand scale.

Monday, September 16 (Moon in Sagittarius to Capricorn 8:04 a.m.) Your little-used talents and skills have a chance to show something today. You can impress loved ones by the way you fix things up in your home. Routine duties can be jazzed up and the more optimistic and positive you are, the more excellent will be your

175

productions. Taurus and Virgo will grant favors. Hot combination numbers: 3 and 5.

Tuesday, September 17 (Moon in Capricorn) Confidential, intimate, and private interests can be pushed. You can make good headway where you avoid publicity and limit participation in discussions. Somebody at the top may want to confide something that is for your ears only. Capricorn and Taurus come front and center. Watch out for the game-playing clones who believe mischief-making is a business requirement. Hot combination numbers: 5 and 8.

Wednesday, September 18 (Moon in Capricorn to Aquarius 8:58 p.m.) You can fall under the spurious charm of a mysterious influence. The exotic can appeal to you. Behind the scenes much is taking place that will have bearing on the decisions that have to be made. The unreal and the illusionary invade the realm of love and marriage. Pisces will relate well to you. Lucky lottery numbers: 16, 25, 34, 7, 18, 30.

Thursday, September 19 (Moon in Aquarius) You can grasp the bright mantle of leadership. Nobody is going to stand in your way. You can attract favorable attention and really make your mark in highly personalized interests. Goals and aims can be announced successfully. Speak up in your own vital interests. At the same time be willing to consider the urgent needs of others. Hot combination numbers: 9 and 2.

Friday, September 20 (Moon in Aquarius) You can begin all over again. You can redirect your personal spacecraft. Personality assets can be tossed into the hopper. It would be easy to become angry at no-shows or slowpokes, but the less said the better under prevailing aspects. You can personally choose your own ways in romance, love, entertainment.

Saturday, September 21 (Moon in Aquarius to Pisces 8:21 a.m.) The public is charmed by your personality. Personal grooming can be a factor in the success you achieve. Your personal world is at the center of things, with loved ones agreeable. You can joyfully sense a wealth of freedom, independence, and will want to be

176

closely associated with other winners. Lucky lottery numbers: 4, 21, 13, 22, 40, 36.

Sunday, September 22 (Moon in Pisces)   You can identify with Pisces and Capricorn. Suddenly you'll sense all that you can do to increase financial take and this optimism can make the week ahead. You gain knowledge now that you will put to good use later on. The ability to track down bargains and good-quality merchandise never was better. What one member of the team doesn't want to sell you, the other will!

Monday, September 23 (Moon in Pisces to Aries 4:56 p.m.)   You get what you want in business transactions and in a friendly chat with your employer or supervisor. You put things the right way, which can lower old barriers and remove some old bias. You can see the mysterious and peculiar ways of money that may not have been revealed to you earlier. You can possess the glamorous. Count on number 1.

Tuesday, September 24 (Moon in Aries)   What takes place in your immediate environment has greater impact upon you than formerly. Watch the mails. Take notes when you come up against things that need fixing or doing. Local problems will crash in on your consciousness even when you try to be more sophisticated and cosmopolitan. Hot combination numbers: 3 and 5.

Wednesday, September 25 (Moon in Aries to Taurus 11 p.m.)   There's an unexpected desire to escape from financial talks, concerns. This is not a good day for signing contracts or making money decisions. Business deals will refuse to go away, however, and afternoon can bring you some support in keeping a door open until you feel like talking turkey. Aries, Leo, and Sagittarius fire your enthusiasms. Lucky lottery numbers: 14, 5, 32, 25, 41, 17.

Thursday, September 26 (Moon in Taurus)   Property values, renovation of home, and preparing everything for winter are in focus. Talks with a spend-thrift relative can clear the air of recriminations. You may resent the need to cater to an in-law. The desire to take charge of a deteriorating situation in your community can be strong. Taurus can be helpful. Hot combination numbers: 7 and 8.

177

Friday, September 27 (Moon in Taurus)   If neighbors pull together, the community can be made safer. You yearn to drop worries about property, break-ins, and dangerous streets and schools. Where you are practical and decisive, you can make good headway in your personal life. Employment matters tend to take a back seat. Virgo makes a suggestion. Your lucky number is 9.

Saturday, September 28 (Moon in Taurus to Gemini 3:26 a.m.)   A strong yen for travel is generated. The desire to see somebody with whom you once were romantically involved can be overpowering. You want to get out of yourself and into groups where there will be much carefree laughter and a sense of belonging. Parent-offspring relationships can be improved. Libra and another Aquarius figure importantly. Lucky lottery numbers: 20, 11, 29, 47, 2, 38.

Sunday, September 29 (Moon in Gemini)   Your responses to the opposite sex will be passionate today. Your intuitive processes serve love, romance, adventure. In work as well as love and play, your involvement tends to be intense, emotional. Ask a few neighbors or friends in this evening. You can count on Gemini. Socializing is good therapy. A feeling of greater personal freedom inspires you.

Monday, September 30 (Moon in Gemini to Cancer 6:59 a.m.)   Fine time for a medical or dental checkup. Excellent for inaugurating an improved regimen of physical exercise. This is the season for walking, for studying the advance of autumn. You come out from under a summer-imposed sense of restrictions and all members of the family tend to mind their own business. Cancer and Capricorn are represented. Hot combination numbers: 8 and 4.

OCTOBER 1991

Tuesday, October 1 (Moon in Cancer)   A new season can call for switches in diet, exercise. The more walking you can get into these pleasant fall days the better. Cancer and Scorpio have roles to play. Work can be burdensome over the afternoon but the chores you tackle this evening will be a piece of cake. Trust humor, wit, a carefree chat with a teenager. Hot combination numbers: 8 and 9.

Wednesday, October 2 (Moon in Cancer to Leo 9:49 a.m.) Probe, search, and question under prevailing aspects. Get to know more about your own prejudices, questionable leanings, and hidden recesses of thinking. Reading for information will hold your attention. You're fascinated with the opinions of a supervisor or other older person. Pisces is in the picture. Lucky lottery numbers: 2, 10, 19, 45, 27, 37.

Thursday, October 3 (Moon in Leo) Marital, public relations, advertising, partnerships, cooperative effort, and agreements are all in focus. You can establish common ground with a critic, opponent. Bridge-building between the various members of your family and community can be worthwhile. Leo has much to say. Conciliate; compromise. Play number 3 to win.

Friday, October 4 (Moon in Leo to Virgo 12:45 p.m.) The glamor and prestige of a colleague can in a sense rub off on you. Ambitions are stimulated. The urge to gather in more goodies is strong. There are opportunities at your elbow, so to speak, and another Aquarius and a Gemini can point to them. Know your own mind before attempting to communicate ideas. Your lucky number is 5.

Saturday, October 5 (Moon in Virgo) You can put things together well. You blend people into an interesting group. This is a good fixit day. What you can't fix should be taken to those specializing in that product. Divorced people are in this picture. Marriage as an institution may require your speaking up for it. Lucky lottery numbers: 16, 25, 5, 43, 7, 34.

Sunday, October 6 (Moon in Virgo to Libra 4:01 p.m.) You work well alone in your own home. Cleanup programs around lawn, yard, sides of your house will improve the scene greatly. Virgo can be counted on. Deteriorating situations can be saved by what you do now. You are able to correct a false impression a neighbor has of you. Liabilities can be transformed into assets.

179

Monday, October 7 (Moon in Libra)   Get close to your offspring; know their fears, insecurities, uncertainties. What you say and do now can be totally constructive and make a big difference. Traditional places where you shop may not be the right ones. It's a good day to reconsider, reinvestigate. Libra and Aries figure prominently. Hot combination numbers: 4 and 5.

Tuesday, October 8 (Moon in Libra to Scorpio 9 p.m.)   Your learning processes are stimulated along with your desire to travel, to get out of yourself and away from what is boring in the familiar. You look beyond the present and well can come up with some good ideas about feathering your nest for the future. You are more perceptive. The longings of others are well within your ken. Your lucky number is 6.

Wednesday, October 9 (Moon in Scorpio)   Push opportunities to advance in your career. Seek wider authority from those who can delegate it. Economic and social status can be upped depending on your attitude and your awareness of what you don't know but can learn. Scorpio comes front and center. Ideas can be transformed into something real and solid. Lucky lottery numbers: 17, 9, 26, 44, 8, 13.

Thursday, October 10 (Moon in Scorpio)   Discussions with your employer or supervisors can net you more usuable information. You could feel angry and thwarted over situations on the job or where you feel automation has been downgrading some of your valuable skills. You sense the spreading of disenchantment across the land. Power builds up in local matters. Your lucky number is 1.

Friday, October 11 (Moon in Scorpio to Sagittarius 4:58 a.m.)   The social side of business and financial activities can tug at you. You may sense severe and extreme changes in the attitudes and philosophies of much older friends. Cliques may appear to be negative influences. Sagittarius has something important to say. Church and club membership becomes more important as autumn waxes. Hot combination numbers: 3 and 9.

Saturday, October 12 (Moon in Sagittarius)   There are wonderful aspects for entertaining kindred spirits, organizing a bridge table, exchanging viewpoints with involved people. Boost your own morale by spending time with people who have something to say. The great outdoors can beckon to you while nature shows off her wares. Lucky lottery numbers: 12, 5, 32, 41, 14, 23.

Sunday, October 13 (Moon in Sagittarius to Capricorn 4:11 p.m.) By being friendly, cheerful, outgoing, and considerate, you can earn a high degree of popularity. Business and pleasure can be combined away from home base. You can sense an increase in social prestige by the way you are treated by new acquaintances. A conversation with an authoritative type can advance some of your career aims.

Monday, October 14 (Moon in Capricorn) In a love exchange or romantic interlude, you can speak of your private dreams and longings. You can dig more deeply into your own psyche and that of your beloved. There can be a summing up of what you have been missing and a parallel resolve to stake claims and deny yourself no longer. Lucky number is 2.

Tuesday, October 15 (Moon in Capricorn) What wasn't revealed earlier in the month can now be taken out from under wraps. You can draw pretty logical conclusions from what you are being told. Capricorn and Taurus are in your corner. By getting a good view of the past, you can more accurately aim your personal spacecraft in a new direction. Hot combination numbers: 4 and 7.

Wednesday, October 16 (Moon in Capricorn to Aquarius 5:05 a.m.) Career matters are speeded up. You can set your own pace and pretty much determine the program and policy of others in your immediate environment. In your higher lunar cycle, you are challenged to show your true mettle. Take charge of situations that are waxing and ignore what is waning, for now. Lucky lottery numbers: 16, 6, 24, 33, 42, 15.

Thursday, October 17 (Moon in Aquarius) Now in your lunar high cycle, you can rearrange things to suit yourself. You can extract the opportunities that you instinctively know are for you more than for any possible competition. Size up the opposition early on so that you can then give your all to the job as it should be done. You can encourage, guide, invite, and attract. Hot combination numbers: 8 and 1.

Friday, October 18 (Moon in Aquarius to Pisces 4:53 p.m.) Stay in first place. Refuse to permit anybody to patronize you or put you down. Speak sharply to interfering, time wasters. Your ability to organize is second to none and will attract the kind of attention that translates itself into support, acquiescence. You are the dominant party in love and marriage and here are opportunities for correcting and improving your own behavior. Your lucky number is 1.

Saturday, October 19 (Moon in Pisces) Originality and creativity are carrying dollar signs. Pisces and Virgo have key roles. Earning power can be increased if you listen more to your own intuitive processes and less to the angry voice nearby. Generosity wars on miserliness and you make certain the positive approach comes out on top. Lucky lottery numbers: 12, 30, 19, 48, 3, 14.

Sunday, October 20 (Moon in Pisces) Push spiritual concepts and tone down material considerations. The desire to be a total person fills your mind and heart. You can increase the confidence of loved ones by the approach you take toward them. Children can be made more cheerful. You know that true value has little to do with money. Another Aquarius has the know-how.

Monday, October 21 (Moon in Pisces to Aries 1:33 a.m.) You're more the activist now, full of stamina, good feelings, and anxious to make your mark. You concentrate and zero in on immediate and pressing matters, and know the real here-and-now picture. There isn't any wasting of time as you move from one chore to another in a dynamic, zestful way. Aries and Leo approve. Lucky number is 9.

Tuesday, October 22 (Moon in Aries) Push hobbies, studies, and keep in close contact with neighbors, siblings, and people you see every day. Know what they are thinking and be willing to speak of your own half-formed dreams for the future. What you set in motion today can prove enduring over the rest of the month.

Read; write; phone. Sagittarius is supportive. Hot combination numbers: 2 and 6.

Wednesday, October 23 (Moon in Aries to Taurus 6:55 a.m.) Full moon forms in Aries and brings enlightenment in studies, learning processes, avocational matters, local involvements, and training. You can improve your position in the areas that count most. Your motivation is more clear, understandable, and your drive in things that interest you unbeatable. Lucky lottery numbers: 40, 23, 4, 13, 39, 36.

Thursday, October 24 (Moon in Taurus) Taurus and Scorpio have the directions. You emphasize the family, familiar, usual, traditional. You are conscious of your place in the scheme of things. What you do to renovate your house will increase its value. National events inspire your patriotic feelings. Your lucky number is 6.

Friday, October 25 (Moon in Taurus to Gemini 10:09 a.m.) Major cleanup programs around the yard, lawn, and garage can absorb you. Taurus is in this scene. Chats with neighbors give you a strong sense of being in the right place at the right time. Local shopping goes well. Community refurbishment, recycling programs, garage sales have their roles. Fun-loving and generous trends are stimulated. Count on number 8.

Saturday, October 26 (Moon in Gemini) There is a feeling of peace and outgoing love permeating your body. You want to be close to your beloved and there is a strong possiblity of one of those memorable experiences that will make you blush even while smiling in the years to come. Invite and accept invitations; scurry to raise your social potential. Gemini has something to say. Lucky lottery numbers: 26, 1, 28, 37, 13, 46.

Sunday, October 27 (Moon in Gemini to Cancer 12:37 p.m.) Your presence is appreciated; your words are approved. There can be gratitude coming your way. You combine good humor with intellectual powers of persuasion. You know well how to combine business with pleasure wherever you happen to be. Libra comes front and center. Hobbies, studies, genuine communications are favored.

Monday, October 28 (Moon in Cancer)   Work is stepped up and more is expected of you today. There can be a sense of panic on some workers and this can annoy you. You have a better sense of proportion than others and dislike seeing the accent placed on something frivolous and meaningless. Cancer and Capricorn have parts to play. You can tackle what others find repugnant. Your lucky number is 7.

Tuesday, October 29 (Moon in Cancer to Leo 3:21 a.m.)   Not a day for dogging it, neglecting, forgetting, being late. You could be judged by your actions and speech. Be practical, reasonable, and meet all duties, responsibilities and obligations. Cancer and Capricorn are prominent. Stick to a good health regimen. There is some peculiar restlessness beneath the surface. Hot combination numbers: 9 and 2.

Wednesday, October 30 (Moon in Leo)   You tend to view partnerships, contracts, and agreements through rose-colored glasses. Things may not be as wonderful as partners and others would have you believe. Distrust expansive viewpoints, extreme promises, and unwise favors. Keep a low profile in money matters, and protect relationships with in-laws. Lucky lottery numbers: 11, 20, 38, 47, 30, 2.

Thursday, October 31 (Moon in Leo to Virgo 6:47 p.m.)   Tell me who your friends are and I'll tell you what you are! The wrong ingredients in any group, cake, or project can cause big problems. Be more realistic in your evaluation of people. Your partner or spouse may be a little edgy. Refurbishment of the spirit is possible through reading, quiet discussions with philosophical types. Trust Aries. Hot combination numbers: 4 and 7.

NOVEMBER 1991

Friday, November 1 (Moon in Virgo)   Virgo and Taurus come front and center. Push savings and investments; talk with your broker; subscribe to a financial publication. The economy as it touches you is becoming too complicated for any potluck approach. Is your house ready for the upcoming colder season? Do you really know what objectionable material is coming to your juveniles via TV? Hot combination numbers: 3 and 4.

Saturday, November 2 (Moon in Virgo to Libra 11:13 p.m.)   An excellent time to make changes, court improvements and corrections. You may find one of your associates painfully materialistic. There's an urge to expand spiritual horizons and to take life more as it presents itself. Not a good time for forcing issues, but evolutionary change can lighten the load. Lucky lottery numbers: 14, 32, 41, 2, 5, 23.

Sunday, November 3 (Moon in Libra)   Libra and Gemini figure prominently. There's additional prestige for you where you take up the slack and move quickly to fill any vacuum. Armchair travel gets good grades. You will enjoy speaking long-distance to a loved one. What's happening far away can give you a sense of adventure. Dine graciously tonight.

Monday, November 4 (Moon in Libra)   Your mind is restless, curious, and anxious to know the truthful trends that are more or less hidden. You're sensitive to changes in the personalities of others. There may be a need for additional tolerance. Not everybody is meeting their responsibilities, which means extra burdens on someone else's shoulders. Your best bet is number 2.

Tuesday, November 5 (Moon in Libra to Scorpio 5:09 a.m.)   The time has arrived when a little string-pulling at the top can improve your economic position. Consult Scorpio and Gemini. The questions you ask may not have definite, easy answers. Career complexities are in focus and there is much unfair opposition and competition set free. Write; read. Hot combination numbers: 4 and 1.

Wednesday, November 6 (Moon in Scorpio)   The new moon illuminates a professional quandry or career impasse. Prepare to take a great leap forward in the way you handle assignments. Cancer and Sagittarius are in the picture. Automation can't be kept out of business and office procedures. New time, labor, and money-saving devices may not save anything. Machinery breaks down. Lucky lottery numbers: 15, 24, 42, 6, 33, 18.

Thursday, November 7 (Moon in Scorpio to Sagittarius 1:22 p.m.)   Push special talents which have previously endeared you to your employer. Buy items that may assist you in career ambitions. Wherever you see a need or developing problem, suggest ways to combat these. Taurus and Virgo are on your side. Exciting improvements and corrections can get under way. Hot combination numbers: 8 and 4.

Friday, November 8 (Moon in Sagittarius)   Some friends are genuinely sensitive; others are merely touchy. But both require tactful and diplomatic handling. It's not too early to blueprint plans for Thanksgiving. A real bargain could be found in the advertising pages. Admiration, gratitude, favors, and compliments are in the picture, along with Pisces. Your lucky number is 1.

Saturday, November 9 (Moon in Sagittarius)   Socialize, spend time with true and dear friends. A show of genuine responsibility will excite the special feelings that a member of the opposite sex has for you. Groups, gatherings, lectures, places where you can learn by listening and observing are well aspected. You are lucky in the conclusions you draw. Cancer and Leo are front and center. Lucky lottery numbers: 12, 3, 48, 39, 9, 16.

Sunday, November 10 (Moon in Sagittarius to Capricorn 12:17 a.m.)   Summarize, draw conclusions, consider all the facts and then make up your mind. Dealings with organizations, with the problems or worries of your mate are well aspected. You see through the mist and excel in cutting red tape and clearing away the debris. Facts not fancies have priority. Keep abreast of recent government legislation which may have bearing on your business. Capricorn is helpful.

Monday, November 11 (Moon in Capricorn)   No matter what your age, show special consideration and respect for those born in the last century for upon their problems and sorrows some of your goodies were constructed. Read World War I literature or nonfiction to gain a better understanding of present times. Business demands attention. Sales and advertising are well aspected. Virgo and Taurus make contributions. Your lucky number is 9.

Tuesday, November 12 (Moon in Capricorn to Aquarius 1:07 p.m.) Your secret admirers are out in force. What is going on behind the scenes can be of some value and help. Don't permit another to push simplistic solutions to complex problems. Rumors and gossip are making the rounds. Libra knows the truth. Consider the position of a small child who requires chastisement. Play number 2 today.

Wednesday, November 13 (Moon in Aquarius) Step to the center of the stage. You can have what you deserve. Speak up, share your ideas, and air your hopes for the future. The initiative belongs in your hands. The desire for greater freedom and independence is compulsive. Another Aquarius, Gemini, and Libra are in the scenario. You are that majority of one, however. Lucky lottery numbers: 13, 40, 4, 22, 31, 19.

Thursday, November 14 (Moon in Aquarius) You can use your charm and charisma effectively today. Friends want to know your secret, highly personal side. But you still may be playing your cards close to your chest. By opening up a bit, you can persuade others to your point of view. You can lower the intensity of criticism coming your way from those who don't really know you. Lucky number is 6.

Friday, November 15 (Moon in Aquarius to Pisces 1:34 a.m.) Push your earning power and income; dispose of possessions you no longer want. You can raise money in peculiar ways. The peculiarities of buying and selling are represented. Pisces is in the script. There can be some good pointers on how to fund unpopular projects. Veils are lifted so that you understand what is going on behind the scenes. Hot combination numbers: 8 and 1.

Saturday, November 16 (Moon in Pisces) Guard valuables. Where possible stick to budgets even though somebody may try to inveigle you into spending too much. Know what the price of an entertainment will be before you go along with the merrymakers. Exciting financial news can arrive before the day ends. Ignore unpleasant rumors. Lucky lottery numbers: 10, 28, 37, 1, 46, 16.

187

Sunday, November 17 (Moon in Pisces to Aries 11:08 a.m.)   Generosity may be a pitfall. You could receive an invitation with a quirk or hook in it. The feeling that older loved ones are taking advantage can be strong. Know where your youngsters are and with whom they are conniving. Peace of mind may be rather elusive, and you could find mere acquaintances rather evasive. Retire early.

Monday, November 18 (Moon in Aries)   You pull loose ends together efficiently. Aries is helpful. You know where to put the emphasis as more than one responsibility is faced. Neighbors, siblings, and their youngsters are in this script. You would like to deal with something new and can become bored easily with the expected and familiar. Move about your own neighborhood. Your best number is 7.

Tuesday, November 19 (Moon in Aries to Taurus 4:49 p.m.)   Plant feet firmly where you are and refuse to be budged from a conviction. There are those who can't stand your disagreeing with their bias for a short-range view. Communications are flowing freely punctuated now and then with a rumor or mere supposition. Powerful types make ridiculous promises with small chance of being able to abide by them. Take a chance on number 9.

Wednesday, November 20 (Moon in Taurus)   You may wish to escape from the confusion outside your home. There can be rumors about property values and community-action groups. Your desire to be friendly with somebody very different from you can be rebuffed. Taurus has important information. Consider what you can do personally to fight neighborhood deterioration and crime. Lucky lottery numbers: 11, 20, 31, 38, 47, 2.

Thursday, November 21 (Moon in Taurus to Gemini 7:23 p.m.)   Virgo and Pisces have key roles. It's a day of pleasant chores that have to be done this month. Family and friends figure prominently. Reunions, celebrations, and laying foundations for greater family interactions are all favorably represented. You could be censored behind your back for an attitude of possessiveness. Hot combination numbers: 4 and 8.

Friday, November 22 (Moon in Gemini)   You can have the feeling that things are as they should be. Old memories can be stirred and nostalgia and sentimentalism enter the picture. Gemini has much to say. Your affections are intense and you tend to overlook even glaring faults in a loved one. Things seem worthwhile, and you can hug situations to your breast. Hot combination numbers: 6 and 2.

Saturday, November 23 (Moon in Gemini to Cancer 8:26 p.m.)   Creativity and flexibility make this a day of great vitality and achievement potential. You socialize effectively and impress others with your charm and talents. Entertain in your own home this evening. Writing, other forms of artistic expression, are well within your scope. Sagittarius and Libra are your best audience. Lucky lottery numbers: 17, 8, 23, 35, 44, 8.

Sunday, November 24 (Moon in Cancer)   Let Capricorn and Cancer have their due. Protect all aspects of health, and be cautious while climbing and descending. There can be some leftover work that is not exactly to your liking, but a coworker of your choice can prove entertaining. You may also dislike the antics of neighborhood children and their pets.

Monday, November 25 (Moon in Cancer to Leo 9:38 p.m.)   There is a sense of urgency about making your day count. Work hanging fire for some time can rise up to haunt you. Trying to meet all the dietary and exercise musts that keep coming at you from all directions may seem too much. Cancer and Scorpio have important roles to play. Organization of details can give them more importance than they deserve. Hot combination numbers: 6 and 8.

Tuesday, November 26 (Moon in Leo)   Working in close cooperation and understanding will achieve much. Diplomacy and tact in marriage and other partnerships will pay off. You may suddenly wish that you had the key to an improved relationship with in-laws. Your image in the minds of coworkers may not be to your liking. You reach out, extend your thinking, but there can be cold aloofness. Hot combination numbers: 8 and 3.

Wednesday, November 27 (Moon in Leo)   What's wrong with wearing rose-colored glasses in marriage? Even when you're naked? If you look for those silver linings, you won't be disappointed. It's not enough to know that things are wrong in society—do something about it. Leo makes an announcement. In your own mind you can resolve doubts and uncertainties. Lucky lottery numbers: 1, 27, 28, 37, 10, 46.

Thursday, November 28 (Moon in Leo to Virgo 12:12 a.m.)   The extras you give your career and all professional matters won't be wasted. The potential for taking great leaps forward to higher prestige and status is activated. But social commitments can be pressured. Keep close tabs on savings, investments, and overall security interests. Virgo knows. Your lucky number is 3.

Friday, November 29 (Moon in Virgo)   In marriage, there can be a veritable second honeymoon without leaving your boudoir. Partnerships are pleasant, productive. Virgo and Taurus figure prominently. Be public-spirited and avoid those who can't seem to help being mean-spirited. In many ways, you are the giver of gifts, the source of much happiness. Hot combination numbers: 4 and 9.

Saturday, November 30 (Moon in Virgo to Libra 4:47 a.m.)   Keep on the move today. Change your scene and you invite good luck. Libra has an important role. There is a search for warm memories amid half-forgotten scenes. Travel, nostalgia, intellectual activity are strongly represented. Contact a former neighbor and somebody who moved far away. Evoke pleasant and sentimental rememberances. Lucky lottery numbers: 14, 32, 41, 5, 30, 11.

DECEMBER 1991

Sunday, December 1 (Moon in Libra)   Before this holiday month gets crowded with chores, take off on an escapist holiday. Your career is at a standstill. Visits with kindred spirits, sightseeing, dining out, and viewing a resort's preparation for Christmas are all good possibilities. Libra is in the picture. You can please members of the opposite sex without half trying. Enjoy.

Monday, December 2 (Moon in Libra to Scorpio 11:34 a.m.)   Socializing, spontaneous ideas, and enjoyment of the newcomers and strangers in your midst are favored today. Gemini and Aquarius brighten your day. You look ahead and refuse to become trapped in the present. Your mind is stimulated by fascinating people, places, and ideas. You can count on genuine relaxation because you are where you want to be. Hot combination numbers: 1 and 4.

Tuesday, December 3 (Moon in Scorpio)   Your career picks up a little steam, but some are not where you would expect to find them. The bottleneck is on hand, however, and things can become confused. You may not have much patience with a supervisor or coworker. This evening favors spontaneous socializing and a bit of shopping. Hot combination numbers: 3 and 9.

Wednesday, December 4 (Moon in Scorpio to Sagittarius 8:33 p.m.)   Your awareness of what you want and want to do is strong. Ideals can get in the way of practical progress. You are more spiritual and emotional than the physical Taurus and Scorpio on the scene. Your powers of persuasion increase. A conference, quiet business discussion, and working out a holiday budget will be appropriate. Lucky lottery numbers: 14, 5, 23, 41, 32, 16.

Thursday, December 5 (Moon in Sagittarius)   It's an excellent time for preholiday parties, entertainments, annual banquets. Fine for activities associated with charitable and humanitarian efforts. Check with church and club to see what you can do for the needy and homeless. You will enjoy moving about a shopping mall and looking your own community over. Your lucky number is 7.

Friday, December 6 (Moon in Sagittarius)   Today's new moon illuminates social plans and volunteer work and helps you understand friends and their motivation. Excellent for issuing invitations, mailing greeting cards, or Xeroxing work. Being diplomatic when such tact is required, can save a friendship. Give others the benefit of every doubt and distrust rumors and gossip. Sagittarius and Leo figure prominently. Play number 9 to win.

191

Saturday, December 7 (Moon in Sagittarius to Capricorn 7:41 a.m.)   Entertain in your own home today. Invite coworkers and neighbors in for a bit of holiday cheer. You may mix a few close friends with this mob. Slow starters will appreciate your holiday push. There are good trends for finalizing plans for the remainder of this month. But hold off heavy shopping. Lucky lottery numbers: 11, 20, 2, 29, 38, 7.

Sunday, December 8 (Moon in Capricorn)   Complete, finish up, write notes and help your mate or another with some project that disinterests you but which you still feel obligated to do. Late afternoon can hang on your hands and children can interfere. It's time to question what might be going on in lives of small children and what may be happening behind the scenes. Gemini helps out.

Monday, December 9 (Moon in Capricorn to Aquarius 8:27 p.m.)   There can be a strong sense of accomplishment when you finish jobs you never wanted to begin in the first place. You have heard just about enough from that big mouth. You could suspect or even witness the beginning of a romantic attachment in your place of business. Libra stands tall and ready. Hot combination numbers: 9 and 5.

Tuesday, December 10 (Moon in Aquarius)   Conferences with your employer, employees, and coworkers should clear the atmosphere of uncertainties and suspicions. Plans for a holiday entertainment can be pushed successfully. Aries and Gemini make contributions. There is some flexibility in projects and plans, and programs may be required due to weather or some other interference. Hot combination numbers: 1 and 5.

Wednesday, December 11 (Moon in Aquarius)   People you used to work with and who have been on your mind of late should be contacted. Have lunch in some unusual place with a kindred spirit, who really knows and understands you. Intellectual curiosity is strong. As the evening meanders along, you can become somewhat more social. Shopping is enjoyable. Lucky lottery numbers: 12, 30, 48, 3, 21, 39.

Thursday, December 12 (Moon in Aquarius to Pisces 9:20 a.m.)   Hold the initiative throughout the day.

Charm, charisma, and self-confidence are opening new doors for you. Speak up; air your hopes for the future; let the world see you at your best. Dress to the nines. You can have your own way in some bartering or buying operation. Another Aquarius is helpful. Gemini and Cancer have the answers. Your lucky number is 5.

Friday, December 13 (Moon in Pisces) Step lively and finish up some jobs that make you look good. Spruce up your personal appearance today. Contests, self-reliance, and contacting business people are all favored. As the day moves along there can be some unexpected financial opportunities. Evening is fine for having close friends in for preholiday celebration. Hot combination numbers: 7 and 8.

Saturday, December 14 (Moon in Pisces to Aries 8:07 p.m.) Push finances: collect what is due you, sell, advertise, hold special sales. Review budgets and allocate what you need for holiday expenses. Shopping potential is good and gifts that have been elusive so far suddenly can appear. Self-expression opportunities are first rate. You can sense much agreement and understanding coming from an older friend. Lucky lottery numbers: 18, 36, 27, 14, 9, 45.

Sunday, December 15 (Moon in Aries) Trust Virgo and Pisces. Asking questions will offset the possibility of making erros. There can be too much talk about expenses or money generally. Much can be gained in prestige and status from the way you dress, enter and leave a room. Courtesy will prove to be money in the bank, checks you can cash later on. Cleverness is represented.

Monday, December 16 (Moon in Aries) Concentration powers are excellent. You can zero in on opportunities as soon as you identify them. Phone, write, and keep in touch for there is much bridge-building potential here. Former critics can be persuaded to your points of view. Aries and Sagittarius figure prominently. Hobbies and greeting cards in the mail are favored routines. Your lucky number is 6.

Tuesday, December 17 (Moon in Aries to Taurus 3:10 a.m.) Gather your wits about you today and you can

193

achieve, even win big. Know the score; keep your weather eye on the prize and on what is transpiring in your immediate environment. Taurus comes front and center. An excellent day for creative, household decoration and getting your home ready for major entertainment. Your lucky number is 8.

Wednesday, December 18 (Moon in Taurus) Social plans pick up steam. What couldn't be done earlier in the month is child's play today. Domestic interests are featured, along with real estate, family, home, property, catering, and ownership. You are rather possessive of what you have put together, what you have built up in life. Virgo and Capricorn are prominent. Lucky lottery numbers: 10, 28, 37, 46, 18, 1.

Thursday, December 19 (Moon in Taurus to Gemini 6:22 a.m.) This is a real love day. Affection, passion, creativity, flexibility, closeness to parents and offspring are all to the fore. You can win many points today, including a great deal of approval and appreciation. Love is related to friendship, companionship, as well as fabulous gender response. Another Aquarius and a Gemini are in the picture. Hot combination numbers: 3 and 7.

Friday, December 20 (Moon in Gemini) A special closeness to your beloved marks this day. Try to steal away with the one and only for a few hours at least. Be prepared for some interference, however, even rumor-mongering and gossip. You are stimulated intellectually by a romantic interlude. This evening is ideal for partying on the grand scale. Open your doors as well as your heart. Hot combination numbers: 5 and 9.

Saturday, December 21 (Moon in Gemini to Cancer 6:55 a.m.) You may be a little slow in getting started today. But a good breakfast and the companionship of a wise shopper and entertaining personality can make your day. You can get many pesky holiday tasks out of the way. Get a few hours napping before taking off for a spectacular evening. Lucky lottery numbers: 16, 25, 35, 7, 21, 43.

Sunday, December 22 (Moon in Cancer) Information from a distance boosts your morale. It's a good day for putting the finishing touches on some social plans. Don't attempt too much in the way of hard work. Watch your intake of food and liquids. No casual jeans today; you can catch many an interesting roving eye if you dress up, with attention to style. Check with Libra.

Monday, December 23 (Moon in Cancer to Leo 6:39 a.m.) Sharing, cooperative effort, and joint endeavors will make the day ring. Unite with those around you. Make sure others agree before beginning anything. Know the plans of all members of your household before setting up Christmas schedules. Glamor and illusion give extra sparkle to the day. Your lucky number is 4.

Tuesday, December 24 (Moon in Leo) Excellent parent–child relationships are possible now. Your sense of being part of a team is giving you and the other person most concerned a real lift. Relax, talk, laugh; if it isn't done by now, let it go until next year. Your marital relationship, public relations, your own place in the big scheme of things are all favored. Hot combination numbers: 6 and 7.

Wednesday, December 25 (Moon in Leo in Virgo 7:24 a.m.) You are not alone. When others reach out to you for special love, understanding, consideration, you won't be lacking. Your personality assets are doubled under prevailing aspects. It is a fabulous radiant, golden Christmas, full of treasures, jewels, and flowers. Walk or drive about your own locality to see the lights this evening. Lucky lottery numbers: 17, 26, 8, 35, 44, 31.

Thursday, December 26 (Moon in Virgo) A generous approach to these events is recommended. The more you please others, the more money you are putting in the love bank. Virgo and Taurus come front and center. A project will be easier to fund than you may have realized—if you go about it in a pleasant, cheerful, optimistic, and enthusiastic way. Count on number 1.

Friday, December 27 (Moon in Virgo to Libra 10:38 a.m.) You could be chastened a little by what you are told. There can be some unusual revelations. Your desires may get out of hand now and then and surprise you. Grandoise ideas are in the air. Leo opens the door. You are rather dramatic and intense not only in love but in all social pastimes, partying, entertaining. Your lucky number is 3.

Saturday, December 28 (Moon in Libra)   You are more free to take a little trip than you were earlier. Be back before the evening of the 31st. Checking into a hotel or motel that is known for its holiday spirit would do a lot for you and your companion. Dining in an unusual restaurant also is part of this medicine. Scorpio and Cancer can help you see the joys of life. Lucky lottery numbers: 14, 23, 28, 41, 32, 5.

Sunday, December 29 (Moon in Libra to Scorpio 5:04 p.m.)   An excellent time to appreciate the season with church and club participation. The more formal the event, the more you are going to respond to it. Libra and Gemini play major roles. Dancing, singing, unusual ethnic foods, are all possibilities under these aspects. Special festivals, fêtes, and musicals connected with the holiday season will add just what you wanted.

Monday, December 30 (Moon in Scorpio)   You can tackle major projects and get the drop on the competition. You will make quicker and greater headway if you deal with those in authority. You can find the day more exciting than others do, which is part of the secret of your current success. Scorpio and Capricorn figure prominently. Your lucky number is 2.

Tuesday, December 31 (Moon in Scorpio)   Push distribution, circulation, and consider new sources of supply. A new kind of training may be required because more modern equipment soon will be introduced. Sagittarius takes a leading role. Conferences, interviews, alternatives, and substitutes are part of the action. Be especially wary of marital disagreements. Take a chance on number 4.

JANUARY 1992

Wednesday, January 1 (Moon in Scorpio to Sagittarius 2:30 a.m.)   Oh what a friendly day! Social, amiable, pleasing trends mark the day. Group activities, church and club membership and participation matters are favored. Money turnover is slow. Avoid dealings with large organizations and institutions for the time being. Listen to Capricorn. Lucky lottery numbers: 1, 10, 5, 14, 46, 28.

Thursday, January 2 (Moon in Sagittarius)   If you don't feel you are able to take over for your spouse or business partner, say so. This is not a good time to handle unfamiliar work or to stir up smoldering embers. You could feel that groups are trying to take advantage of you. Your most productive time is spent outdoors. Take a chance on number 3.

Friday, January 3 (Moon in Sagittarius to Capricorn 2:09 p.m.)   You could feel rushed and bothered today. Business and government are complaining and seemingly in turmoil. The upcoming eclipse patterns invite mistakes, errors, nagging, and complaints. Distances seem too far. There's rough going on that final series of steps. Hot combination numbers: 5 and 9.

Saturday, January 4 (Moon in Capricorn)   Eclipse patterns create annoyances. What is rooted in the past can demand your attention. It's not a good day for traveling, dealing with large organizations, or helping your mate with unfamiliar work. Sagittarius and Pisces come front and center. Prices are higher, or at least they seem to be. Lucky lottery numbers: 7, 16, 11, 25, 34, 43.

Sunday, January 5 (Moon in Capricorn)   Tackle household chores that have been hanging fire since the holidays. Finish, complete, summarize, file away, and keep good notes. Organize income-tax information. Take care of social relationships that you neglected during the busy holidays. Someone may feel you have forgotten him or her. Champagne is your color. Consult Capricorn. Your lucky number is 9.

Monday, January 6 (Moon in Capricorn to Aquarius 2:59 a.m.)   Stand tall, speak up, and take the initiative on a day when you can win big. Be yourself—be free, independent, and ready to back up your claims and announcements. A Leo and another Aquarius come front and center. Arrange a Twelfth Night funfest or involve others in the arranging. Old rose wins for you. Play number 2 to win.

Tuesday, January 7 (Moon in Aquarius) Take care of personal interests. Be open, warm, cheerful, and thoroughly honest. You can count on good friends, Gemini and Libra. Your independent ways are admired under prevailing aspects. People don't offer obstacles. Ebony, amber, and tan are winning colors. Hot combination numbers: 4 and 7.

Wednesday, January 8 (Moon in Aquarius to Pisces 3:52 p.m.) Push on into the future. Changes, adaptations, adjustments, and advancements are all favored under these trends. You can expand your thinking, your social life, and your concepts of your job. Make way for the future in all your thinking and doing. Virgo and Capricorn come front and center. Lucky lottery numbers: 15, 6, 12, 24, 33, 42.

Thursday, January 9 (Moon in Pisces) Optimism is related to the money you spend and the traveling you undertake. Pisces and a Cancer have the answers. You could be attracted to a strongly spiritual person. What happens behind the scenes intrigues you. Wear off-white and jet. Hot combination numbers: 1 and 9.

Friday, January 10 (Moon in Pisces) Matters rooted in the past are speeded up and it's a case of what goes around comes around again. A Scorpio and a Gemini will see the problem differently. You can increase your earning power if you take positive action. Scarlet and black will invite and attract for you. Your lucky number is 3.

Saturday, January 11 (Moon in Pisces to Aries 3:22 a.m.) Concentrate on what has to be achieved today. Zero in on advantages and opportunities without making a federal case of it. Know your strengths and weaknesses in relationship to a big project connected with your career and future. Off-white and a little gold will work wonders for you. Lucky lottery numbers: 14, 5, 11, 18, 23, 41.

Sunday, January 12 (Moon in Aries) Studies, hobbies, and enjoyable conversations with relatives or neighbors can make this a pleasant cycle. Stay in your neighborhood so you'll be at home when the others arrive. Serve a light lunch that will please and impress a critical person. Aries is in command. Mocha and marmalade are winners. Count on number 7.

Monday, January 13 (Moon in Aries to Taurus 12 noon) Come down to earth, and do what has to be done. Deal in the usual, practical, familiar, and local. Siblings, a Libra, and a Sagittarius can dominate. Pleasant information can arrive. Romantic illusions are very much represented. The desire to force change should be distrusted. Lavender and ivory are winning colors. Your lucky number is 2.

Tuesday, January 14 (Moon in Taurus) Rentals, mortages, and changes of address are part of the big scene. What you own is increasing in value. The desire to change your residence and possibly move across the country is one of your secrets under prevailing aspects. Taurus may not agree. Emerald and powder blue are winning colors. Pick six: 4, 7, 1, 4, 9, 3.

Wednesday, January 15 (Moon in Taurus to Gemini 4:55 p.m.) There are good aspects for making love in some unusual way, and for sensing the strange needs of a lover. There are also fine trends in understanding, compassion, sympathy as well as passion. But beware of pity—it is not love. Domestic interests may require more than you want to give them. Trust Scorpio. Lucky lottery numbers: 15, 6, 24, 33, 19, 42.

Thursday, January 16 (Moon in Gemini) Gemini can make your day. There's a lot of love in your soul today and your personality wins you much attention and popularity. Be romantic, considerate, and open new social doors. Join a club or group. Magenta, white, and olive are your lucky colors. Hot combination numbers: 8 and 1.

Friday, January 17 (Moon in Gemini to Cancer 6:26 p.m.) A love affair may suddenly demand more of your time. There's not as much forgiveness as there should be in the larger scene. Sagittarius has some questions to ask you. You can find solace and a sense of personal worth in a creative project. Earth and olive are your colors. Hot combination numbers: 1 and 5.

Saturday, January 18 (Moon in Cancer) Charitable and humanitarian involvements will do you proud.

Weather and tension can work against your health. Work may pile up due to absenteeism; and where you require review and evaluation, the person you report to may not be available. A Cancer and a Pisces are anxious. Wear navy blue. Lucky lottery numbers: 3, 12, 18, 25, 30, 39.

Sunday, January 19 (Moon in Cancer to Leo 5:57 p.m.) The full moon in Cancer illuminates work projects, health improvements, services others expect from you, and ways you can protect the health of your family and household. The community may be up in arms over some rumors of new buildings. Mace and eggshell are your colors. Your lucky number is 5.

Monday, January 20 (Moon in Leo) Leo and another Aquarius are represented. Listen to your intuition about marital, legal, and public relations changes. Optimism and positive thinking will save the day. Personal relationships may require even more of your time. Burgundy and lavender are winning colors. Hot combination numbers: 7 and 1.

Tuesday, January 21 (Moon in Leo to Virgo 5:22 p.m.) Counsel with your spouse and business partner. Inspire and guide your mate to take on more interesting responsibilities. Leo and Gemini come front and center. Gains can be chalked up in love, understanding, and compromises. Focus on improvements. Sky blue and white are a good combination. Hot combination numbers: 2 and 6.

Wednesday, January 22 (Moon in Virgo) Taurus and Virgo offer definite and genuine help in financial matters. More money may be a better approach toward your kitchen budget. Eat better for less is a popular motto today. Savings and security interests get good grades under these aspects. Wheat and jet will invite luck for you. Lucky lottery numbers: 40, 4, 13, 22, 26, 31.

Thursday, January 23 (Moon in Virgo to Libra 6:43 p.m.) Discuss drains in household and allied expenses that must be plugged. Money may be slipping away from a carefree, generous, good-hearted Aquarius. A Scorpio has helpful suggestions for transforming wishes into facts. Your aspirations are admired by others. Eggplant and old gold will invite and attract for you. Hot combination numbers: 6 and 3.

Friday, January 24 (Moon in Libra)   Libra and another Aquarius make definite contributions to your day. Don't ignore the essentials, but make allowances for the illusions. You may have a strong wish to change your scene. But there are obstacles and perhaps there's no one to really pinch hit for you. Olive and purple are winning colors. Your lucky number is 8.

Saturday, January 25 (Moon in Libra to Scorpio 11:32 p.m.)   Weather permitting, get outdoors. Shop, have lunch in an interesting restaurant, meet an old friend for a chat. The library, museum, and newer outlet malls are all good possibilities. Buy maps, travel guides, and pick up brochures at travel bureaus. Ruby and snow are your lucky colors. Lucky lottery numbers: 10, 1, 25, 32, 28, 37, 14.

Sunday, January 26 (Moon in Scorpio)   Plan your work week ahead. A professional approach will serve you best under these aspects. It's a fine day for quiet entertainment in your own home; invite your boss and cooperative coworkers. Pave the way for seeking an increase in salary and perhaps a change of assignment. Seek responsibilities and obligations. Your lucky number is 3.

Monday, January 27 (Moon in Scorpio)   Scorpio and Pisces impact your day. Push your career, and hold interviews and conferences. Take problems to the front office. Your status and prestige can be put on display. Don't hesitate to review the good work you have been doing for some time. Navy blue and beige are winning colors. Hot combination numbers: 5 and 8.

Tuesday, January 28 (Moon in Scorpio to Sagittarius 8:20 a.m.)   Continue to focus on your career. Discuss personal career interests with those in authority. Encourage your department to do better. Bring together feuding factions at your office. Shop for items that will help you do your job better. A Cancer and a Taurus are helpful. Pick six: 7, 2, 4, 1, 6, 5.

Wednesday, January 29 (Moon in Sagittarius)   Church and club involvements will move along well. Friendships can make your day. You'll feel at home wherever you happen to light under existing aspects. Good news is on its way, and information flows freely. A Sagittarius and a Cancer make their contribution. Know the score before contradicting. Lucky lottery numbers: 2, 11, 20, 33, 38, 47.

Thursday, January 30 (Moon in Sagittarius to Capricorn 8:07 p.m.)   It's a fine time for parties, collecting what is due you, helping in a charitable or humanitarian cause. Enjoy outdoor activities but dress appropriately. Consider the social side of your job and do something constructive about coworkers. A Gemini and an Aries figure prominently. Hot combination numbers: 4 and 7.

Friday, January 31 (Moon in Capricorn)   Complete tasks; put January away before midnight. It's a good time for phoning and letter writing, especially about business matters. Deal with large organization and institutions. Help your mate and others finish up odd jobs. Summaries, inventories, and organizational matters will go well. Hot combination numbers: 6 and 1.

FEBRUARY 1992

Saturday, February 1 (Moon in Capricorn)   If you haven't finished last month's chores, get to them right away. Government legislation and announcements can be upsetting. What you are told and what you hear will not make much sense under these aspects. Still, power is building up for you in highly personalized interests. Trust Virgo and Taurus. Lucky lottery numbers: 5, 14, 23, 41, 9, 18.

Sunday, February 2 (Moon in Capricorn to Aquarius 9:09 a.m.)   Business ideas and anxieties can encroach more than they should. It's a good day for staying at home and entertaining drop-in friends, coworkers, and neighbors. You could be called upon to cheer up others. A Leo and an Aries have key roles. It's not too early to plant seedlings indoors. Apricot and indigo are winning colors. Your lucky number is 7.

Monday, February 3 (Moon in Aquarius)   The new moon illuminates highly personalized interests. Your personality assets will work wonders for you. Spruce up your appearance with greater attention to your hair and wardrobe. Concentrate on what is easy to do. A little gold, turquoise, and jade green will invite and attract for you. Hot combination numbers: 9 and 3.

Tuesday, February 4 (Moon in Aquarius to Pisces 9:51 p.m.) Stick to work that makes sense to you. What comes to you naturally and easily under existing aspects will be right. Pisces and a Cancer figure prominently. There are some indications that you are preferred, chosen, and accepted in high places. Organize your time well. Azure and mocha are winning colors. Pick six: 3, 5, 7, 2, 4, 5.

Wednesday, February 5 (Moon in Pisces) You can earn more money today than you counted on. Expand your financial and commercial thinking. Seek favors and ask questions. Consult ultra-successful people. Pisces, Cancer, and Scorpio figure prominently. Move quickly. White and chocolate are your colors. Lucky lottery numbers: 5, 10, 15, 6, 33, 42.

Thursday, February 6 (Moon in Pisces) Hold financial and business conferences. Listen for a valuable idea that can surface now. Your earning power and income are favored. It's not a day to toe the line on the job. You'll make progress by shaking things up a bit. Consult Aries. Gold, bronze, and black are winners. Hot combination numbers: 8 and 3.

Friday, February 7 (Moon in Pisces to Aries 9:15 a.m.) Simplify situations, projects, and ideas for best results. Knock big ideas, suggestions, and plans down to manageable size. There's a good connection between new money and what is immediate and pressing. You can learn new financial tricks under prevailing aspects. Wear pink, silver, and white for success. Pick six: 1, 7, 5, 8, 1, 2.

Saturday, February 8 (Moon in Aries) Aries, Leo, and Sagittarius have key roles. It's a fine day for local, here-and-now, immediate, familiar, and usual interests. Brothers, sisters, and neighbors can be helpful. Studies, hobbies, avocational matters, cooking, and baking are all in focus. Almond and ivory are winners. Lucky lottery numbers: 12, 3, 8, 16, 30, 21.

Sunday, February 9 (Moon in Aries to Taurus 6:36 p.m.) Read the financial pages of your newspaper, and listen to a business forecast on television. Discussions about the economy, cost of living, and standard of living with neighbors can be productive. It's a day for people to show they know as much as the so-called experts. Amber and yellowish-browns are winners. Play number 5 to win.

Monday, February 10 (Moon in Taurus) Avoid giving the impression that you are overly competitive or possessive. Household chores can be handled with dispatch. It's a fine time for getting estimates on any work you want done on your residence. Taurus and Capricorn have key roles. Plan a Valentine's Day party. Wheat is your color. Hot combination numbers: 7 and 1.

Tuesday, February 11 (Moon in Taurus) Entertainments in your own home can turn this drab month around. Make decisions slowly and get input from those in the know. Avoid arguments with a rebellious teenager. An animal can be obnoxious. There is much gossip and rumormongering in the air. Community obligations are being neglected. Pick six: 9, 3, 6, 2, 8, 4.

Wednesday, February 12 (Moon in Taurus to Gemini 1:08 a.m.) Spend time with someone who inspires and thrills you. Ecstasy is a good possibility under existing romantic trends. Be loving, fastidious, passionate, outgoing, and be realistic about love. Stick with your own contemporaries for best results. Generation gaps are widening. Wear rust. Lucky lottery numbers: 2, 12, 17, 22, 4, 40.

Thursday, February 13 (Moon in Gemini) Parties, entertainments, and relaxation with loved ones are indicated. Creativity, imagination, and inventiveness are strong trends. Gemini and another Aquarius come front and center. Dress stylishly; they're watching you. Champagne and fuchsia are colors that invite and attract good luck. Pick six: 4, 8, 1, 2, 4, 5.

Friday, February 14 (Moon in Gemini to Cancer 4:31 a.m.) Give a few compliments as Valentine's Day gets underway. Later, work tends to pile up, and someone may be complaining about stomach upsets. An older person may be critical of you for some task left undone. There is a great deal of jealousy separating the various generations. A Scorpio knows what it's all about. Amber and sauterne are your colors. Your lucky number is 8.

Saturday, February 15 (Moon in Cancer)   New ways of doing old jobs, innovations, alternatives, and substitute methods are accented. Improvements and corrections can be handled well. A Pisces and a Cancer come front and center. There are fine rays for getting on top of a chore that generally is repugnant to you. Green and Wallis blue are your colors. Lucky lottery numbers: 10, 28, 46, 1, 15, 23.

Sunday, February 16 (Moon in Cancer to Leo 5:15 a.m.)   Joint efforts, compromises, combined operations, marriage, business partnerships, meeting all duties, responsibilities, and obligations are onstage—along with Leo and another Aquarius. Contracts and agreements can be honored, bettered. Spiritual ideas are present. Venetian gold is your lucky color.

Monday, February 17 (Moon in Leo)   Money matters are progressing. Dynamic coworkers can lead you into improved financial potential; there's assistance, support, and someone to run interference for you. A Cancer and a Scorpio are in the picture. A leadership role can be yours. Ruby and taupe are winning colors. Hot combination numbers: 7 and 4.

Tuesday, February 18 (Moon in Leo to Virgo 4:47 a.m.)   Today's full moon illuminates marriage, other partnerships, legal contracts, agreements, what others expect from you, and new ways that you can increase the cooperation you give willingly. Trust Leo to give you the map. Satisfaction comes easily in true love. Old rose and rust are your colors. Pick six: 9, 3, 6, 9, 1, 2.

Wednesday, February 19 (Moon in Virgo)   Pisces and Virgo are in the picture. Push for more remunerative investments and greater savings. Talks with a banker and broker may be helpful. This may be a good time to make switches and to push alternatives and substitutes. Keep your self-confidence up. Angry reds are your colors. Lucky lottery numbers: 2, 20, 19, 24, 11, 38.

Thursday, February 20 (Moon in Virgo to Libra 5:04 a.m.) Get away from boring situations and people who complain and nag. Change your scene for best creative results; Libra and Aries can spur you on. There's nothing like good companionship to turn a day like this into an event. Venetian gold and cherry are your colors. Hot combination numbers: 4 and 7.

Friday, February 21 (Moon in Libra) Some interesting challenges are coming to the fore. Special assignments will offer rare opportunities to show what you can do. Gemini, Libra, and another Aquarius are in the picture. What's taking place at a distance can affect your future. Your winning colors are bronze and charcoal. The lucky number is 6.

Saturday, February 22 (Moon in Libra to Scorpio 8:11 a.m.) An urge to do things differently can dominate your thinking. You may want to break away from limiting rules and regulations. The travel bug is biting and there is a tendency to think that everything is done better far away. Taurus and Virgo hew to the established and practical. Lucky lottery numbers: 17, 8, 26, 22, 31, 35.

Sunday, February 23 (Moon in Scorpio) Work behind the scenes rather than out in the open for best results. Take care of household chores that have to be done before spring. Career interests can be served in a quiet and unobtrusive way. Spend some time with a coworker who is well disposed toward your ultimate advancement. Plum is your lucky color. Play number 1 to win.

Monday, February 24 (Moon in Scorpio to Sagittarius 3:26 p.m.) Tackle the work that no one else wants to do; a little volunteer work can hold you in good stead later on in the year. Those in high places love peace and those who help promote it in the workplace. Scorpio has the answers. Rust and raspberry are winning colors. Your lucky number is 3.

Tuesday, February 25 (Moon in Sagittarius) Your hopes and aspirations are given a genuine boost under these aspects. Diplomacy and tact will win you laurel wreaths. Friends are helpful. Group activities boost your morale. Invite a Sagittarius and a Gemini. Your awareness is particularly strong this evening. Wear mocha and ivory. Hot combination numbers: 7 and 2.

Wednesday, February 26 (Moon in Sagittarius)   Aries and Leo come front and center. Parties and entertainments are strongly indicated. The desire to please many people and to prevent a group from breaking up is strong. Invite people for a light supper and lots of exciting conversation. This drab neutral month requires some jazzing up. Lucky lottery numbers: 9, 27, 26, 31, 36, 45.

Thursday, February 27 (Moon in Sagittarius to Capricorn 2:33 a.m.)   Protect your family and personal secrets in the face of much prying. You may not realize how attracted a coworker happens to be and how much this person would appreciate an invitation to your home. Deal with large organizations and institutions without fear or intimidation. Cash registers and computers make errors. Take a chance on number 2.

Friday, February 28 (Moon in Capricorn)   It's an excellent day to close the files on some project, sum up, make lists, shut one business door so that another one can be opened. Capricorn has much to say about what is going on. Your mate or business partner may want assistance but not want to ask. Your colors are powder blue and purple. Your lucky number is 4.

Saturday, February 29 (Moon in Capricorn to Aquarius 3:34 p.m.)   Odd chores can get in the way of something more important. A Capricorn and a Virgo collaborate successfully. Summarize, submit work, and finish up odd chores about the house. Make decisions and then convey them to those who will be impacted by them. Your winning colors are white, magenta, and crimson. Lucky lottery numbers: 15, 6, 37, 24, 33, 18.

MARCH 1992

Sunday, March 1 (Moon in Aquarius)   Seize and hold the initiative and the ascendancy while you are in your high lunar cycle. Take the wraps off your projects and make your announcements. Another Aquarius and a

Gemini are in the picture. Stand tall in any situation and let people know that you mean business. Cerise, lime, and lemon are winning colors. Your lucky number is 7.

Monday, March 2 (Moon in Aquarius)   It's a good day for facing up to the impossible and for tackling the more difficult jobs. Arise early and take control of situations. Libra figures prominently. A friendly attitude will open doors and clear away interference. You work well with groups. Eggshell, ivory, and silver are your winning colors. Hot combination numbers: 9 and 4.

Tuesday, March 3 (Moon in Aquarius to Pisces 4:11 a.m.)   Push your wealth production hard. Talks with a banker and broker will go well. Money is flowing freely; there are good aspects for special sales, advertising, and business conferences. The value of your property is rising. Trust Pisces. Beet, white, and scarlet are your best colors. Pick six: 4, 8, 4, 1, 2, 5.

Wednesday, March 4 (Moon in Pisces)   Today's new moon illuminates earning power, income, ways of increasing your financial take, and discovering new sources of capital. A Cancer and a Scorpio have key roles. It's a fine day for interviews, conferences, and discussing money potential. Make appointments. Fuchsia and magenta are winning colors. Lucky lottery numbers: 15, 24, 6, 10, 42, 33.

Thursday, March 5 (Moon in Pisces to Aries 3:07 p.m.)   Local, pressing and immediate matters, studies, and hobbies are all proceeding rapidly. Your personality was never more effective. Money flows freely and your earning power can be pursued successfully. Aries and Pisces come front and center. This is a good day for funding projects. Indigo and gold will win for you. Hot combination numbers: 8 and 9.

Friday, March 6 (Moon in Aries)   Communications, information, research, and short-distance travel get high grades. Taurus and Virgo figure prominently, as does another Aquarius. You are free, friendly, liberated, and emancipated under prevailing aspects. Distant places can beckon. Puce and taupe are your colors. Hot combination numbers: 1 and 4.

Saturday, March 7 (Moon in Aries)   Family, home, community, property, and ownership interests can be served by a happy-go-lucky attitude, much self-confidence, and enthusiasm for what you are doing. Capricorn and Sagittarius have key roles. Spend some time outdoors—walking, hiking, especially with children, will prove rewarding. Lucky lottery numbers: 3, 12, 30, 16, 21, 48.

Sunday, March 8 (Moon in Aries to Taurus 12:05 a.m.)   Be patient and calm if another tries to make a mountain out of a molehill. You may find people edgy and irritable. Keep an open mind and don't permit a propagandist for some strange cause to annoy you. Your home is more than your castle; it's your haven, port, and escape hatch. Ask Gemini. Your lucky number is 5.

Monday, March 9 (Moon in Taurus)   Relatives are very much in the picture today. You may have to cancel some public commitment in order to meet your family obligations. You cater services well under these aspects. Community needs or property obligations may make demands on your time. Consult a Cancer and a Scorpio. Azure and beet are your colors. Your lucky number is 9.

Tuesday, March 10 (Moon in Taurus to Gemini 7:03 p.m.)   Things are looking up. Prepare for a rewarding love evening; phone your beloved around 2:00 P.M. and arrange a date for tonight, wherever you can have the most privacy. There are fine trends for creative effort, adaptability, and being spontaneous and flexible. Silver and pink are winning colors. Pick six: 2, 6, 4, 2, 1, 9.

Wednesday, March 11 (Moon in Gemini)   Love, romance, socializing, and entertainment get good grades and green lights. Dress up, look your best, be outgoing, cheerful, enthusiastic, and pleasing. Generation gaps can be bridged well now. Settle any difference of opinion right away. Cerise and plaid are your colors. Lucky lottery numbers: 13, 4, 11, 17, 9, 27.

Thursday, March 12 (Moon in Gemini to Cancer 11:50 a.m.)   Gemini and Libra are in the picture. This is an excellent time for parties, entertaining spontaneously, and meeting the needs of parents and offspring. Your ability to mix business with pleasure will win you new

209

respect under these trends. Your winning colors are coral, lilac, and red. Your lucky number is 6.

Friday, March 13 (Moon in Cancer)   Work may be slipping away from you, especially if done amid pleasant or unpleasant distractions. You could have an advance case of spring fever and lose things in the bottleneck. Consult Virgo and Capricorn. Wear a little lavender or orchid. Hot combination numbers: 8 and 5.

Saturday, March 14 (Moon in Cancer to Leo 2:20 p.m.)   Someone may be out of step and interested in giving others a rough time. Do what you can to improve harmony at work. Neighbors may voice their complaints. Fences may need mending; trim shrubbery, clean up in outdoor areas, and prepare for some fertilization. Sand and tan are your colors. Lucky lottery numbers: 28, 46, 14, 23, 1, 10.

Sunday, March 15 (Moon in Leo)   The ides of March warn against making sarcastic remarks to your spouse, lover, or someone who wants you to be almost perfect. Leo and Gemini come center stage. Children can behave obnoxiously, and an older relative may be jealous of the time you spend with another. Lemon and lime are colors, mixed with a bit of brown or taupe. Your lucky number is 3.

Monday, March 16 (Moon in Leo to Virgo 3:13 p.m.)   Joint investments and adventures can make this a memorable day. You could enjoy a meeting with a much older person, who has been everywhere and done everything. A kindness you do for a difficult in-law now will be long remembered and appreciated. Wear tan and light browns. Count on number 5.

Tuesday, March 17 (Moon in Virgo)   You can confide in Virgo and put another Aquarius on the right track. Savings, investments, and budgets receive green lights. Someone who was short-tempered with you last week may want to make amends, without actually referring to the past. Of course, green is your color on St. Patrick's Day. Your lucky number is 9.

Wednesday, March 18 (Moon in Virgo to Libra 3:55 p.m.)   The full moon enlightens you in finances, savings, insurance, and tax-shelter matters. It's a good day for refurbishment and replenishment of body, mind, and soul. It's also an excellent time for improvements, making do, correcting, and spreading the ideals that are influencing you. Taurus wants to know. Lucky lottery numbers: 2, 20, 18, 24, 11, 47.

Thursday, March 19 (Moon in Libra) Libra and Aries may seem to be at cross-purposes. Today's fine cycle begins in travel, taking care of long-range and long-distant involvements, and opening your heart to a homeless person who needs a helping word and hand. Charitable and humanitarian ideas abound under prevailing aspects. Burgundy is your color. Hot combination numbers: 4 and 8.

Friday, March 20 (Moon in Libra to Scorpio 6:20 p.m.) As spring begins, your thoughts can wander. Old times, other places, and other faces come into focus. A desire to see winter recede is stronger than usual. Lean toward what is fair, just, balanced, and symmetrical under prevailing aspects. Pink and coral are your colors. Count on number 6.

Saturday, March 21 (Moon in Scorpio) Aries and Scorpio will prove helpful and cooperative. Spend some time with a supervisor or coworker with whom you will be working closely during the week ahead. Express yourself so that nothing is left unsettled. Your colors are watermelon and beige. Lucky lottery numbers: 8, 17, 26, 44, 21, 30.

Sunday, March 22 (Moon in Scorpio to Sagittarius 12:13 a.m.) Church and club membership and participation matters are accented. A friendly approach to charitable and humanitarian types will improve not only this day but the rest of the month. Taurus and Pisces have much to say. Write a few social notes, and phone an older loved one. Your colors are purple and taupe. Your lucky number is 1.

Monday, March 23 (Moon in Sagittarius) Your social life is given a real boost. Parties, reunions, entertainments, and the social side of your job are all well aspected. Spend some time outdoors, studying the advance of spring. Friends, former neighbors, and the friends of your relatives are all favorably represented. Sagittarius and Leo have the answers. Sunflower yellow is a winning color. Your lucky number is 3.

Tuesday, March 24 (Moon in Sagittarius) There are excellent trends for celebrations, annual banquets, and parent-child socializing. Group activities permit you to shine, and kindred spirits will boost your morale. Plan social programs and events. You can favorably influence the lives of friends under these aspects. Peppermint stripes are lucky. Hot combination numbers: 5 and 1.

Wednesday, March 25 (Moon in Sagittarius to Capricorn 10:08 a.m.) You self-confidence and enthusiasm will make this a wonderful day. Your long-term aspirations are getting the proper attention. Capricorn and Virgo are impacting situations. Write business letters this evening. Indigo and marigold are winning colors. Lucky lottery numbers: 31, 9, 45, 25, 36, 18.

Thursday, March 26 (Moon in Capricorn) Patience and perseverance are valued highly. Take your time before responding in anger. People may have their own way of doing the things at which you excel. What happens behind the scenes may be more influential in the long run than what is visible. Taurus knows the answer. Hot combination numbers: 2 and 7.

Friday, March 27 (Moon in Capricorn to Aquarius 10:44 p.m.) Investigate, research as you enter your high lunar cycle. Take charge. You can take your personal ambitions as far as you want. Be sure to look your best on a day when the eyes of the world can be on you. Dress to the nines, avoid the casual, I-don't-care look. Old gold is your color. Your lucky number is 4.

Saturday, March 28 (Moon in Aquarius) Another Aquarius and a Gemini are in control. Laughter and gossip ring loud and clear. Challenge, compete, contest, and remain self-confident enough to win big. You know how to avoid problems today. Yellow and white are your colors. Lucky lottery numbers: 15, 33, 42, 6, 28, 37.

Sunday, March 29 (Moon in Aquarius) Take strong stands where you are sure. Set the pattern, let others know you mean business; you're in control today. Another Aquarius, a Leo, and Gemini can make important contributions. Establish goals and discuss aims. Dress to the nines. Beige and mocha are winning colors. Count on number 8.

Monday, March 30 (Moon in Aquarius to Pisces 11:23 a.m.) If you look the part, people will go along with you. There's money to be made where you set the pace, invite, court, and attract good luck. A Libra and an Aries figure prominently. Sort, sift, pick, and choose. Make decisions and stick to them. Mauve and old rose are unbeatable colors. Hot combination numbers: 3 and 8.

Tuesday, March 31 (Moon in Pisces) Pisces and Scorpio will be willing hands; Gemini has the vocal advice. Establish the parameters of the discussion and make sure that others respect them. Money is flowing freely, and you can increase your earning power and improve routine assignments under prevailing aspects. Supervisors and coworkers want to know how you feel. Your lucky number is 5.

APRIL 1992

Wednesday, April 1 (Moon in Pisces to Aries 10:04 p.m.) A good money cycle begins. Discussions with your banker and broker will produce results. Show self-confidence and enthusiasm for difficult situations in order to get what you want. Domestic situations tend to produce some good luck. Scorpio and Virgo are ready to be helpful. Kelly green and coffee are winning colors. Lucky lottery numbers: 4, 13, 22, 8, 40, 31.

Thursday, April 2 (Moon in Aries) Settle down. Consolidate and stabilize. Studies and hobbies are favored. Siblings, neighbors, and immediate and pressing matters get the go-ahead. Aries and Sagittarius can be consulted successfully. Speak up, phone, and write necessary letters. Off-whites and raspberry are among your lucky colors. Hot combination numbers: 6 and 9.

Friday, April 3 (Moon in Aries) The new moon illuminates the significant matters that require immediate attention. Learning processes have green lights and good marks under prevailing aspects. Taurus and Capricorn figure significantly. Organizational matters can be pushed well. Keep in close touch with what's perking. Pick six: 9, 5, 2, 8, 1, 3.

Saturday, April 4 (Moon in Aries to Taurus 6:18 a.m.)   Push hard, and keep things moving. Attend to what you have on the front burners. Don't let anything important slide under these trends: anticipate, project, and program. Younger men can be lucky for you. Courtesy will pay off. The genders should stick to their normal roles. Wear angry reds. Lucky lottery numbers: 1, 10, 28, 37, 46, 14.

Sunday, April 5 (Moon in Taurus)   Spring cleaning plans can be formulated today. Browse about seed and feed stores, checking out the wide variety of plants that can be started outdoors at this time. Family and community gossip can add pleasure to a routine day. Consult Virgo. Blueberry and white are your colors. Your lucky number is 3.

Monday, April 6 (Moon in Taurus to Gemini 12:33 p.m.)   Taurus and Scorpio are collaborating. Domestic, property, and real estate interests can be handled well. The family at large has a corporate opinion that is worth considering. There are fine trends for buying and selling real estate, contemplating the purchase of acreage far from the city. Wear gold. Your lucky number is 5.

Tuesday, April 7 (Moon in Gemini)   The local situation becomes more to your liking. Your love life is strongly stimulated; romance, courtship, and opportunities to be with your adored one are all represented. Gemini has much to say. Offspring are more considerate and parent-child understanding grows. Amber and cerise are your colors. Count on number 7.

Wednesday, April 8 (Moon in Gemini to Cancer 5:18 p.m.)   Consult Libra and another Aquarius. Creativity, imagination, and flexibility make it easy for others to love you. Your fan club is growing. Moments can be precious under these aspects. You can impress members of the opposite sex with your innate understanding of people and their personality problems. Your winning colors are chocolate and white, beige, and lime. Lucky lottery numbers: 9, 18, 16, 45, 36, 27.

Thursday, April 9 (Moon in Cancer) A more direct approach in money and business matters is recommended. Setting up a new diet or preventive-medicine routine will go well. Work may pile up if you can't be enthusiastic about it and handle it competently. There can be many complaints coming from dissatisfied workers and neighbors. A Cancer and a Pisces play significant roles. Russet and old rose are winning colors. Hot combination numbers: 4 and 7.

Friday, April 10 (Moon in Cancer to Leo 8:46 p.m.) Scorpio comes front and center. It's a good day for reading literature about health, youth restoration cosmetics and activities, and nutritional matters. It's also a fine time for encouraging youngsters, listening to the ravings of coworkers, and attempting to be sympathetic. Salmon and tan are winning colors. Pick six: 1, 6, 4, 6, 8, 2.

Saturday, April 11 (Moon in Leo) Marriage, partnerships, contracts, agreements, and public relations matters get the nod. Leo and Libra have key roles. Consult, consider, ponder, listen carefully, and then make up your mind on anything meant to be lasting. Avoid ultimatums and showdowns. A calm aporoach will work wonders. Lucky lottery numbers: 17, 11, 21, 8, 35, 44.

Sunday, April 12 (Moon in Leo to Virgo 11:09 p.m.) Blessed are the peacemakers. Bring feuding factions together, and do what you can to restore harmony in your own or another marriage. It's a good day for building bridges from the social to the economic, and for cashing in on favors and kindnesses you did much earlier. Ask those questions of Pisces. Azure and rainbow are your colors.

Monday, April 13 (Moon in Virgo) New starts in new directions are indicated. There are fine aspects for gardening, landscaping, and clearing away debris on the lawn and in the yard. It's also good for doing odd jobs about garage, attic, basement, and patio. Vigor and vitality are high. A Virgo and a Taurus come center stage. Silver and strawberry are your colors. Count on number 5.

Tuesday, April 14 (Moon in Virgo)   Local, familiar, and routine matters are speeded up. Transform ideas into something solid. The changes you make now are going to mean big improvements and impressive corrections. Money turns over well. You could save a little time and money by taking a new approach to work. Capricorn has the message. Hot combination numbers: 7 and 3.

Wednesday, April 15 (Moon in Virgo to Libra 1:11 a.m.)   Strike a good balance between work and play. The desire to get away from the madding throng can catch up with you this P.M. What you have perking favorably at a distance can produce good results. People at or from a distance have much to teach you. Your ideas about love, sex, and marriage can be changing. Lucky lottery numbers: 18, 9, 15, 22, 36, 45.

Thursday, April 16 (Moon in Libra)   You are more ambitious and visible so that others notice. Still, you may dislike the recommendations that come your way. Travel, long-range interests, taking on more work, new avocational efforts, hobbies, and studies are all possibilities. Libra has the ideas. Amber and olive are winners. Your lucky number is 2.

Friday, April 17 (Moon in Libra to Scorpio 4:10 a.m.)   Today's full moon illuminates long-range and long-distance matters. The yen to travel can be strong. There is a blending of past experiences and present aspirations. What is rooted in the past can be used and in a sense milked dry. Your life makes more sense to you than usual. Libra is front and center. Your lucky number is 9.

Saturday, April 18 (Moon in Scorpio)   A hobby or avocational interest is not a career at this time and should not be permitted to interfere with career advancement. Keep your nose to the grindstone for best results, and avoid giving anyone the impression that you are disinterested in what is taking place. Plaid is your color. Lucky lottery numbers: 2, 11, 18, 28, 33, 6.

Sunday, April 19 (Moon in Scorpio to Sagittarius 9:40 a.m.)   Be constructive in your criticism or say nothing. You may have the feeling that a younger person is testing you, trying to see just how much aggravation you will accept. Plans may be upset temporarily. Scorpio and Pisces have key roles. Wear lavender, indigo, or emerald for luck. Count on number 4.

Monday, April 20 (Moon in Sagittarius)   Taurus and Sagittarius figure prominently. Expand socially and spend time with kindred spirits. It's an excellent time to organize a party or entertainment for later on in the month. Friends, companions, and coworkers tend to enjoy your suggestions. The desire to please is first rate. Mauve is your color. Play number 6 to win.

Tuesday, April 21 (Moon in Sagittarius to Capricorn 6:41 p.m.)   Taurus and Sagittarius have key roles on a day that is perfect for happiness, socializing, friendship, parties, entertainments, and closeness to kindred spirits. See coworkers after working hours, and expand socially. People you haven't heard from in some time can suddenly descend on you. Mocha and kelly green are winning colors. Hot combination numbers: 5 and 8.

Wednesday, April 22 (Moon in Capricorn)   Capricorn stands tall and knows what it's all about. What happens behind the scenes can prove beneficial to you. Deal with large organizations and help your mate with tasks you don't usually share. In-laws are strongly represented. Old rose and salmon are winning colors. Lucky lottery numbers: 16, 7, 22, 29, 34, 14.

Thursday, April 23 (Moon in Capricorn)   Protect family secrets and beware of prying eyes and ears. What was withheld in the way of information at work can suddenly be made available to you. Information flows much more freely. Taurus and Virgo have their own ideas about what is right and wrong. Antique white and marmalade are your colors. Play number 9 to win.

Friday, April 24 (Moon in Capricorn to Aquarius 6:38 a.m.)   In your high lunar cycle, you take charge, command attention and respect. Hold the initiative throughout this weekend. Explain, prove, assure, teach, and instruct. Others will follow if they know where you are leading them. You can win big in the matters that really count today. Silver and white are your colors. Your lucky number is 2.

Saturday, April 25 (Moon in Aquarius) Keep on the go; what you want you can get. Self-confidence, a warm, winning personality, and enthusiasm for what you are doing will make this day yours. Opportunities and advantages burst forth, and it's up to you to seize them. Another Aquarius and a Libra impact your day. Lucky lottery numbers: 25, 35, 4, 40, 13, 49.

Sunday, April 26 (Moon in Aquarius to Pisces 7:20 p.m.) Rise to the occasion and to the challenges. This is no time to hide your brilliant light, talents, or skill under that proverbial bushel. Speak up, stand tall, and let the world know that you are present and want your due. Read, study, and listen—valuable information is coming your way. Mauve and beige are your colors. Your lucky number is 6.

Monday, April 27 (Moon in Pisces) Your earning power increases and you can uncover a new source of income. Your enjoyment of wealth production is more than half the battle to greater security. Pisces and Virgo are helpful. Social skills and talents are carrying large dollar signs. The more popular you are, the more difficult types will accept you. Nectarine is your color. Your lucky number is 8.

Tuesday, April 28 (Moon in Pisces) While money is flowing in, it might be a good idea to save a little more. Plug drains on your household, transportation, and entertainment budgets. Are there items in your basement, attic, or garage that might be sold? A Scorpio and a Cancer have key roles. Cherry is your color. Pick six: 4, 3, 8, 1, 2, 5.

Wednesday, April 29 (Moon in Pisces to Aries 6:13 a.m.) Be precise, hit the mark, and go where you have to go to make your point. Pioneer, explore, and give relatives the benefit of every doubt. Real estate, ownership, and property matters are favored. An Aries and a Leo have important roles. Peach, emerald, whites, and blacks are lucky colors. Lucky lottery numbers: 5, 14, 29, 36, 23, 41.

Thursday, April 30 (Moon in Aries) Cleanup programs around your home and grounds will go well. Gardening, landscaping, and taking care of overgrowth are well aspected. It's a fine day for talks with nursery and hardware personnel. Mend fences and dig out weeds and stubborn roots between cracks in driveway concrete. Making things look well brings happiness. Your lucky number is 7.

MAY 1992

Friday, May 1 (Moon in Aries to Taurus 2:09 p.m.) Be kind and considerate of employees, and avoid giving anyone the feeling that you are unduly possessive or nosy. Open up some new doors in business and money matters. Your family is cooperative, and there are good aspects for minor entertainments and special dinners in your own home. Trust Leo and Sagittarius. Wear olive and ivory. Hot combination numbers: 7 and 2.

Saturday, May 2 (Moon in Taurus) Today's new moon illuminates household projects and ownership and property interests. Taurus, Virgo, and Capricorn have significant roles. Joint projects with a relative will turn out well. Reading, letter writing, and asking questions are well aspected. Earth and puce are winning colors. Lucky lottery numbers: 18, 27, 13, 9, 36, 45.

Sunday, May 3 (Moon in Taurus to Gemini 7:28 p.m.) Push domestic interests. Stand by relatives who want moral support. Cleanup programs around the grounds of your home can really achieve. Plant, trim, water, and set seedlings outdoors. Community matters are favored. Discuss domestic interests with practical Virgo or Capricorn. Wear shades of pastel—orange, tangerine, lemon, and lime. Your lucky number is 2.

Monday, May 4 (Moon in Gemini) Give proper attention to your love life. Spend time with your beloved, who sends your moral soaring. Avoid the critics, the bores, and others who merely sap your energies. Be youthful, creative, imaginative, and flexible. Gemini and another Aquarius play significant roles. Sky blue, baby pink, and coral are your colors. Play number 6 to win.

Tuesday, May 5 (Moon in Gemini to Cancer 11:09 p.m.) Love conquers all problems, worries, and uncertainties under prevailing aspects. You will be rewarded for the flexibility you demonstrate. Your lover has excellent advice after lovemaking but not before. Romantic interludes and overtures won't be denied. Orange, gold, and tangerine are your colors. Pick six: 5, 4, 2, 8, 1, 9.

Wednesday, May 6 (Moon in Cancer)   Watch what you eat and drink—people are less conscious of cleanliness, hygiene, and sanitation than they were in the past. Be on guard while climbing and descending. The health of an older loved one can cause some concern. Know the routines of your children, which may be questionable. Lucky lottery numbers: 10, 1, 14, 28, 37, 46.

Thursday, May 7 (Moon in Cancer)   Consult a Scorpio or a Cancer. Work tends to bow to pleasant distractions. On-the-job discussions can get out of hand. The battle of the sexes is represented. Isolation, peace and quiet, and privacy can all be therapeutic. Amber, puce, and mauve are winning colors. Hot combination numbers: 3 and 8.

Friday, May 8 (Moon in Cancer to Leo 2:07 a.m.) Leo and another Aquarius are in the picture. New contracts and agreements can be formulated. There can be expansion in business and financial agreements. Public relations, advertising, and property transactions are favored. The rules, regulations, standards, and ethics of the situation must be honored. Your lucky number is 5.

Saturday, May 9 (Moon in Leo)   Marriage and business partnerships can be improved, and relationships are given a real shot in the arm. There are fine trends for reaching business as well as social and emotional agreement. Plans, programs, and projects shared with your beloved will succeed beyond your highest hopes. Trust Gemini and Leo. Antique white, yolk, and silver are winning colors. Lucky lottery numbers: 7, 25, 16, 20, 43, 15.

Sunday, May 10 (Moon in Leo to Virgo 4:56 a.m.) Financial and economic readings and conversations can be productive. Ponder the changes you would like to make as spring moves toward summer. Budgets can be improved under these aspects. Angry reds, toned down by a bit of ivory, will boost your ego and the impressions you make on others. Your lucky number is 9.

Monday, May 11 (Moon in Virgo) Push savings, insurance, tax, collections, payments, and investments. It's a fine day for financial interviews and conferences. Virgo and Taurus come front and center. Begin to make improvements and corrections at the office. Furniture-fixing or replacement get good grades. Wheat and old rose are winners. Take a chance on number 2.

Tuesday, May 12 (Moon in Virgo to Libra 8:05 a.m.) Take a methodical, consistent, and practical approach toward money—saving it, spending it, and re-placing anything you "borrow" from yourself. Capricorn has some good ideas for you. Animals, gardening, and minor landscaping are in the big picture. A relationship can be saved. Tawny beige and mauve are your colors. Hot combination numbers: 4 and 5.

Wednesday, May 13 (Moon in Libra) Libra is a pleasant companion on a short-distance trip, even on a long-distance one. You may want to extend yourself on the job to catch up or breeze ahead of the competition. The desire to please authorities is strong. Stick to the facts. Celery and eggplant are winning colors. Lucky lottery numbers: 8, 17, 13, 21, 44, 35.

Thursday, May 14 (Moon in Libra to Scorpio 12:15 p.m.) There are wonderful aspects for getting away from the grind, changing your scene, and anticipating. Gemini has a story to tell you. Another Aquarius would rather you wouldn't. It's a fine day to follow illusions, fancies, and enjoy yourself. Put yourself where the action is. Wear white and pink. Your lucky number is 1.

Friday, May 15 (Moon in Scorpio) Career demands can be on the increase. You may feel that coworkers are somewhat jealous. Authority is disputed under existing aspects. Protect your status and the prestige you've won the hard way. Scorpio and a Cancer have key roles. Pistachio and pineapple are lucky colors. Hot combination numbers: 3 and 8.

Saturday, May 16 (Moon in Scorpio to Sagittarius 6:22 p.m.) The full moon illuminates your career or professional life. You'll discover ways of increasing your prestige and reputation, or winning greater responsibility on the job. You can transform some ideas about buying and saving into a real trend. Pisces will tell you. Lucky lottery numbers: 14, 5, 16, 27, 32, 41.

Sunday, May 17 (Moon in Sagittarius) Sagittarius and Aries hold center stage. There are indications that new friendships can be cemented. It's a wonderful day to move about socially, see lots of people, party, entertain, and enjoy the social side of your job and career. Church and club participation fare well. Azure and orchid are your colors. Your lucky number is 7.

Monday, May 18 (Moon in Sagittarius) Listen to what Leo and Gemini have to say. Socialize, be friendly, chat, visit shut-ins, and spread goodwill. There are fine aspects for evaluating a group or club that someone has suggested you join. Test, investigate, and ask questions. Various shades of green will invite and attract. Hot combination numbers: 9 and 5.

Tuesday, May 19 (Moon in Sagittarius to Capricorn 3:13 a.m.) Help your mate with work you don't ordinarily do. What's going on behind the scenes can affect your life. Deal with very large organizations and institutions. Complete, finish up, amend, file away, summarize, and submit reports. You may be able to extract something extra from a finished project. Capricorn is center stage. Your lucky colors are coral and emerald. Pick six: 2, 8, 4, 9, 1, 2.

Wednesday, May 20 (Moon in Capricorn) Clear the deck for future actions. Prepare, plan, and program. Follow through on work that has been hanging fire too long. Stay in close touch with a former neighbor who has been having a rough time. Taurus is helpful; and Virgo can lead. Tan and rust are winning colors. Lucky lottery numbers: 4, 13, 22, 40, 20, 28.

Thursday, May 21 (Moon in Capricorn to Aquarius 2:43 p.m.) Gemini and Capricorn can compromise under these aspects, which might surprise you. Plans and projects come out from under their wraps, and there can be some surprises in the news. It's a fine day for winding up one task so that you will be free to tackle new ones. Yolk, canary, and celery are winning colors. Your lucky number is 8.

Friday, May 22 (Moon in Aquarius)   Now with your lunar cycle high, you can be a winner, especially if you have been keeping your nose to the grindstone. Rewards and awards are in the picture. Leo and Libra impact your day. Your personality assets run interference for you and no one is better at minimizing your liabilities. Crimson and earth are your colors. Hot combination numbers: 1 and 6.

Saturday, May 23 (Moon in Aquarius)   Another Aquarius and a Cancer can make a major contribution to events and situations. Express yourself simply and calmly for best results. Dress up and aim for that rich, royal look. Your social skills are going to open new doors for you. Magenta and beige are winning colors. Lucky lottery numbers: 12, 3, 23, 34, 48, 30.

Sunday, May 24 (Moon in Aquarius to Pisces 3:25 a.m.)   Know how much you have to spend and abide by your own knowledge. Ways of protecting and possibly increasing your earning power can occur to you while reading or viewing television. Virgo is assertive of your rights. Prepare for a busy work week. Bronze and coral are winning colors. Count on number 5.

Monday, May 25 (Moon in Pisces)   You can achieve a higher production rate. Be steady, stable, and dependable, for these traits offer money-making potential. Your personality and the relationship between personal habits and appearance and career success stands out. Review reports and bring them up to date, but withhold criticism for the time being. Ivory and venetian gold are lucky colors. Your lucky number is 9.

Tuesday, May 26 (Moon in Pisces to Aries 2:53 p.m.)   Gemini makes a hit with your circle, and Virgo has more practical advice on money matters. The impact of your locality, the here and now, on your earning power is acute. Rumors abound, and they tend to be concerned with employment, the national economy, and shortages. Fuchsia and taupe are lucky colors. Hot combination numbers: 2 and 8.

Wednesday, May 27 (Moon in Aries) Love matters, romantic overtures, and interludes burst forth. Socializing is a must, but you don't have to go far to find pleasure. The accent is on the familiar, dependable, the tried and tested. Siblings and neighbors are in the picture, together with Pisces and Aries. Lucky lottery numbers: 40, 4, 13, 27, 35, 22.

Thursday, May 28 (Moon in Aries to Taurus 11:16 p.m.) Zero in on split-second opportunities, and concentrate on what has to be done now. Studies, hobbies, avocational interests, and the learning processes are in focus. Leo and Sagittarius have key roles. Communications and short-distance travel signify. Cocoa and platinum are your colors. Pick six: 6, 2, 1, 6, 8, 4.

Friday, May 29 (Moon in Taurus) Pay attention to family matters. Sprucing up the appearance of your home and its grounds will be time well spent under prevailing trends. Taurus and Virgo make their contributions. A practical and methodical approach toward work will bring results. Community responsibilities won't go away. Your lucky number is 8.

Saturday, May 30 (Moon in Taurus) There are splendid rays for getting a lot of work out of the way before this afternoon; then, the social beckons. Friendships, companionship, and social expansion get good grades. Your beloved has the right plans, so go along with them. Offspring can be directed properly, and advised well. This evening favors dressing formally, dancing, and joy. Lucky lottery numbers: 41, 5, 30, 14, 32, 17.

Sunday, May 31 (Moon in Taurus to Gemini 4:19 a.m.) Your love life is strongly stimulated. Be everything you can be to the person you love most, but don't let outside influences make inroads in romance, marriage, or erotic love. Your offspring may be testing you. Stand tall and hold firm to your own principles. Play it safe with number 3.

Monday, June 1 (Moon in Gemini)   Take advantage of the illumination and enlightenment available to
you in love matters. Be spontaneous in relationships with
younger people and in social commitments. You may feel
that things are moving slowly, especially where your responsibilities and obligations are concerned. Wear rainbow colors. Trust number 4.

*Tuesday, June 2 (Moon in Gemini to Cancer 6:58
a.m.)*   Trust a Pisces and a Cancer all the way. Work
gives you opportunities for creativity. Be flexible in family relationships and spiritual matters. Good luck can be
realized in savings and investments and where you are
dealing in financial changes. Wear taupe, eggshell, and
chocolate. Hot combination numbers: 6 and 8.

Wednesday, June 3 (Moon in Cancer)   Abide by
the usual preventive-medicine routines. Tackle the more
difficult jobs first, especially those that irk or bore you.
Then, enjoy putting frosting on the cake. Scorpio has the
answers now. It's a fine cycle for tackling the interests
that are important to your partners. Mauve and beige are
winning colors. Lucky lottery numbers: 17, 8, 12, 26, 35,
44.

*Thursday, June 4 (Moon in Cancer to Leo 8:35
a.m.)*   You can get a lot of work out of the way if you
start it early in the day. Reading health, dietary, and
nutritional brochures can be useful. The desire to keep
active, youthful, and attractive is strong throughout the
day. Pisces and Aries come front and center. Count on
number 1.

Friday, June 5 (Moon in Leo)   An improved investment program is represented. Be patient and persistent,
but don't try to force events. Cooperative ventures where
you combine your skills with another's talents will succeed. Taurus and Gemini come front and center. Silver
and salmon are your colors. Your lucky number is 3.

Saturday, June 6 (Moon in Leo to Virgo 10:28 a.m.)
Your popularity can be increased, and an outgoing and
jovial attitude will draw much praise. You are viewed as

sexy by a newcomer and chances are you will find this person difficult to understand. An Aries is in the picture and can be quite critical of the company you keep. Mace and beige are your colors. Lucky lottery numbers: 14, 5, 41, 6, 18, 23.

Sunday, June 7 (Moon in Virgo)   You provide the saving graces in difficult and discordant exchanges. There are larger profits than you counted on in some investments. You can improve food budgets, but may have to persuade others in your household to cooperate on keeping costs down. Pisces wants to know. Your lucky number is 7.

Monday, June 8 (Moon in Virgo to Libra 1:33 a.m.) Your own horizons can be expanded by the positive attitudes and approaches you choose. Don't be overly impressed by a proud but uncompassionate type. Well-meaning people can sap your energies if you don't take steps to keep them at arm's length. Another Aquarius is helpful. Play number 9 to win.

Tuesday, June 9 (Moon in Libra)   It's a fine day for traveling, and for keeping in close touch with what you have perking positively at a distance. There is an expanded point of view at work now, and it is inviting progress and profits. Libra has the answers. People at or from a distance are lucky for you. Burgundy and eggplant are winning colors. Hot combination numbers: 4 and 9.

Wednesday, June 10 (Moon in Libra to Scorpio 6:27 p.m.)   This is not a day for limitations or obstacles. Surmount these. Stick to your point of view and lifelong convictions. Discuss matters only with those at the top who understand the big picture. An Aries and a Leo figure prominently. Don't let a third party ruin a relationship that is for two. Lucky lottery numbers: 15, 10, 19, 24, 33, 42.

Thursday, June 11 (Moon in Scorpio)   Don't insist on rights and privileges that may be questionable. Be willing to hug the sidelines if you sense explosive emotional outbursts. Career progress can be assured if you listen more than you speak. A Scorpio and a Cancer come front and center. Plaid and orange are winning colors. Hot combination numbers: 8 and 3.

Friday, June 12 (Moon in Scorpio) The more you smile, the happier and more popular you will be under existing trends. A Pisces wants to tell you something. Improve relationships with executives and others in authority. Buy what your job requires. Various shades of pink and coral are your colors. Your best number is 1.

Saturday, June 13 (Moon in Scorpio to Sagittarius 1:29 a.m.) Social expenses are rising. Know what you are getting into before buying something recommended by a friend, or contributing to some cause you know nothing about. The price can be much higher than you anticipated. You could question the motivation of a friend. Parties may be a little overwhelming. Wine and burgundy are lucky colors. Lucky lottery numbers: 25, 30, 3, 48, 39, 12.

Sunday, June 14 (Moon in Sagittarius) Show your flag. Patriotic programs will do well, but the cost of tickets, license fees, incidentals can be higher than you expected. Be diplomatic and tactful for best results. Avoid arguments, bickering, and gambling under these aspects. Aries and Leo make good companions. Ivory and jet are lucky colors. Your lucky number is 5.

Monday, June 15 (Moon in Sagittarius to Capricorn 10:50 a.m.) Don't foist changes upon yourself or on friends. Church and club membership and participation matters can be pressured. Attempts to link the social to the economic are not favored. Travel carries a minor accident-producing potential. Social expansion can boomerang. Off-white and platinum are inviting colors. Hot combination numbers: 7 and 1.

Tuesday, June 16 (Moon in Capricorn) Some freakish accident-producing potential is a result of the lunar eclipse patterns of yesterday. A friend may do the reverse of what you expected. Eccentricities are indicated where people socialize. There can be a distraction and interruption if you are on the last stage of a job. Taurus is helpful. Play number 9 today.

Wednesday, June 17 (Moon in Capricorn to Aquarius 10:19 p.m.) Mysteries can be solved and puzzles can

227

be worked out. Exotic and fabulous people and events come front and center. Romantic secrets have their moments. You may feel that records are being broken in what you do under prevailing aspects. Virgo and Libra are represented. Raspberry and plum are colors that attract for you. Lucky lottery numbers: 7, 25, 17, 4, 31, 40.

Thursday, June 18 (Moon in Aquarius)   With your lunar cycle high, you make good decisions. Your personal ideas, hopes, aspirations, and ambitions are all illuminated by the moon close to your natal sun. Things work out in your favor. Your enthusiasm and optimism pay off. Another Aquarius and a Capricorn can do business. Mauve and beige are your colors. Hot combination numbers: 6 and 3.

Friday, June 19 (Moon in Aquarius)   Stand tall, and let the world know you are present. Your popularity and personal magnetism were never greater. Spruce up your personal appearance now. Trust Gemini and Libra to have your best interests at heart. Quick thinking can make your day memorable. Wear dynamic colors—lemon, lime, and coral. Hot combination numbers: 8 and 1.

Saturday, June 20 (Moon in Aquarius to Pisces 11:00 a.m.)   Shop for wardrobe items and accessories that will boost your morale and attract favorable attention. You feel in the pink, emancipated from useless worries, breaking free of inhibitions and hidebound traditions. As the day meanders along, some good money ideas occur. Cerise and ecru are lucky colors. Lucky lottery numbers: 10, 28, 20, 32, 1, 46.

Sunday, June 21 (Moon in Pisces)   Budget some home improvements into your available cash reserves. Peace of mind can't be bought, but you can create the proper atmosphere by adding light and color to your surroundings. The advantages of being loved emerge strongly as the day advances. Pisces and a Cancer will give zest to the gathering. Gold and gray are winners. Your lucky number is 3.

Monday, June 22 (Moon in Pisces to Aries 11:03 a.m.)   Your financial and economic situation is improving. Count your personal blessings when you hear malingerers complaining. Interference, ignorance, and prejudice cannot upset the ideals under which you are advancing causes. Virgo and Gemini add spice to the day. Your winning colors are pine needle and dove gray. Count on number 5.

Tuesday, June 23 (Moon in Aries) Narrow your sights, concentrate, and stick to what is possible. You can relate well to your coworkers, brothers, sisters, and neighbors. Schedule short-distance travel only as eclipse patterns begin to form. Take care of those chores others are complaining and nagging you about. Aries may have had enough. Hot combination numbers: 7 and 1.

Wednesday, June 24 (Moon in Aries) Be content with what you have and where you happen to be. Divine discontent enters most pictures under prevailing aspects, but this is not the time for foisting changes upon yourself or on others. Studies are boring, hobbies fall apart at the seams, and youngsters want to stop what they're doing. Lucky lottery numbers: 9, 18, 24, 33, 38, 11.

Thursday, June 25 (Moon in Aries to Taurus 8:28 a.m.) You could encounter some aggressive behavior and it would be advisable to ignore it. An abrasive person may not realize just how unacceptable such an attitude can be under prevailing trends. Aries comes front and center. Begin hugging the financial sidelines as eclipse patterns form. Play it safe with number 4.

Friday, June 26 (Moon in Taurus) The community, corporation, or group gets the emphasis. Real estate transactions do well. Domestic situations may need careful diplomatic handling. Older women can help with any difficult situation. Taurus will offer good advice. Your colors are emerald and jade green. Hot combination numbers: 6 and 1.

Saturday, June 27 (Moon in Taurus to Gemini 2:14 p.m.) Leo and Virgo take a bow. Keep jobs that have to be finished before the end of the month on the front burner. But postpone signing an actual financial or business contract until next month. Beach and water sports require greater caution from now until next week. Rainbow is your color. Lucky lottery numbers: 17, 8, 26, 39, 44, 2.

Sunday, June 28 (Moon in Gemini)   Creative projects in your home and backyard are favored, but beware of no careless digging near water or gas pipes. Gossip is enjoyable with the right Gemini. Love is cheerful, fun, and joyful. Children are carefree, but oldsters can complain. Salmon and silver will catch the right eye. Your lucky number is 1.

Monday, June 29 (Moon in Gemini to Cancer 4:42 p.m.)   Social interests, affairs of children, looking attractive, and making a good impression are all part of this scene. Take care of your health—abide by your usual preventive-medicine routines. It's not a good day for travel or unscheduled events. Stay away from the water. Emerald and ruby go well with antique white. Stick with number 5.

Tuesday, June 30 (Moon in Cancer)   Today's total solar eclipse warns against water and beach activities, unscheduled travel, and any showdowns or ultimatums at work. Steer clear of cliques on the job. Avoid dealing in criticism of supervision or employer, because what is said now will be retold and repeated. Guard against freakish accidents and plumbing disasters. Pick six: 7, 1, 7, 5, 3, 4.

JULY 1992

Wednesday, July 1 (Moon in Cancer to Leo 5:15 p.m.)   Do whatever you can to reduce tension in your life. Speak to the overly tense, zealous, touchy persons who share daily routines with you, especially a Capricorn or a Cancer. Your physical attractiveness is enhanced by wearing pastels—lime, lemon, and tangerine. Lucky lottery numbers: 7, 16, 25, 11, 34, 3.

Thursday, July 2 (Moon in Leo)   Leo and another Aquarius understand what can be done with the day's trends in marriage, other partnerships, emotional response, contracts, and agreements. Your legal and public relations interests are advanced. Be willing to consider the other side of the question. Lavender and marmalade are your colors. Pick six: 9, 4, 2, 1, 8, 5.

Friday, July 3 (Moon in Leo to Virgo 5:37 p.m.) You can improve the way you relate to a partner. Talks with a lawyer, judge, or law enforcement agencies will produce desired results. Gemini and Libra come front and center. There's plenty of action represented during the afternoon. Excitement increases this evening. Tan and wine are winning colors. The lucky number is 2.

Saturday, July 4 (Moon in Virgo) Virgo takes charge, and things are going to be done efficiently, practically, and methodically. Also, the costs of this year's celebrations can be cut a little without affecting the outcome. There can be a peculiar physical attraction to someone of questionable character. Don't forget to wear red, white, and blue. Lucky lottery numbers: 22, 40, 4, 17, 31, 13.

Sunday, July 5 (Moon in Virgo to Libra 7:27 p.m.) Pay attention to your household expenses, especially kitchen and transportation budgets for your family. You can be somewhat emotional about a member of the opposite sex. Strange overtures and interludes are associated with these aspects. Taurus is in the picture. Sand and rainbow are winning colors. Your lucky number is 6.

Monday, July 6 (Moon in Libra) Libra enjoys a good flirtation. Travel or just the desire to be far away tempts you. It would be a good time to take off on a summer vacation. Business-pleasure combinations show up. Take a long-range view of the interests you want to pursue. Azure, sky blue, and powder blue are your colors. Hot combination numbers: 8 and 4.

Tuesday, July 7 (Moon in Libra to Scorpio 11:53 p.m.) New goals can be reached provided you ignore those who limit, diminish, and detract from your self-confidence. Your sense of responsibility to yourself and to your treasured goals is first rate. Another Aquarius will understand. Rainbow and peppermint stripe are your colors. Hot combination numbers: 1 and 7.

Wednesday, July 8 (Moon in Scorpio) Taurus and Scorpio come front and center. Career demands may be

231

stepped up. Even if you are away on vacation, the ties that bind you to work and upsetting employment problems can be tugging. Work submitted at this time may be overlooked. Plaid and pistachio are winning colors. Lucky lottery numbers: 12, 3, 30, 8, 18, 48.

Thursday, July 9 (Moon in Scorpio) A professional, authoritative approach is best. Your sense of status and prestige may be somewhat offended when a stranger insists on using your first name. The situation is all the more aggravating when the culprit is younger and engaged in service work. When you offer help, make sure you are not going to be used. Capricorn may complain. Hot combination numbers: 7 and 3.

Friday, July 10 (Moon in Scorpio to Sagittarius 7:17 a.m.) It's a fine day to visit the home office of your employer. It's also good for talking with people who do your kind of work. Pisces and Scorpio have opinions that may not agree with yours. Good grooming and a fashionable appearance will impress the people you want to startle or excite. Plum and ivory are your colors. Hot combination numbers: 9 and 5.

Saturday, July 11 (Moon in Sagittarius) Gemini and Sagittarius are center stage. Parties, entertainments, and stopovers at beautiful resorts are indicated. A holiday atmosphere can engulf you. Beach and water activities beckon. Talks with older people expose you to rare wisdom. Your personal philosophy can be tried out on a receptive listener. Emerald is your color. Lucky lottery numbers: 11, 2, 24, 29, 38, 19.

Sunday, July 12 (Moon in Sagittarius to Capricorn 5:19 p.m.) Friendly approaches, talks with your clergyman, and a sense of being exposed to a spiritual influence are all indicated. There can be considerable soul-searching under prevailing aspects. Aries and Leo figure prominently. You can enjoy a sense of peaceful relaxation. Platinum and tawny are your colors. Your lucky number is 4.

Monday, July 13 (Moon in Capricorn) It's an excellent day for getting boring detail work out of the way. It's fine for tackling jobs ordinarily repugnant to you.

Some people have to be told the truth about their performance, but choose the right moment in privacy. Capricorn plods away. Important changes are brewing. Amber and purple are your colors. Your lucky number is 8.

Tuesday, July 14 (Moon in Capricorn)   Leo is for love, and under these trends people are wearing their hearts on their sleeves. You do well where you review what you have going for yourself in love, work, and achievement potential. Taurus has something to say. Emerald and wine are your colors. Hot combination numbers: 1 and 6.

Wednesday, July 15 (Moon in Capricorn to Aquarius 5:03 a.m.)   With your lunar cycle high, you can step lively and take the lead; you can pretty much write your own ticket. Accent personality assets and tone down whatever might be considered a liability. Another Aquarius is in the picture. Wear pastel stripes. Lucky lottery numbers: 12, 3, 30, 15, 25, 39.

Thursday, July 16 (Moon in Aquarius)   Make decisions, keep on top of personal responsibilities, and look your best while the world is watching you. You can step up the ladder of success. Your personality is electrifying and you can see many people at the same time. You can push off into the future with self-confidence. Pick six: 4, 5, 2, 8, 1, 4.

Friday, July 17 (Moon in Aquarius to Pisces 5:44 p.m.)   Friends can be counted on today. Gemini and Libra are listening to you. Make announcements, give your side of the story, and engage in charitable and humanitarian projects. It's important that you leave your imprint on the day. Off-white and silver make a fine combination for you. Your lucky number is 7.

Saturday, July 18 (Moon in Pisces)   Import-export matters surface and you can obtain some lovely gifts from island countries. You're cheerful and feel quite secure financially, even when others are crying the economic blues. Your financial intuition is good. Pisces is leading. Lavender and light yellow are lucky colors. Lucky lottery numbers: 18, 9, 27, 31, 36, 45.

Sunday, July 19 (Moon in Pisces)   A Virgo and a Cancer have key roles. Be sure you have all the facts before taking action. A lazy person may not mean to delay things. Secrets require more than ordinary protection. Be ultra-careful about parking your vehicle in a dark or unfamiliar area. Raspberry and mace are your colors. Play it safe with number 2.

Monday, July 20 (Moon in Pisces to Aries 6:07 a.m.) There are bottlenecks in law, public relations, and partnerships. Concentrate on the minuscule, on what can be done today, on the little things of life. Aries and Leo are in the picture. Siblings and neighbors will be glad to hear from you. Lemon and antique white are winning colors. Count on number 4.

Tuesday, July 21 (Moon in Aries) You can battle your weight in wildcats while adventures in faraway places beckon to you. You want a new scene, a new scenario, and may look to a Scorpio and another Aquarius for help. Young men, knightly types, are in the picture. Your learning processes are stimulated. Sky blue and canary are your colors. Pick six: 8, 4, 3, 7, 2, 1.

Wednesday, July 22 (Moon in Aries to Taurus 4:36 p.m.) Restlessness continues to gnaw away at you, and it's easy to become bored. Older people seem selfish and jealous. You will be angry if you are exposed to aggression and abrasive behavior. Leo and Sagittarius have key roles. Puce, olive, and earth are your colors. Lucky lottery numbers: 1, 10, 22, 32, 28, 46.

Thursday, July 23 (Moon in Taurus) Members of your family are strongly represented. Any possible point of deterioration in home construction could show up under these aspects. Examine locks on doors and windows, check screens, plumbing, roof, and any damp or musty spots. Outdoor beautification programs are favored. Taurus has the reins. Mauve and beige are your colors. Your lucky number is 3.

Friday, July 24 (Moon in Taurus) Community responsibilities can be aggravating. Private rather than public life may require attention. Know where your children are and what they are doing; investigate their associates. Entertain grandparents, aunts, uncles, and senior members of your family. Wheat is your color; 5 is your number.

Saturday, July 25 (Moon in Taurus to Gemini 11:44 a.m.) Things are looking up. Love, romance, socializing can make this a red-letter day. You're daring, original, imaginative, adaptable, flexible, and creative. A Gemini and another Aquarius can make you happy. You have a marvelous enthusiasm for enjoying kindred spirits. Peppermint stripes are for you. Lucky lottery numbers: 2, 11, 38, 43, 7, 25.

Sunday, July 26 (Moon in Gemini) Romantic overtures and interludes dominate. Dress to the nines today; look rich, royal, and vital. Success is connected with attitude—be positive, jovial, and encourage children. You are the perfect guide and you can inspire others to do better. White and black combine to make you look chic. Your lucky number is 9.

Monday, July 27 (Moon in Gemini to Cancer 3:08 a.m.) A Cancer and a Pisces figure prominently. You can get plenty of work done today. Your intuitive processes tell you how to please your boss and keep coworkers busy. This is a good day for serving the needs of loved ones, for bringing the various generations in the family together. Love and pleasure are therapeutic. Play number 2 to win.

Tuesday, July 28 (Moon in Cancer) Be practical and methodical in meeting the demands of your job. The desire to get close to the water may be strong, but you could be criticized for anything omitted now. Pets, dependents, and wardrobe needs are all represented, and the day is a busy one. Old rose is your color. Pick six: 4, 1, 2, 6, 4, 9.

Wednesday, July 29 (Moon in Cancer to Leo 3:39 a.m.) The other point of view must be considered. Marriage and business partnerships require some self-effacement; let your partner lead. A Leo and a Libra have key roles. Harmonize your plans with others, and defer to the wishes of your companion if you are traveling at this time. Ecru and coral are lucky colors today. Lucky lottery numbers: 39, 44, 8, 17, 35, 29.

Thursday, July 30 (Moon in Leo) This is a perfect time for a short honeymoon—perhaps right back to where it all began. Pillow talk, and positive approaches to the simple things of life are in the picture. Gemini is entertaining; and Virgo will confide in you. Relaxation and rest will replenish and refurbish. Your colors are plum and melon. Hot combination numbers: 1 and 7.

Friday, July 31 (Moon in Leo to Virgo 3:01 a.m.) Security interests, a discussion about taxes and tax shelters, and a new look at budgets are all represented. But your sense of values can be off-track; make sure you are not functioning with a depression-scarred mind. The foundations of your love life, marriage, and job are accented. Rainbow is your color. Your lucky number is 3.

AUGUST 1992

Saturday, August 1 (Moon in Virgo)   There is an expansive quality in your thinking and working as though you are emerging from the limitations imposed upon you by others. Virgo is helpful. A methodical, practical approach will work wonders, but above all comes the saving graces of kindness and consideration. Sauterne and beige are your colors. Lucky lottery numbers: 11, 2, 15, 20, 29, 47.

Sunday, August 2 (Moon in Virgo to Libra 3:17 a.m.)   The accent falls on people at or from a distance, long-range plans, and changes of scenery. If travel is out, then rearrange furniture in your home. Give yourself a change of scenery. Libra and another Aquarius figure prominently. Wear nectarine and powder blue. You may enjoy a spiritual discussion. Your lucky number is 4.

Monday, August 3 (Moon in Libra)   If you keep on the go today, much can be accomplished. Plan some upcoming event. There are rewards and awards forming in this picture. Gemini has a lot to say about the future. Your prestige and status are shaping up and you can build solidly upon past achievements. Amber and canary are winning colors. Hot combination numbers: 6 and 1.

Tuesday, August 4 (Moon in Libra to Scorpio 6:16 a.m.)   Scorpio and Taurus have your best interest at heart even though it would be wishful thinking to believe that they agree with you. Your career can benefit from a little pushing. Speak up in your own behalf. Be more daring in some changes you bring about that can save time, money, and energy. Pick six: 8, 3, 2, 1, 5, 8.

Wednesday, August 5 (Moon in Scorpio)   Go to the front office and deal with higher-ups, who can make decisions and help with problems. There are changes, new directions, and fascinating turns in life under prevailing aspects. Scorpio is in charge. Make do with some of the materials you have on hand. Lavender and charcoal are your colors. Lucky lottery numbers: 16, 7, 12, 3, 30, 11.

Thursday, August 6 (Moon in Scorpio to Sagittarius 12:57 p.m.)   Savings, investments, and budgets can be served well. The practical side of things is represented. You can build upon past experiences and realize some good savings. Your household, particularly culinary budgets can be improved. Insurance, taxes, license fees, may add to expenses. Emerald and fuchsia are your colors. Hot combination numbers: 5 and 8.

Friday, August 7 (Moon in Sagittarius)   Luck can play a big role in what you receive and achieve. Be jovial, enthusiastic, and positive for best results. Optimism carries a big dollar sign. Sagittarius and Aries come front and center. Friendships can make this a pleasant evening. Amber and melon are your colors. Hot combination numbers: 7 and 2.

Saturday, August 8 (Moon in Sagittarius to Capricorn 11:00 p.m.)   Be generous, diplomatic, and tactful. Personal relationships are rewarding. Meet friends of your friends and of your parents. Write letters to old friends who have moved to another part of the country. Church and club involvements are favored. Earth and olive are winning colors. Lucky lottery numbers: 9, 18, 45, 22, 36, 27.

Sunday, August 9 (Moon in Capricorn)   Largess, expansion, the feeling that you have some time on your hands, the urge to be generous to your mate and others are activated. "Do good and disappear . . . ," states an old religious adage. Work behind the scenes in private to improve situations. Capricorn and Virgo have key roles. Mulberry is your color. Your lucky number is 2.

Monday, August 10 (Moon in Capricorn)   Get in touch with large organizations and institutions, and don't be overwhelmed by size in any situation. It's a fine day for finishing up odd chores, writing summaries, reports, and closing one door so that new one can be opened up in the middle of the week. Taurus is onstage. Eggplant and bronze are your colors. Count on number 4.

Tuesday, August 11 (Moon in Capricorn to Aquarius 11:07 a.m.)   Conclude, know when to cut things off and to end conversations and interests abruptly. Avoid people who tend to depress you mentally and make allowances for anxiety in older people. Gemini comes forward. There are fine trends for dressing up and going places. Burgundy and old gold are your colors. Hot combination numbers: 6 and 1.

Wednesday, August 12 (Moon in Aquarius)   Begin anew, and start the ball rolling in the right direction. With your lunar cycle high, you can make good decisions, persuade others to see your point of view, and make visible as well as not-so-visible progress. Another Aquarius and a Libra have key roles. Indigo and deep purple are your colors. Lucky lottery numbers: 17,26, 12, 23, 44, 35.

Thursday, August 13 (Moon in Aquarius to Pisces 11:51 p.m.)   Today's full moon illuminates personal quandries and enlightens you in highly personalized matters. Hold the initiative as you discuss matters with people, including a Gemini and a Leo. Marital and business partnership matters are picking up steam. Contracts and agreements can be amended. Magenta and orange are your colors. Your lucky number is 3.

Friday, August 14 (Moon in Pisces)   Push financial and economic interests for all they are worth. Financial conversations with your banker and broker will produce good results. Earning power, income, and locating of new sources of capital are favored. You can enjoy your possessions. Pisces and a Cancer have important roles. Mauve is your color. Play number 5 to win.

Saturday, August 15 (Moon in Pisces) The spiritual side of your nature is accented. Pisces and Scorpio are front and center. The funding of some special but hard-to-explain projects may be difficult, but possible under prevailing aspects. Beach and water activities attract you. Flesh and florentine gold are your colors. Lucky lottery numbers: 16, 7, 15, 29, 34, 12.

Sunday, August 16 (Moon in Pisces to Aries 12:11 p.m.) Bargains can be found in strange out-of-the-way places. Antiques, books, and roadside junk shops are all represented. If you look in unlikely places, you could find some money or valuable items today. Taurus and Virgo have the plans put together already. Wear a little silver. Count on number 9.

Monday, August 17 (Moon in Aries) Everything is real, visible, and rather logical; you can reach out and touch. The immediate and the pressing may be demanding attention. School plans and projects are pushing into your consciousness. Everyday routines, the usual, familiar, and local are all front and center. Aries and Leo meander in and out. Hot combination numbers: 2 and 5.

Tuesday, August 18 (Moon in Aries to Taurus 11:10 p.m.) You could encounter aggressive and abrasive behavior today—young men are especially difficult. Siblings and neighbors come in for their share of your attention. Studies, hobbies, and getting annoying jobs out of the way are possibilities. Sagittarius has flights of fancy. If you organize your time well, you can make the day count. Pick six: 4, 7, 2, 4, 1, 6.

Wednesday, August 19 (Moon in Taurus) Domestic, household, community, property, and ownership trends are favorable. A member of your family may be spending too much money, and this could bother you enough to mention the subject. Be prepared for opposition and resentment; your best defense is a patronizing smile. Champagne is your color. Lucky lottery numbers: 15, 6, 19, 30, 35, 8.

Thursday, August 20 (Moon in Taurus) Taurus and Virgo are center stage. You could feel that your family and home are standing between you and genuine relaxation. But it's the mountains and inland areas rather than water and seashore that are beckoning. A little village at the foot of the hills would be suitable for Aquarius. Your lucky number is 1.

Friday, August 21 (Moon in Taurus to Gemini 7:36 a.m.) Discuss measures that might be taken within your home to reduce tampering with budgets. Cost-of-living increases have to be recognized by all members of the family. Capricorn and Taurus are in the picture. Orange and ebony is a good combination for beach wear. Hot combination numbers: 3 and 6.

Saturday, August 22 (Moon in Gemini) Concentrate on what has to be done prior to early afternoon. The desire to socialize later on can be strong. Gemini and Leo come front and center. Your love life is activated as the day moves along, and this could be the night! Get away from the familiar. Wear amber and ivory for luck. Lucky lottery numbers: 14, 5, 22, 34, 41, 32.

Sunday, August 23 (Moon in Gemini to Cancer 12:36 p.m.) Spend time with your beloved, away from crowds, and avoid any topic on which you happen to disagree. A parent-offspring relationship can be improved by a day away from each other. Beach and water activities can be boring. If the group is too large, forget it! Lemon is your color. Your lucky number is 7.

Monday, August 24 (Moon in Cancer) Don't volunteer for extra duties. Meet responsibilities and obligations that long have been yours, but don't take on anything new. Cancer and Capricorn are the solar groups demanding action. Work can be aggravating and shared responsibilities can tire you. You'd rather do a few things alone. Pink and coral are your colors. Hot combination numbers: 9 and 3.

Tuesday, August 25 (Moon in Cancer to Leo 2:15 p.m.) Abide by your usual preventive-medicine routines. Americans don't make good servants, and you will be strongly aware of this today. Getting cooperation isn't all that easy. Ask Scorpio for advice under these aspects. Matters may seem to be more urgent than they really are. There's plenty of gossip and rumormongering about.

Old rose is your color. Hot combination numbers: 4 and 6.

Wednesday, August 26 (Moon in Leo)   Replenish and refurbish your soul and body. Security matters are accented. Evaluating the work you are called upon to do and the amount of cooperation you aren't receiving are worthy ventures. Leo and another Aquarius are in the picture. You can hold on to more money than you may realize. Lucky lottery numbers: 15, 6, 26, 37, 24, 42.

Thursday, August 27 (Moon in Leo to Virgo 1:46 p.m.)   Aries and Sagittarius cooperate well. It's a fine day for marriage, legal matters and public relations, but the results of your hard work may not be sufficient. Joint ventures are better than solo efforts. Check the way you view money, knowing not only its advantages but its limitations. Plaid is your color. Your lucky number is 8.

Friday, August 28 (Moon in Virgo)   Virgo takes charge. Be practical about the way you handle finances. Methodical, logical, step-by-step ways are best under these aspects. Investments can show some action and savings are under protective configurations. Late-summer adjustments, changes, improvements, and corrections can get underway. Hot combination numbers: 1 and 6.

Saturday, August 29 (Moon in Virgo to Libra 1:11 p.m.)   You may feel that items are overpriced while shopping. Surely, your cost of living is increasing. Still, you are optimistic about personal matters and about the improvements and corrections you have in the back of your mind. Intellectual challenges are in the picture, along with a Scorpio and a Pisces. Lucky lottery numbers: 29, 43, 12, 3, 30, 39.

Sunday, August 30 (Moon in Libra)   Travel, enjoying cultural sights within a 100-mile radius, and trying out a distant restaurant are all possibilities under existing aspects. Libra and another Aquarius are good companions. You may wish that a former neighbor would return to your area. Strawberry and off-white are your colors. Count on number 5.

Monday, August 31 (Moon in Libra to Scorpio 2:38 p.m.)   There may be some modification of your long-range plans. The urge to do something unusual and to get away from people who sap your energies by their very presence can permeate your entire being. There may be too much scheduling for the week ahead. Stay away from hot beaches. Play number 7 to win.

SEPTEMBER 1992

September 1 (Moon in Scorpio)   You will advance in your career and find that you are able to build upon the foundations of established prestige and status. Scorpio and Cancer come front and center. Although material ambitions are strongly represented, you never really toss ideals away. Antique white and fuchsa are your colors. Your lucky number is 8.

Wednesday, September 2 (Moon in Scorpio to Sagittarius 7:50 p.m.)   A little boldness would not be amiss under existing aspects, especially on the job. You could convince a supervisor to see your point of view about work that is falling behind. It's a good time to begin new time-, energy-, and money-saving activities. Self-confidence is your most valuable commodity. Wear ivory and yellow for happiness. Lucky lottery numbers: 14, 2, 10, 29, 38, 47.

Thursday, September 3 (Moon in Sagittarius)   Sagittarius and Leo are holding firm. You are quick to grasp the subtleties in social relationships. A friend may be interested in something more than friendship. Social obligations are strongly represented. You could feel that your friendship circle may be hurt by the development of a romantic triangle. Salmon and mocha are winning colors. Your lucky number is 3.

Friday, September 4 (Moon in Sagittarius)   Church and club involvements are picking up steam after summer. A busybody may attempt to pile too many responsibilities on you, but your mood is such that you may permit this for the time being. Groups are beckoning to you. Aries enters the picture. Your colors are azure and coral. Count on number 5.

Saturday, September 5 (Moon in Sagittarius to Capricorn 5:06 a.m.)   Problems are solved quietly, privately, and possibly behind the scenes. Secrets kept from you earlier in the year suddenly can be taken out from under wraps. Deal with large organizations and institutions, even though you could feel somewhat hemmed in by the prejudices and hangups of others. Lucky lottery numbers: 7, 25, 20, 34, 13, 19.

Sunday, September 6 (Moon in Capricorn)   Visit those who are confined to their own home or hospital. Be especially kind to the unpopular types; try to understand how unattractive people feel in any group of svelte, fashionable types. It's a good day for going out of your way to please people. You operate well behind the scenes. Your lucky number is 9.

Monday, September 7 (Moon in Capricorn to Aquarius 5:08 p.m.)   Close one door so that another one can be opened. There can be some shifting of ideas and approaches. You are preparing to say more and want to know just how to go about it. Capricorn and another Aquarius are in the picture. Finish useless projects. Your winning colors are beige, ecru, and magenta. Play number 2 to win.

Tuesday, September 8 (Moon in Aquarius)   In your high lunar cycle, you can make strong impressions, hold the initiative, and turn your personal goals in whatever direction makes sense to you. Make announcements, state your objections, and take over where you see deterioration and waste. Goldenrod and wine are winning colors. Your lucky number is 4.

Wednesday, September 9 (Moon in Aquarius)   You're relaxed, pleased with yourself, and conscious of both the intuitive and learning processes. Leo and Libra have key roles. You can make plans without much interference, and your self-confidence is high enough for decision making. Do some shopping for glamorous items—it's imperative that you look well now. Lucky lottery numbers: 8, 17, 21, 44, 26, 35.

Thursday, September 10 (Moon in Aquarius to Pisces 5:56 a.m.)   Are your earning power and income keeping up with the increased costs of living? If not, a good down-to-earth discussion with your supervisors and employers would be appropriate. Pisces and Cancer come front and center. Some possessions you no longer require may be disposed of under existing trends. Marigold and rust are winning colors. Hot combination numbers: 1 and 4.

Friday, September 11 (Moon in Pisces)   Promote your skills and talents. Review the areas of work where you have been most rewarded. Be clever, shrewd, and dig deeply for the financial answers. The accent falls on money you have, money you are earning, and money you want. Beige and various shades of blue are your colors. Trust Scorpio. Count on number 3.

Saturday, September 12 (Moon in Pisces to Aries 6:02 p.m.)   You can write an effective, productive business letter under these aspects. You can draw the attention of a powerful person to something that has to be done pronto. Speak up when you are sure you are in the right. Business deals can be cemented. Special moneys can be earmarked for you. Lucky lottery numbers: 14, 5, 12, 27, 23, 41.

Sunday, September 13 (Moon in Aries)   Move about your own neighborhood with self-confidence and a smile. Neighbors are favorably represented. What is pressing and immediate can be taken care of today. Your learning processes are perking, and information is flowing freely. Aries and Pisces are front and center. Cerise and beige are your colors. Count on number 7.

Monday, September 14 (Moon in Aries)   Leo and Sagittarius have the answers and directions. You're able to concentrate effectively, and work done under prevailing aspects tends to be first rate. You lean toward the usual, familiar, and scheduled. Students, teachers, and fellow travelers are favored as you keep on the go. Hyacinth blue and aqua are your colors. Play number 2 to win.

Tuesday, September 15 (Moon in Aries to Taurus 4:47 a.m.)   Taurus and Virgo have questions for you. Avoid disagreements with relatives over something silly. You may resent the way a former dependent is so quick to assert complete independence in everything except money.

244

There's pleasure in talks with older loved ones. Champagne is your color. Today's number is 4.

Wednesday, September 16 (Moon in Taurus) Household chores can be handled with dispatch. Cleanup programs around the grounds of your home are a must as summer ends. Happy times are recaptured as you plan autumn festivals, hay rides, lawn fetes, Octoberfests. Discuss the old days with a sibling, aunt, or uncle. Magenta's your color. Lucky lottery numbers: 15, 6, 16, 28, 33, 42.

Thursday, September 17 (Moon in Taurus to Gemini 1:40 p.m.) It's a fine day to buy and sell real estate, help with community charitable and humanitarian programs, have lunch in an unusual tearoom or restaurant with a former neighbor or real estate agent. As the day advances, you are stimulated strongly by nostalgia and sentimental ties. Your lucky number is 8.

Friday, September 18 (Moon in Gemini) Passionate responses are indicated. All the beautiful illusions and fantasies of love are possible when romance goes into high gear. Socializing is spontaneous and all the more fun. Parent-offspring relationships are favored. Creativity makes sex revitalizing. Amber is your color. Play number 1 to win.

Saturday, September 19 (Moon in Gemini to Cancer 7:09 p.m.) Know where your children are, what they are doing, and who they are spending time with. Secretive types should not be trusted. A party that you arrange now will be more successful than those arranged in the past. Your skills and talents, are holding you in good stead socially. Purple and melon are your colors. Lucky lottery numbers: 12, 3, 19, 34, 39, 21.

Sunday, September 20 (Moon in Cancer) What you have perking at a distance is speeded up; so are legal interests. Chores may be piling up in and around your home. There are fine rays for making changes and turning things around so that there can be some plugging of financial drains. Yellow and plum are your colors. Your number is 5.

Monday, September 21 (Moon in Cancer to Leo 11:19 p.m.) You may want to do things differently today,

245

but not for any good rhyme or reason. Possibly a change in pace and pattern could bring some adventure into your life. Coworkers may be less interested in cooperation now and under existing aspects, there can be some disagreements about the work itself. Stick with number 9.

Tuesday, September 22 (Moon in Leo) Every marriage can be improved, and this is the right kind of day to set corrections and changes in motion. Legal involvements may require more discussion. You could find a business partner greedier than you realized. Dependents may give snappy, flippant responses. Celery and fuchsia are your colors. Hot combination numbers: 2 and 6.

Wednesday, September 23 (Moon in Leo) Leo and Libra are favorably represented, together with marital harmony and intellectual contacts. If you defer to the wishes of a partner, you'll increase your chances of success and high achievement. Open new lines of communication with someone you used to love. Wear silver and salmon. Lucky lottery numbers: 13, 4, 23, 35, 40, 22.

Thursday, September 24 (Moon in Leo to Virgo 12:08 a.m.) Adjustments in family and home routines can mean more contentment. You can improve the base of your economic security. Feathering of your retirement nest is activated by prevailing aspects. Changes, switches from one opinion to another, the desire to improve the lot of an older loved one will all go well. Hot combination numbers: 6 and 9.

Friday, September 25 (Moon in Virgo to Libra 11:55 p.m.) Scorpio is center stage. Your responses in romance and love are more passionate than usual. Fantasies during love's prologue can surprise even you. Be agreeable and value all the saving graces in your relationships with others. Set money aside where possible, because higher expenses are on the horizon. Your lucky number is 8.

Saturday, September 26 (Moon in Libra) Today's new moon illuminates distant involvements, travel plans and possibilities, and enlightens you where you want to improve your appearance and the impact you have on others. Fascinating projects and stimulating people come front and center. While traveling you could find your heart's desire. Lucky lottery numbers: 1, 10, 26, 41, 46, 37.

Sunday, September 27 (Moon in Libra)   Someone you haven't seen in a long time can appear suddenly. You could hear some surprising but pleasant news. People at or from a distance are lucky for you. You can discover truths about yourself under prevailing aspects that amaze you. Libra and Aries have key roles. Ecru is your color. Play number 3 to win.

Monday, September 28 (Moon in Libra to Scorpio 12:44 a.m.)   Career progress is evident; talks with top executives can give your morale a real boost. Use authority carefully but don't forget to utilize it. Dress stylishly, pay attention to your hair, and aim for the regal impression, because you are being evaluated secretly today. Aquamarine and ecru are your colors. Your lucky number is 5.

Tuesday, September 29 (Moon in Scorpio)   It's a good time to make progress on the job. Professional and authoritative approaches will work wonders. Scorpio and a Cancer figure prominently. Be daring and courageous in the way you meet challenges. Mace and cherry are your colors. Hot combination numbers: 9 and 3.

Wednesday, September 30 (Moon in Scorpio to Sagittarius 4:33 a.m.)   Business-pleasure combinations fare well. You relax in group situations and have a deep appreciation of your friends. Popularity is yours under existing circumstances. In positive ways you will be reaching a greater number of people. Sagittarius is tactful. Burgundy and Wallis blue are your colors. Lucky lottery numbers: 2, 30, 42, 11, 20, 38.

OCTOBER 1992

Thursday, October 1 (Moon in Sagittarius)   Church, club, and group involvements are favored. Step lively to keep social situations moving along. A change of programs may be just what the group and project require at this time. Be daring and bold in the social suggestions you make, for you could be dealing with many old fogies. Sagittarius has much to say. Kelly green and magenta are winning colors. Your lucky number is 2.

Friday, October 2 (Moon in Sagittarius to Capricorn 12:29 p.m.) Aries and Gemini figure prominently. Emphasize courtesy and understanding in all social relationships. Old and trusted friends can have an off-day and drain your emotions. You may find older loved ones irritable and have difficulty tracing this to the source. Life is dealing with others. Taupe is your color. Count on number 4.

Saturday, October 3 (Moon in Capricorn) Capricorn takes over and will take umbrage if you sidestep rules, regulations, or traditions. But it's a good day to complete work that may have been hanging fire too long. It's fine for summing up, but no audacious moves under these trends. Orchid and venetian gold are your lucky colors. Lucky lottery numbers: 19, 24, 6, 15, 42, 33.

Sunday, October 4 (Moon in Capricorn to Aquarius 11:53 p.m.) A doubting Thomas can upset a business or social applecart. Your enthusiasm can persuade others to see things from your point of view. Private matters may require more protection under these aspects. Where you are practical, there can be some unanticipated dividends. Consult Virgo and Taurus. Your lucky number is 8.

Monday, October 5 (Moon in Aquarius) People will enjoy doing you favors with your lunar cycle high. Compliments are coming your way, and your personal appearance attracts members of the opposite sex even if you are dissatisfied yourself. You're in the driver's seat and can make strong impressions with the work you do. Another Aquarius and a Gemini come front and center. Ruby's your color. Count on number 3.

Tuesday, October 6 (Moon in Aquarius) There are excellent trends in highly personalized interests. You can take great leaps forward toward important goals. You have all your ducks gathered together and can turn this into a momentous cycle. Libra has some answers. Widen your circle of friends while you look so magnificent. Place your chips on number 5.

Wednesday, October 7 (Moon in Aquarius to Pisces 12:38 p.m.) Your career interests are strong. You can make progress through talks with higher-ups and cooperation with coworkers and underlings. Your personality enables you to get along with just about everyone, which makes you a valuable employee. Antique white and powder blue are your colors. Rust, russet, and marigold are your winning colors. Lucky lottery numbers: 7, 16, 11, 25, 34, 32.

Thursday, October 8 (Moon in Pisces) Earning power and income are favored. You can double your output if you inaugurate new technologies and methodologies. Don't hold back when there is big money to be made. Move along with the times; new equipment is a must. Discuss time-, labor-, and money-saving devices with supervisors. Pick six: 9, 1, 4, 2, 8, 5.

Friday, October 9 (Moon in Pisces) Try to make do rather than spending on something you can do without. Help older loved ones to manage their budgets more effectively. The accent falls on earning power, income, and wealth production generally. A Pisces and a Cancer have key roles. Speak up, know your rights. Crimson and canary are winning colors. Your lucky number is 2.

Saturday, October 10 (Moon in Pisces to Aries 12:36 a.m.) Sign contracts, make decisions, and express yourself in ways you enjoy. Hunting, fishing, and hikes through the woods are favored. You feel young, really alive today, and will want to show the world how good you look. Aries, Leo, and Sagittarius are in the picture. Reddish browns are your colors. Lucky lottery numbers: 4, 13, 10, 26, 22, 31.

Sunday, October 11 (Moon in Aries) Get away from dull, boring, old fogies. The great outdoors is beckoning to you. Take a drive in a rural area and trace the advance of fall. Stabilize your home situations and know the value of what you own. Gains can come from listening to an authority. Wheat, russet, and fuchsia are your colors. Play number 6 today.

Monday, October 12 (Moon in Aries to Taurus 10:48 a.m.) You have visible moral and physical courage, which is going to impress others, especially the confident way you speak. What you have going for yourself locally will matter today. Studies, hobbies, communciations, and short-distance travel get green lights. Discuss situations with siblings. Hot combination numbers: 8 and 3.

Tuesday, October 13 (Moon in Taurus)   Can you think of any way to make your home return a little income to you? Do you have space, machinery, or tools to rent or lease? Household expenses can be somewhat aggravating, and budgets may have to be revamped. There is special closeness to loved ones now. Marigold and magenta are your colors. Hot combination numbers: 3 and 9.

Wednesday, October 14 (Moon in Taurus to Gemini 7:08 p.m.)   Taurus and Virgo have key roles. Family endeavors and investments can do well. Family unity is an unbeatable strength under prevailing aspects. Concentrate on the positive ideas, appraoches, and attitudes of loved ones. Sentiments, affections, and genuine love rays are dominating. Lucky lottery numbers: 14, 5, 18, 23, 41, 27.

Thursday, October 15 (Moon in Gemini)   Parties and entertainments can be organized well. You're in the mood for love, and your responses to romantic overtures and interludes are memorable. The opposite gender is very much aware of your presence. Flirtations are accented. Conversation flows freely. Wheat, sauterne, and tan are your colors. Your lucky number is 7.

Friday, October 16 (Moon in Gemini)   Gemini and Libra have the right ideas. Your love life is rewarding and you tend to mend social fences with in-laws and friends of your beloved. Dress fashionably and know that the eyes of both admirers and critics are on you. Go places and see things. Hyacinth and aqua are your colors. Hot combination numbers: 9 and 5.

Saturday, October 17 (Moon in Gemini to Cancer 1:36 a.m.)   A Capricorn and a Cancer are helpful. There's more work involved in the day's projects than you may believe at the outset. Some questionable food may be put on the table. Focus on new methods, new directions, and improved ways of performing old tasks. Buy items that will help you on the job. Lucky lottery numbers: 24, 29, 11, 2, 38, 47.

Sunday, October 18 (Moon in Cancer)   Stick to your usual routines. There can be some evidence of the generation gap in home matters. Your sense of responsibility is strong, but be aware of recent obligations and burdens that small fry may attempt to transfer to you. Pisces and Virgo are watching. Sand is your color. Your lucky number is 4.

Monday, October 19 (Moon in Cancer to Leo 6:01 a.m.)   Rely on the advice of someone who has known you for a long time. Your partners, mate, and people you see every day on the job are accented. How you can improve these relationships is illuminated for you. Publicity matters, advertising, and legal interests are favored. Leo and Sagittarius play important roles. Olive and earth are your colors. Hot combination numbers: 6 and 1.

Tuesday, October 20 (Moon in Leo)   Conferences, interviews, joint endeavors, and investments are featured. Gains can be made through the intervention of your spouse, in-laws and friends of your spouse. You do well where you are open-minded, easy to get along with, and where you avoid sullen, morose types. Hot combination numbers: 8 and 7.

Wednesday, October 21 (Moon in Leo to Virgo 8:27 a.m.)   Partnerships can be increased, decreased, and changed, and contracts can be amended and improved under prevailing aspects. Deal with an in-law who has your welfare at heart along with good money and business ideas. As the day meanders along, you can realize some savings you haven't anticipated. Lucky lottery numbers: 25, 7, 30, 3, 12, 46.

Thursday, October 22 (Moon in Virgo)   Virgo and Taurus have major roles. There are good trends in savings, investment, and overall security interests. It's a fine day to make changes, improvements, and corrections. You can begin things all over again and this time avoid mistakes that hampered you in the past. The relationship of love and sex is accented. Ivory and chocolate are winning colors. Hot combination numbers: 5 and 6.

Friday, October 23 (Moon in Virgo to Libra 9:39 a.m.) Scorpio takes a bow. You can make progress in your career now. Talks with your employer can put you in better stead for a promotion, improved assignment, or an increase in salary. Your employer and supervisor yearn to please you. You may feel that someone you admire is trying to knock you off a favorite social or economic perch. Ruby and Wallis blue are your colors. Your lucky number is 7.

Saturday, October 24 (Moon in Libra) Libra and Gemini are in the picture. You move about with confidence and can enjoy some exciting contacts with dynamic people. Long-range views tend to work well for you and your investments. You're thinking big now and the results are extraordinary. Lucky lottery numbers: 9, 18, 24, 31, 36, 45.

Sunday, October 25 (Moon in Libra to Scorpio 11:04 a.m.) The new moon enlightens you in career, professional, authority, prestige, and status matters. What you can achieve by greater creativity rather than hard work will stand out in bas-relief. Taurus, a Cancer, and Pisces come front and center. You make excellent decisions and can be helpful to others. Jet and off-white are your colors. Count on number 2.

Monday, October 26 (Moon in Scorpio) You have the knack of dealing with the pros and the cons. You can see both sides of the question, which is not true of those with whom you must work. There are many illusions and pretensions in this picture, but if you persevere you can bring these opposing forces into a compromise. Hot combination numbers: 4 and 7.

Tuesday, October 27 (Moon in Scorpio to Sagittarius 2:29 p.m.) Changes that take place in your career aspirations tend to be favorable. The social side of your job can pay handsome dividends. Scorpio and Taurus are in the picture. Interviews go well this afternoon. A conference would tend to enlighten those who aren't knowledgeable. Puce and stripes are in. Your lucky number is 6.

Wednesday, October 28 (Moon in Sagittarius) Sagittarius wants to know what's going on. Social expansion is possible; you can advance your own social position and make some good friends in the bargain. Church and club involvements will pay off in many ways. The urge to see glamorous places is strong. Gold is your color. Lucky lottery numbers: 28, 32, 37, 1, 10, 46.

Thursday, October 29 (Moon in Sagittarius to Capricorn 9:18 p.m.) Sagittarius and Pisces figure in an important way. Distinguish between sensitivity and touchiness. You may feel that some friends are limiting themselves by adhering too much to traditions. The social side of your job can be served well. Subtle and complex situations are developing in social relationships. Play number 3 to win.

Friday, October 30 (Moon in Capricorn) Optimism and positive thinking can ward off depression under existing aspects. It's a good time to finish up projects. There are invisible tangents working away behind and also in front of the scenes. People don't stick to any one point. Capricorn can be helpful in pulling high-blown illusions back to earth. Wear a peppy angry red. Hot combination numbers: 5 and 9.

Saturday, October 31 (Moon in Capricorn) It's a perfect day to draw this month to a close. Summarize, put away, close the doors, pay what you owe, and clear the deck for a new month. Take care of any matter you may have overlooked. Mend social and domestic fences if you have upset anybody's applecart. Old rose and goldenrod are your colors. Lucky lottery numbers: 31, 47, 7, 16, 25, 34.

NOVEMBER 1992

Sunday, November 1 (Moon in Capricorn to Aquarius 7:43 a.m.) Much progress can be chalked up in private. You are permitted to see through the machinations of a difficult person; critics tend to limit the perspective of the worker. A creative approach to highly personal interests will be effective. Rust and wheat are your colors. Trust Taurus. Your lucky number is 6.

Monday, November 2 (Moon in Aquarius)   With your lunar cycle high, you have strong control, a good sense of direction, and the ability to carry others along on the wave of your own self-confidence and enthusiasm. A Libra and another Aquarius have key roles. You're intuitive, psychic, and quick to spot flaws. Pine cone and bronze are your colors. Play number 8 to win.

Tuesday, November 3 (Moon in Aquarius to Pisces 8:13 p.m.)   Follow your agenda and get a lot of work done early. Speak up, and take the lead in any partnership. Be emphatic with a smile on your face and you can't go wrong. Your strong sense of personal freedom wins you points. Azure and blueberry are your colors. Hot combination numbers: 1 and 5.

Wednesday, November 4 (Moon in Pisces)   Pisces and a Cancer figure prominently. Push financial plans and opportunities and reap big rewards. A clever but calculating person may ask too many questions. Know your budget parameters when the big spenders include you in their plans. Possessions increase in value. Lucky lottery numbers: 3, 5, 14, 32, 23, 41.

Thursday, November 5 (Moon in Pisces)   Trust Pisces and Virgo for the right answers. Generosity is your strong suit. Collect information, do research, know where to find the best investments. Correspondence and phone calls can increase your income. What you have purchased over the past two years is increasing in value. Marmalade and cocoa are your colors. Hot combination numbers: 7 and 1.

Friday, November 6 (Moon in Pisces to Aries 8:19 a.m.)   Listen to a financial whiz. Read the business pages of your newspaper. There's money to be made despite cryers of the economic blues who can be everywhere. Discount rumors that are related to your job, profession, career, and place of business. Azure and mauve are your winning colors. Your lucky number is 9.

Saturday, November 7 (Moon in Aries)   Aries and Leo make their point. Time is of the essence and work done amid social distractions will be of little use. Discourage compulsive talkers. Nip some unfair tidbit of gossip in the bud. When something has to be done, bear down hard on it. Short-distance travel is fine. Various shades of light green will win for you. Lucky lottery numbers: 11, 2, 15, 20, 29, 47.

Sunday, November 8 (Moon in Aries to Taurus 6:19 p.m.)   Isolate yourself for a few hours to catch up on work that has been neglected. Siblings and neighbors are favorably represented, along with a Sagittarius and a Libra. Your learning processes are stimulated, and research is enjoyable. Remember the homeless. Raspberry and white is your combination. Your lucky number is 4.

Monday, November 9 (Moon in Taurus)   Charm, charisma, and loving ways are represented and enhance your relationships with others, particularly with the opposite sex. Domestic and community requirements are onstage. You can make progress if you discuss your plans with a Scorpio and a Pisces. Wear hyacinth blue. Play number 8 to win.

Tuesday, November 10 (Moon in Taurus)   The full moon illuminates household, family, residential, ownership, and property matters. Taurus plays a commanding role. Work on closets, drawers, shelves, corners, basement, attic, and garage. You can improve your outlook by improving the looks of your home. Order and organization pay off. Salmon's your color. Count on number 1.

Wednesday, November 11 (Moon in Taurus to Gemini 1:49 a.m.)   Social life slows down and expenses get out of hand. But your love life is stimulated strongly, so you can draw closer to the one you love most at this time. Get away from interference and interruptions, so you can be spontaneous. Don't let greedy, jealous children cause friction. Lucky lottery numbers: 12, 3, 11, 16, 30, 21.

Thursday, November 12 (Moon in Gemini)   Your sense of humor, flashes of genuine wit, and enjoyment of the scene will make this a carefree cycle. Parties and entertainment that you decide to attend on the spur of the moment can make the day memorable. Virgo and Capricorn come front and center. Kelly green is your color. Hot combination numbers: 5 and 8.

Friday, November 13 (Moon in Gemini to Cancer 7:19 a.m.) Creativity, imagination, originality, flexibility, and improved parent-offspring relationships are favored. Gemini and Sagittarius figure prominently. Your closeness to your beloved can make this a red-letter day. Socialize with happily married couples; but avoid divorced people for best results. Hot combination numbers: 7 and 2.

Saturday, November 14 (Moon in Cancer) A Capricorn and a Cancer have key roles. Health improvements and corrections are favored. Busy yourself with work that you enjoy doing. You please others by what you do for them. Dependents and pets figure prominently. Wear a little platinum with mauve and old rose. Lucky lottery numbers: 18, 9, 14, 22, 36, 45.

Sunday, November 15 (Moon in Cancer to Leo 11:23 a.m.) Watch what you eat, especially if you're dining out. What you do for yourself at this time will tell an interesting tale. Replenish and refurbish ideals, aspirations, and hopes for the future. Taurus and Pisces are in charge. The spiritual side of your nature demands equal time. White and ebony are your colors. Your lucky number is 2.

Monday, November 16 (Moon in Leo) Marriage, business partnerships, contracts, agreements, and a good balance between grueling effort and genuine rest and relaxation form today's picture. Joint investments will do well. There may be some illusions in the way you view your beloved, but leave those truths alone. Mocha and antique white are your colors. Stick with number 4.

Tuesday, November 17 (Moon in Leo to Virgo 2:28 p.m.) Public relations, advertising, publicity, and dealing with the public at large are all in the picture. Diplomacy and tact pay handsome dividends. Let things move along at their own pace; don't force issues or foist changes upon others or yourself. The people you see today can be of major assistance. Pick six: 8, 2, 5, 1, 2, 6.

Wednesday, November 18 (Moon in Virgo) Virgo and Taurus have key roles. Security interests can be served. New ways of adding to savings are in focus—is it time to consider a change of brokers? Getting the job done properly should be your main goal. You demand much of yourself. Watch the insidious way taxes are being raised. Lucky lottery numbers: 1, 23, 28, 10, 37, 46.

Thursday, November 19 (Moon in Virgo to Libra 5:03 p.m.) You can count on your personal awareness and the power to transform ideas into talents. There are good rays for insurance, tax matters, tax shelters, and finding the least expensive way to acquire something you need. There's a strong accent on time-, labor-, and money-saving devices, technologies and methodologies. Pisces takes control. Hot combination numbers: 3 and 8.

Friday, November 20 (Moon in Libra) Travel, taking care of matters at a distance, inviting old acquaintances to visit you are part of today's positive picture. Libra and another Aquarius are front and center. Sightseeing, viewing things from away up there, and dealing with creative people will make this a good cycle for you. Your lucky number is 5.

Saturday, November 21 (Moon in Libra to Scorpio 7:52 p.m.) Intellectual activities do well. You can look ahead and make plans for the future. There's a good buoyancy represented, fine esprit de corps, and you are more at home with informed, sophisticated types. Keep on the go; travel within a 50-mile radius is favorable. Taupe is your color. Lucky lottery numbers: 7, 16, 21, 29, 25, 43.

Sunday, November 22 (Moon in Scorpio) Career matters are slowing down, but if you give due thought to them today, you can keep them from sliding backward. Professional and authority considerations are in the picture, together with a Scorpio and a Cancer. Where possible, do business with those who hold important and responsible positions. Your lucky number is 9.

Monday, November 23 (Moon in Scorpio) If you go to the front office and find the person in charge, you'll get what you want. Avoid straw bosses and those who are afraid of their own shadows. You could be instrumental in bringing feuding factions together. Passion heats up any affair of the heart. Wear azure, burgundy, and emerald. Count on number 2.

Tuesday, November 24 (Moon in Scorpio to Sagittarius 12:01 a.m.) Today's new moon illuminates your social involvements, what your friends are thinking, and enlightens you about the social side of your job. Sagittarius and Leo make a good combination. Dreams for the future, desires, aspirations, and hopes are important. Wear raspberry, plum, and celery for luck. Play number 4 today.

Wednesday, November 25 (Moon in Sagittarius) Be part of the group and show loyalty to the organization for best results. Accept all invitations that come your way; and where they aren't forthcoming, scurry them up via the phone, suggestions, or volunteer tactics. Aries is in your corner along with Gemini. Marmalade and cherry are winning colors. Lucky lottery numbers: 30, 35, 8, 17, 26, 44.

Thursday, November 26 (Moon in Sagittarius to Capricorn 6:38 a.m.) As the month winds down, finish chores that would only hold you back in December. Submit reports, pay bills, and collect what is due you. There can be some unexpected visits from relatives, friends, or former coworkers. Confidential information can get out now. Stick with number 1.

Friday, November 27 (Moon in Capricorn) There's a tendency to retreat from anything chaotic, hectic, or confusing. Work alone if people are getting on your nerves. Avoid troublemakers and rumormongers—people who sap your energies by their mere presence. Do what you can to extract additional gains from matters rooted in the past. Wear indigo. Your lucky number is 3.

Saturday, November 28 (Moon in Capricorn to Aquarius 4:19 p.m.) A sense of rejection can be disturbing people—harsh words or glances can often damage sensitive and touchy feelings. Clear the decks for personal action as you move toward your high lunar cycle. By nightfall, you can take over. Lucky lottery numbers: 14, 5, 28, 36, 41, 32.

Sunday, November 29 (Moon in Aquarius) This is an excellent day for taking strong stands, controlling any possible deteriorating situation, and letting the world know that you are very much present. With your lunar cycle high, you can stand tall, come face-to-face with all challenges, and take advantage of split-second opportunities. White and gold are your colors. Take a chance on number 7.

Monday, November 30 (Moon in Aquarius)   Another Aquarius, a Gemini, and a Libra are in the picture. Be sure, swift, agreeable where possible, but keep alert until the job is finished. Clear the slate so that you can be ready for the busy month ahead. Ask questions, use the answers, and assure your followers. Ivory and copper are your colors. Your lucky number is 9.

DECEMBER 1992

Tuesday, December 1 (Moon in Aquarius to Pisces 4:23 a.m.)   Self-restraint is your best strategy. Relationships with much older people are favored. Money-making opportunities are increased as each hour passes. Keep your wits about you as you forge ahead. Your self-confidence impresses those in authority. Aquamarine and dove gray are your colors. Your lucky number is 2.

Wednesday, December 2 (Moon in Pisces)   Pisces and Virgo have key roles. Push for higher earning power. You can find new sources of income under these aspects. Recent aquisitions an be a source of much happiness. A financial break may be hidden under your nose. Plum and rust are winning colors. Lucky lottery numbers: 4, 13, 8, 40, 22, 31.

Thursday, December 3 (Moon in Pisces to Aries 4:49 p.m.)   There are good trends in publishing, printing, letter writing, and what you request by mail. No one is going to get something for nothing under prevailing configurations. What you have achieved so far in life is your takeoff point. Stick to the facts—no enhancements, please. Indigo and beige are winning colors. Hot combination numbers: 6 and 9.

Friday, December 4 (Moon in Aries)   Know what you have to do, and don't want to do as this busy month advances. Put routine and schedule into your greeting card chores, gift-buying, home and lawn decorations. Discussions with siblings and neighbors can pay off. Studies, hobbies, and communications are favored. Olive and snow are winning colors. Your lucky number is 8.

Saturday, December 5 (Moon in Aries)   Opportunities can slip away from you if you don't pounce on them as soon as they show up. Studies, hobbies, and talks with understanding siblings can go well. There are indications that malicious gossip is emanating from an unexpected quarter. Wear a little silver, platinum, or white gold. Lucky lottery numbers: 1, 10, 14, 28, 46, 24.

Sunday, December 6 (Moon in Aries to Taurus 3:16 a.m.)   Taurus and Virgo have key roles. It's an earthy day with little tolerance of pretense or illusions. Domestic, property, ownership, and real estate matters are stimulated favorably. Your own community offers excellent opportunities for charitable and humanitarian projects. Beige and blue are your colors. Count on number 3.

Monday, December 7 (Moon in Taurus)   Push for more family cooperation. Discuss the household budget changes with loved ones to plug up drains on the family coffers. Property you own is increasing in value, but there can be some invisible deterioration at the same time. Older women make good companions. Sand and wheat are your colors. Your lucky number is 5.

Tuesday, December 8 (Moon in Taurus to Gemini 10:37 a.m.)   It's a fine day to gather precious memories. Have an unusual dinner for loved ones; bring a special dessert home with you. Address greeting cards and get them into the mail. Be sure gifts that have to be sent to another part of the country are on their way. Hot combination numbers: 7 and 3.

Wednesday, December 9 (Moon in Gemini)   Gemini and another Aquarius have the prominent roles. A total lunar eclipse in mid-Gemini can pressure your love life. Courtship costs can be up. Your beloved may not be on time or even where you would expect to find him or her. Know where your children are, who they are with, and what they are doing. Lucky lottery numbers: 11, 2, 9, 15, 20, 47.

Thursday, December 10 (Moon in Gemini to Cancer 3:05 p.m.) Don't foist changes upon yourself or on others. There can be some freakish accidents connected with short-distance travel, climbing, descending, where children congregate. You could be misquoted and misinterpreted under existing aspects. Air pollution can be in the news. Dress appropriately. Hot combination numbers: 4 and 5.

Friday, December 11 (Moon in Cancer) Watch what you eat and drink. Hard work may seem especially repugnant. There can be conflicts with pleasant holiday chores. Work can get in the way of a fascinating social invitation. Let the work go this evening; get out on the town or put up holiday decorations. Your lucky number is 6.

Saturday, December 12 (Moon in Cancer to Leo 5:47 p.m.) Don't take chances with your health. Stay out of drafts, and avoid sudden changes in temperature. Services may not be up to your standard, but keep your irritation to yourself. The world is changing and courtesy seems to be taking a last bow. Amber and the angry reds are your colors. Lucky lottery numbers: 8, 12, 23, 28, 10, 1.

Sunday, December 13 (Moon in Leo) Your mate or business partner can have questions for you. Try to keep abreast of holiday plans by doing overtime work at home and elsewhere. Unusual gifts can be found in out-of-the-way places, church stalls, or smaller independent shops. Marriage, contracts, and agreements are favored. Emerald and magenta are winners. Your lucky number is 1.

Monday, December 14 (Moon in Leo to Virgo 7:56 p.m.) Your social life is improving. Joint projects and ventures get top billing. Coworkers may not be as productive as usual and may have many useless discussions about what's wrong with everything. Leo and Gemini have key roles. Mauve and old rose are your colors. Hot combination numbers: 3 and 8.

Tuesday, December 15 (Moon in Virgo) Stick to your holiday budgets as closely as possible. You could be appalled by an increase in the price of food and clothing.

Much shoddy merchandise is on the market. Costs, standards, and saving graces are in focus, along with Virgo and Pisces. Wear softer reds with white or ivory. Hot combination numbers: 5 and 6.

Wednesday, December 16 (Moon in Virgo to Libra 10:33 p.m.)   Savings and investments are pressured as available cash runs out. Expenses are higher than anticipated. Information from a distance gives your morale a boost. Involve small fry in household chores. Organize your work so that it takes less of a toll on your nerves and patience. Lucky lottery numbers: 16, 7, 22, 34, 1, 43.

Thursday, December 17 (Moon in Libra)   If you are planning on any preholiday traveling, take off today but be back by December 22 or 23, before eclipse patterns form in the dungeon of your horoscope. Keep in close touch with loved ones at a distance; write, or better still, phone. Annual banquets and get-togethers do well this evening. Red and kelly green are your colors. Hot combination numbers: 2 and 7.

Friday, December 18 (Moon in Libra)   Sightseeing, spending time with loved ones who live at a distance, and delivering holiday gifts are all in focus. Plans are turning out better than you may have hoped. It's a good evening for entertaining in your own home; mix neighbors with coworkers and friends. Cherry and off-white are your colors. Play number 4 to win.

Saturday, December 19 (Moon in Libra to Scorpio 2:20 a.m.)   How many careers and jobs in the United States are neglected during this week before Christmas? If you give what you can to your job now and during the next day and a half, you will have increased your chances for a promotion later on. There are excellent aspects for office parties away from the office. Cherry and crimson are your colors. Lucky lottery numbers: 15, 6, 19, 28, 33, 42.

Sunday, December 20 (Moon in Scorpio)   Scorpio and Pisces are supportive. It's an excellent time for sheer labor, meeting many demands of yourself, your family, and others. Professional and authority situations are accented. The reputation of a business or profession can be at stake. You'll have to be organized to meet requirements. Champagne and emerald are your colors. Your lucky number is 8.

Monday, December 21 (Moon in Scorpio to Sagittarius 7:44 a.m.) Today's emphasis is on doing the job differently in order to save time and energy. More work is accomplished because others are in a good mood, but some warning signs may indicate that there can be troubles ahead because of rising social costs and unexpected situations. Some of the day will have to be played by ear. Sagittarius is wondering. Hot combination numbers: 3 and 6.

Tuesday, December 22 (Moon in Sagittarius) The band plays on and everybody goes about his or her business. People and situations seem to be computerized. There are many smiles and the greed in the hearts of children multiplies by leaps and bounds. Today's accent is on the great outdoors and the last-minute rush. Gemini and another Aquarius are shaking their heads. Pick six: 4, 1, 2, 8, 4, 5.

Wednesday, December 23 (Moon in Sagittarius to Capricorn 3:04 p.m.) Prices are being lowered, and shoddy merchandise is being offered. Business is complaining and government hides its many faces. Only within yourself can you find something to feel good about. Express the spiritual side of your nature. Capricorn and Taurus step aside. Lucky lottery numbers: 16, 7, 23, 29, 34, 14.

Thursday, December 24 (Moon in Capricorn) Somehow the old traditions aren't the same this Christmas Eve—they are pressured and eclipsed. You may feel that you are on an uncharted desert. There is dissatisfaction with gifts and half-hearted attempts to celebrate. See if Gemini, Libra, and another Aquarius can't liven things up. Reds and greens predominate. Stick with number 9.

Friday, December 25 (Moon in Capricorn) Travel is full of mixups, bottlenecks, and slowdowns. There is some accident-producing potential also. It's as though earth is protesting the billions of tons of plastic about to be imbedded into it. Older people can be somewhat depressed, but the managerial generation knows that the show must go on. Your lucky number is 2.

Saturday, December 26 (Moon in Capricorn to Aquarius 12:43 a.m.) Swinging back into your lunar high, you can do much to jazz up what's left of the holiday season. Let it all explode from your loving heart and you can't go wrong. Love is the great healer, together with joy, freedom, and a sense of being able to move about freely. Another Aquarius comes front and center. Lucky lottery numbers: 40, 26, 35, 4, 22, 31.

Sunday, December 27 (Moon in Aquarius) Spread yourself thin, see many people, keep busy, lead, control, develop, and nurture. Friends can make your day. Give groups some of the pleasure they have given you during the year. Entertainments and parties will do well if you give them strong support. White and gold are your colors. Your lucky number is 6.

Monday, December 28 (Moon in Aquarius to Pisces 12:28 p.m.) Maintain control, arrange, rearrange, encourage, guide, and be daring in the way you bring people together to create the right ambience. Dress up, because others like to see you looking your best. Group activities, church and club involvements are all favored. Leo and Libra have key roles. Play number 8 to win.

Tuesday, December 29 (Moon in Pisces) Restful hours can be followed by material considerations. While others are away from their jobs, you may be asked to do some pinch-hitting. The cost of living is a big consideration, but the search for bargains can be productive. A Pisces and a Scorpio are in the big picture. Various shades of brown will attract for you. Count on number 3.

Wednesday, December 30 (Moon in Pisces) Virgo and a Cancer come front and center. If you push for material gain, you are going to earn more than you anticipated. You will do well where you are seeking the funding for a special project. Review bills you committed yourself to during December. Some adjusting of budgets may be a good idea. Burgundy and beige are winning colors. Lucky lottery numbers: 30, 36, 5, 14, 23, 41.

Thursday, December 31 (Moon in Pisces to Aries 1:07 a.m.) Narrow your sights and zero in on some last-minute opportunities. The old year wants to add to your security. Your learning processes are good and can serve you during the week ahead. Some freakish accident potential exists close to home, in parking lots, and where illegal parking is a factor. Darker greens and eggshell are your colors. Hot combination numbers: 7 and 2.

ABOUT THIS SERIES

This is one of a series of
twelve Day-by-Day Astrological Guides
for the signs in 1992
by Sydney Omarr

ABOUT THE AUTHOR

Born on August 5, 1926, in Philadelphia, Omarr was the only person ever given full-time duty in the U.S. Army as an astrologer. He also is regarded as the most erudite astrologer of our time and the best known, through his syndicated column (300 newspapers) and his radio and television programs (he is Merv Griffin's "resident astrologer"). Omarr has been called the most "knowledgeable astrologer since Evangeline Adams." His forecasts of Nixon's downfall, the end of World War II in mid-August of 1945, the assassination of John F. Kennedy, Roosevelt's election to a fourth term and his death in office . . . these and many others are on record and quoted enough to be considered "legendary."

"...I do not walk alone!"

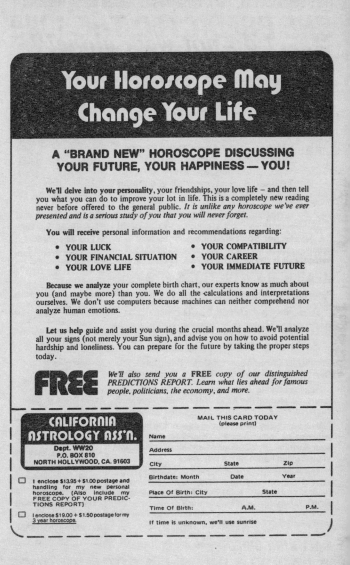

LET THE INCREDIBLE "SIXTH
BRING YOU WEALTH AND LOVE

JOYCE JILLSON MAKES NEWS!

Perhaps you've seen Joyce with Merv Griffin, Mike Douglas and John Davidson. You may have caught her on the *CBS Evening News* with Dan Rather, with Ted Koppel on *Nightline* or on *Entertainment Tonight*. You may be one of the millions who read her perceptive column every day in over 100 newspapers across North America. And books by Joyce Jillson have made the New York Times best-seller list.

In the past 20 years, the world of astrology has undergone great changes. Since all the math necessary to interpret the charts is done by her computer, **Joyce's psychic knowledge and advice is now available to you!**

Now thanks to Joyce Jillson, you will receive your personal **Lucky Numbers**, **Lucky Days** and **Lucky Signs**!

"Put my name in lights. I went on a trip to Las Vegas. I taped my Lucky Number to the flap of my purse. I won $1,111.00!" —J.C., Black Creek, Wisconsin.